MODERN WORK AND THE MARKETISATION OF HIGHER EDUCATION

Gerbrand Tholen

P

First published in Great Britain in 2022 by

Policy Press, an imprint of
Bristol University Press
University of Bristol
1–9 Old Park Hill
Bristol
BS2 8BB
UK
t: +44 (0)117 374 6645
e: bup-info@bristol.ac.uk

Details of international sales and distribution partners are available at
policy.bristoluniversitypress.co.uk

British Library Cataloguing in Publication Data
A catalogue record for this book is available from the British Library

ISBN 978-1-4473-5527-4 hardcover
ISBN 978-1-4473-5528-1 paperback
ISBN 978-1-4473-5530-4 ePub
ISBN 978-1-4473-5529-8 ePdf

Cover design: Clifford Hayes
Front cover image: Clifford Hayes

Contents

About the author   iv

1   Introduction   1

2   Dimensions of marketisation   15

3   Policymaking in higher education: understanding the economy   28

4   Policymaking in higher education: understanding work and the labour market   43

5   Policymaking in higher education: human capital   55

6   Graduate work in modern capitalism   70

7   The graduate labour market   81

8   Earnings   91

9   The misinterpretation of graduate work   101

10   Conclusion   117

References   125

Index   167

About the author

Gerbrand Tholen is Senior Lecturer in Sociology at City, University of London. He is the author of *Graduate Work: Skills, Credentials, Careers, and Labour Markets* (2017).

1

Introduction

In early 2020, the UK government announced a plan to introduce Ofsted-style rankings for English universities. A key measure of quality would be graduate earnings. Courses associated with lower salaries would be labelled as failing by the Office for Students. The Department for Education commented: 'The government subsidises around 50% of the cost of higher education and it is only fair that this funding is used as efficiently as possible, so students can be confident they are getting good value for money' (Fazackerley, 2020). In 2022, Minister for Higher and Further Education Michelle Donelan commented on the idea that students unhappy with their course should be able to apply for a refund of their tuition fees, stating: 'Absolutely. They are consumers, at the end of the day. They're paying a substantial amount of money that's an investment in their own lives. They deserve that appeal right' (Tominey, 2022).

It is now accepted that those who pay for higher education (HE), both the government and student, can make demands on providers to uphold quality standards. Regulatory control of the HE sector is thought to help ensure competition and consumer protection akin to regulation in other markets. It is also accepted that graduates' labour market outcomes are essential quality indicators of the education that they have received. Universities are held accountable if their students' investments lead to relatively low wage returns. This type of reasoning would have made far less sense to anyone involved in HE 50 years ago. Yet, in 2022, HE is now increasingly treated as driven by a market for education and its courses seen as economic investments. Specifically in England, the rise of tuition fees to over £9,000 a year and the near elimination of direct government funding for university teaching has transformed the HE landscape. The removal of the cap on student numbers and more direct competition for students have likewise been experienced as key changes in how HE functions. How did we get to this situation?

This book is about the much-maligned marketisation of HE, that is, the greater reliance on the use of markets in its management and functioning, applying economic theory of the market to the provision of education (Brown, 2011a, p 1). This means that supply and demand for university activities, most markedly education, are expected to be balanced through a price mechanism, where possible. In this line of thinking, students become in the first place consumers and are expected to choose between the educational options on offer based on perceived value for them (including price, quality and availability). They will experience HE as a consumption good, or an investment product. HE institutions will act as market providers, vendors of educational programmes. Concerns about marketisation have been part of the debate on the HE sector for decades within the UK and many other countries (Gibbs, 2001; Bragg, 2007; Slaughter and Cantwell, 2012). Specifically, the dominance of market rationales in the management of HE and increasing competition to drive up quality have been met by expressions of great concern worldwide (Baldwin and James, 2000; Wright and Ørberg, 2017; Zaloom, 2019).

Marketisation has fundamentally changed the English HE sector. A key example is the altered relationship between the state and the HE sector. Instead of HE being fully controlled by market forces, the government heavily regulates institutions, imposing markets and competition measures, and reducing the autonomy of HE institutions. Journalist and commentator Peter Wilby made an interesting observation on the current state of English universities:

> Today every university operates as a business, making its living in a globalised marketplace. Every university has remodelled its governing bodies along corporate lines. Every university gets most of its income from private sources. Paradoxically, every university is also, mainly through the funding agencies and their 'quality' indicators, subject to a degree of state control that would have been unthinkable 50 years ago. (Wilby, 2020)

Marketisation also has changed how we understand university education and the degrees it awards. The discourse of marketisation positions HE as a private good, and other meanings become largely suppressed. In particular, policymakers and politicians emphasise that a degree should be considered an investment made by the students. As a result, growing concerns continue to emerge on whether the investments are sound and hold HE institutions responsible for the labour market outcomes of their graduates. As Tory MP Neil O'Brien commented: 'Too many students are effectively being mis-sold a university education' (Sellgren, 2019b).

Despite the growing chorus of critical voices against more marketisation (for a wide range of reasons), including from the Labour Party, most clearly expressed in its 2019 manifesto, HE has been driven towards further marketisation instead of a reduction. How can we understand this ongoing support for the idea that HE should be (further) driven by competition, choice and the price mechanism? The ongoing marketisation of HE is regularly regarded as part of a wider trend of neoliberal reform of the public sector and public services. Others disagree and see it as a logical outcome of a long-term process to sustain mass participation in HE. This book argues that we need to look more closely at how marketisation has been rationalised by governments. Specifically, we need to understand a specific narrative on the nature of modern work and labour markets supporting the arguments for marketisation. This narrative highlights the role of HE for so-called individual human capital investment. It actively builds on ideas on the nature of Western economic development, globalisation and the importance of high-skilled work within the economy. The desire to create a more educated workforce helped improve HE access and increase participation. But in the English context, it also led to policies to increase competition between HE institutions, with students increasingly positioned as consumers and institutions working to improve according to 'consumer demands'. Once the HE sector had been framed as the key facilitator of economic success and individual labour market opportunity, the need for increasing competition, choice and personal responsibility made sense.

This book will help explain how the understanding of work and the labour market actively shaped the arguments used to support marketisation, delineating crucial political and economic contexts to which the perceptions about the need for a market and competition within HE occurred. The purpose for universities to foster human understanding through open-ended inquiry has been overshadowed by the idea that they foremost should actively help promote the knowledge-based economy and, subsequently, the opportunity for young people to master the skills to succeed in the new economy. Over time, HE was seen increasingly as a solution to broader economic and social problems, and HE policies became a central part of an economic strategy. The promise of the knowledge-based economy made the continuous growth of HE needed for the economy and provided the premise to recognise HE participation principally as a sound economic investment. A condition for *optimal* human capital investment was an HE system based on choice, competition and personal responsibility. HE institutions were positioned as market suppliers of education and should be managed and incentivised as such. The competition for students would drive efficiency, quality and, equally importantly, their utility in developing the human capital employers need. Students over time were expected to pay for their own education and to act and make decisions upon labour market signals. Their market interests were seen as aligned with the interests of both employers and the state. Market choice and competition would improve and enhance the role HE could play within the economy. Influential human capital theories provided the scientific underpinning, confirming how we should understand the nature of HE and who should pay for it.

The book also shows that the conceptualisations of graduate work and the graduate labour market, which has driven the marketisation project, are flawed and based on an idealised relationship between HE and high-skilled work. It will do so by assessing the assumptions made by policymakers alongside some of the existing empirical evidence on the graduate labour market. The book demonstrates that this evidence does not support the policy understanding of graduate labour and, thus, there is a clear need to question the current rationale for further marketisation.

A sizeable body of scholarly works has dedicated itself to describing and explaining how and why marketisation is changing the HE landscape (Molesworth et al, 2011; R. Brown, 2013; John and Fanghanel, 2015; Watts, 2017). I aim to contribute to this literature by proposing a renewed understanding of how marketisation has been justified and rationalised. Although the role of, for instance, human capital's influence in HE marketisation has been observed before (for example, Holmwood, 2016), a detailed account of how skills and the labour market are presented discursively is missing. In addition, a coherent evaluation of the assumptions will strengthen the existing critiques of the justification of HE marketisation. Although many factors shape political decisions, some being idiosyncratic and opportune, I will demonstrate that settled assumptions about the nature of the role of HE in the economy and individual opportunity drive HE policies and underpin the need for marketisation within the English context. As such, the main argument of the book questions conventional wisdom that marketisation is mainly a logical outcome of affordability concerns in a mass HE society or as a natural phenomenon caused by a general right-wing or neoliberal political force affecting the public sector and HE.

In this book, I will predominantly write about 'universities'. A university is of course a type of institution, and other HE providers such as further education (FE) colleges represent important actors in the UK's HE landscape. Yet within the debates on HE, universities are often singled out. Also, this book will mainly look at marketisation within the educational role of the HE institution rather than research, which also has been affected by the drive for marketisation (R. Brown, 2013; McCaig, 2018). Yet the argumentation about the need for markets and competition in the organisation and funding of research by universities would require a much wider assessment, which is not within the scope of this book. The focus of the analysis is mainly on England. It has less relevance for the other nations of the United Kingdom (in particular Scotland). After creating devolved assemblies in 2000, government policy for HE in Wales, Northern Ireland and Scotland received separate jurisdiction. Recent drastic marketisation reforms apply primarily to England. However, many of the pressures of marketisation arguments are felt all over the globe. To what extent these debates draw on the understanding of graduate work will depend on the national context. This book concentrates on the English HE system as a unique case of marketisation, but it will also aim to draw parallels with other HE systems and review evidence from other countries.

Marketisation

What do we mean by marketisation? Marketisation is different from commercialisation (running HE primarily for financial gain) and privatisation (a growing influence of private capital and ownership on running HE), although they often go hand in hand. It is also distinct from commodification (the transformation of education into a product acquired and marketed like other commodities); although this should be seen as part of marketisation in my view (see Chapter 2). Ultimately, it is the dominance of the market mechanism, which we find in the free market, that defines marketisation. Jongbloed (2003) explains: 'In market-driven systems, individual choice behaviour is stressed. More emphasis is placed on the individual entity (i.e., the student, university and college). Marketisation policies try to push for self-steering and accountable entities that decide on the basis of reliable information' (p 114). Marketisation is expressed through some key market principles that have permeated much of the HE system in England:

- pursuit of markets and competition between universities and courses;
- private sector managerialism and rationalism in the governance of universities;
- transferring the cost of HE to students;
- student choice concept of customer–provider relationships in HE between students and institutions;
- the drive for value for money towards students and the taxpayer.

We will go into more detail for each of these in the next chapter.

Across the world, national HE sectors have experienced a gradual process of the introduction of markets over the last decades (Williams, 2004; Foskett, 2011). Many governments have introduced reforms to increase market-led coordinating of HE, balancing its provision through the price mechanism. The marketisation of HE is not a uniform phenomenon and some countries, despite growing pressures, have largely stayed free from marketisation. Yet in no country is HE completely opened up to free market competition. Also, the market in the HE system is far from free in the English context. As Brown (2013, p 25) points out, a 'pure' market would have legally autonomous institutions, little or no regulation of market entry and no regulatory limits on the prices charged (fees) or the numbers enrolled (among others). This is currently unthinkable for the UK at least. For many countries, a form of marketisation occurred alongside the growth of HE itself. Alongside marketisation, internationalisation is a key characteristic that has defined HE in both Western and non-Western countries.

Within the academic literature as well as in the media, marketisation as a driving force in HE is not only well documented but also frequently evaluated

(Brown, 2011a, 2013; Molesworth et al, 2011; John and Fanghanel, 2015; Willetts, 2017). Some have welcomed marketisation as providing better value for its users, that is, students and the taxpayer. Proponents see it as the most sensible route to run and finance mass HE, improving accountability and being more likely to aid economic development (Brown, 2011a). Others feel that market forces are destroying HE as we know it and turning it into a commodified institution that no longer holds integrity and substance (Deem, 2001; Gibbs, 2001; Barnett, 2003). To satisfy an economic model of education, students' educational achievement loses its intrinsic value of higher learning for an instrumental one (Collini, 2018). Others have argued that HE has lost its public role as a social institution due to increasing marketisation and commercialisation (De La Fuente, 2002; Heller, 2016).

Three key rationales for marketisation are outlined by Brown (2015). First, the market is deemed to know best where the resources need to be allocated. Paying students are thought to be financially motivated actors who are incentivised to optimise decisions on their HE investments. Markets are deemed to stimulate the raising of standards, delivery and achievement (Dill, 1997; Williams, 1997). HE will have to respond to students' needs and preferences or lose business. HE institutions must continuously seek to gain an advantage in the market in terms of quality of service (or in theory price), and as a result, they become more attentive to students. Second, marketisation aligns with the notion that those who use and profit from a good or service need to pay for it. Mass HE has led to an increasing cost burden to the taxpayer who is (or is thought to be) less willing or able to fund it. Meanwhile, HE participation leads to a wide array of private benefits, including higher wages, job quality and positive health effects (Willetts, 2017). Therefore, it is only fair that the students should contribute a reasonable share of the costs. Third, marketisation is also thought to lead to greater value for money for students and the taxpayer, as institutions can compete on price due to variability in tuition fees. Competition for students is also thought to lead to superior responsiveness to the needs of students and promoting innovative educational approaches and methods to attract new customers.

Policy background

How did the growing reliance on markets and competition happen? We need to avoid any historical determinism here. The current state of HE in Britain results from a long and changeable history in which various agents, students, university staff members and policymakers have transformed HE. To avoid any teleological fallacy, we need to see the transformation of HE as the outcome of many independent processes and actions of individual groups, each with their own interests, views and understandings. It is very much open to change, and the direction that it has taken is not set in stone.

A key reason for this is that there is limited agreement on the aims of HE, what needs to be taught, who should be able to access it, and who should pay for it. As Coates (2016, p 75) reminds us, 'there is no agreement – and not even significant conversation – about the appropriate scale, funding and expectations for universities'.

Marketisation has been a gradual process in the UK context. Over time, marketisation increased incrementally through policy and statutory changes (Foskett, 1996; Williams, 2004; Brown, 2013; McCaig, 2018). Various governments, both Labour and Conservative (including the coalition) have contributed to it and supported the consensus on the need for market competition in improving and managing the HE sector in England. I will, in brief, highlight some key policy moments, focusing in particular on changes in student finance, access and quality control.

In the 1980s, the UK HE sector showed strong remnants of an elite system. The UK had one of the lowest participation rates in HE of any advanced industrial country. The taxpayer covered the cost of it almost completely. Tuition costs were primarily funded through block grants to institutions and through students' Local Education Authorities, then reimbursed by central government. Full-time UK domiciled students studying for a first degree also received maintenance grants. By the 1990s, the pressure on HE made the calls for forms of marketisation stronger, although some had already taken shape in the Thatcher governments, as we will see in the next chapter. By then, the student numbers kept increasing and the HE sector suffered from severe underfunding, with decreasing funding per student leaving universities stretched. Universities and polytechnics were unified by 'The Further and Higher Education Act' in 1992. Funding Councils were created to allocate government grants to individual institutions. In 1997, the National Committee of Inquiry into Higher Education, appointed by the Conservative government and chaired by Ronald Dearing, published 'Higher education in the learning society'. It made 93 recommendations in all. A key message was that students themselves should contribute towards the cost of their tuition. All full-time undergraduates should contribute £1,000 per year of study after graduation on an income-contingent basis. It also argued for the expansion of student numbers and that the government should increase funding for research. It was a watershed moment as it fundamentally changed the relationship between HE institutions and their students. Increasing participation was deemed necessary, and the positioning of students as paying users paved the way for further market-inspired policy change. The report demonstrated an awareness that marketisation in public policy in general was there to stay:

> There have been moves towards the stronger interplay of market forces, in order to increase competition between providers and thereby

encourage efficiency, and an emphasis on standards and accountability. These general trends have been reflected in higher education through the introduction of new funding methodologies, new approaches to quality assurance and an emerging focus on the 'consumer' rather than the 'provider'. Although the emphasis and the mechanisms may change over time, we expect there to be a continuing concern to promote efficiency, informed choice, quality and accountability over the next twenty years. (NCIHE, 1997, p 50)

For the first time in HE policy history, the virtues of student choice were extolled. Institutions were encouraged to respond to maintain or increase recruitment and income. The report claimed that student choice would drive institutional responsiveness. The contribution towards tuition would drive students to be more demanding of their institutions. Yet it was reasonable that the level of contribution should not deter anyone from participation and the report recommended financial support for those with limited means.

The newly elected Labour government brought in the 'Teaching and Higher Education Act' in 1998 and introduced annual flat-rate up-front tuition fees of £1,000, together with income-contingent loans. Means-tested maintenance grants for living costs were changed into maintenance loans for all. The Labour government believed the Act would widen participation and fairness. We now make a five-year jump to 2003, in which a new proposal emerged to share further the costs of HE between student and taxpayer in 'The future of higher education' white paper. The Higher Education Act 2004 provided for 'top-up', variable tuition fees to replace the existing up-front fees. Institutions could choose to charge students a fee of between £0 and £3,000 per year. The maximum would be capped at £3,000, rising with inflation. It also introduced loans to cover the cost of tuition fees, repayable on an income-contingent basis with any outstanding debt written off after 25 years, as well as more maintenance loans and maintenance grants for students with limited means. The newly created Office for Fair Access (OFFA) was to ensure fair access to HE for under-represented groups, monitoring how institutions would promote fair access, particularly to students from poorer backgrounds, through bursaries and outreach activities. It would also regulate fees. Yet price competition never appeared. The hope that HE institutions would set variable fees for their students to compete on price and offer discounts through bursaries and scholarships was unfounded as all universities charged the full £3,000 a year for all their courses. There was a strong sentiment in government that these changes were grounded in a fair distribution of costs in relation to the benefits of HE without becoming a deterrent from participation in HE. But it is also clear that expansion of student choice leads to great improvement in efficiency and management; the demands from the student as consumers would drive higher quality education.

Six years later, the 2010 Browne Review called for increasing and widening HE participation and improving HE quality. It also planned for new funding models to reduce the sector's reliance on the taxpayer. It repeated the points made in the earlier policy documents that those who directly benefit from HE should be more responsible for its costs. It rehearsed the arguments around the importance of student choice for quality and value for money. Yet here, the review radically aimed to link student choice to its funding proposal. It envisioned a free-market competition between HE institutions for students based on price and quality and recommended the withdrawal of almost all government funding to HE institutions and for students to pay for higher tuition fees via loans. There would be no upper limit as to how much could be charged but those charging over £6,000 would be required to pay a levy to the government. Kernohan (2020a) reminds us that none of the Browne Review recommendations were implemented, and its conclusions ignored. The Browne Review does, however, offer an important policy moment in government thinking about greater student choice and marketisation as it imagined a fully functioning competitive market in HE.

As a response to the Browne Review, the 2011 white paper 'Higher education: Students at the heart of the system' announced that the government would drastically reduce government funding to HE institutions and install significantly higher tuition fees repaid via loans. It applied a cap of £9,000 per annum for full-time courses and £6,500 for part-time courses, giving the institution the freedom to charge what they wanted within the upper boundary. It is the spirit of the free market competition, and the reliance on student choice to improve the quality and quantity, that is noteworthy. It directly ties student finance regime support to student choice, trusting that student choice drives price and quality competition. It was argued that the demand for HE was still larger than the number of places available. Unmet demand is both unfair as well as economically unsound:

> However, the current system of controls limits student choice, because institutions are prevented from expanding in response to demand from applicants. That in turn protects institutions with lower levels of demand, which fill their places with students who cannot get to their first-choice institution. If left unchanged, the current system would also prevent new providers from entering the market, as they have no means to get access to a student allocation – this would need to be taken from an existing provider. Reform is essential if we are to secure the benefits of improved competition and diversity. Another issue is unmet demand from the growing number of prospective students unable to find places at any higher education institution. (DBIS, 2011, p 48)

The market would decide the demand for and supply of education: 'We have no target for the "right" size of the higher education system but believe it should evolve in response to demand from students and employers, reflecting particularly the wider needs of the economy' (DBIS, 2011, p 61). In September 2012, HE institutions in England were permitted to triple their annual tuition fee from £3,000 to £9,000. With the reduction in the teaching grant the government's control over student numbers was loosened. Universities could enrol unlimited students achieving at least AAB A-level grades or equivalent (extended to ABB the next year). Maintenance grants for students from low-income homes were replaced by loans announced in July 2015 by the then Chancellor, George Osborne, in his Budget. Osborne defended the change based on the notion of a 'basic unfairness in asking taxpayers to fund grants for people who are likely to earn a lot more than them' (BBC, 2016). In 2014, the government removed all controls on domestic student numbers (in England).

The 2016 white paper titled 'Success as a knowledge economy' marks another important milestone in HE reform. It is the point where arguably marketisation has become fully accepted, and most of the policies are centred on improving the accessibility and quality of HE through market and choice. It proposed to make it easier to set up 'high quality' universities which would offer more consumer choice in order to give students more choice. It also tried to improve quality through the quality of teaching and ensure labour market outcomes through the Teaching Excellence and Student Outcomes Framework (TEF). Institutions' relative performance in this assessment would have consequences for setting higher fees. The paper argues that what is needed is greater competition between providers, which improves efficiency and teaching quality within the marketplace and offers students more choice in the type of education they want.

The Higher Education and Research Act 2017 that followed made it again clear that competition is the best option to improve quality, participation and responsiveness. A key aim was to establish a regulatory 'architecture' for an HE market built on competition and choice, replacing existing HE regulatory systems with a new single regulator. The Office for Students (OfS) was created to regulate the new student market and oversee whether competition and choice are expressed in the system and assess quality and standards. It unapologetically defended the interest of consumers (that is, the student), with taxpayers and employers coming in a close second. Although it set itself the task to protect the institutional autonomy of HE providers, the interest for students was defined by greater choice, quality and competition between English HE providers, and the need to promote value for money in the provision of HE by English providers. The Teaching Excellence and Student Outcomes Framework (TEF) also became a reality for England. The new exercise was expected to drive up quality as underperforming institutions would seek to raise their teaching standards in order to maintain student numbers and raise fees. It assesses universities on the quality of the student experience, teaching standards and labour market outcomes for graduates. It includes contact hours students receive and the class sizes in which they are taught. Courses and institutions with successful assessments would see greater demand. Courses that were unable to raise standards or differentiate themselves in the sector would eventually withdraw. McCaig (2018) observes that the Act introduced new forms of risk which shifted from the state to institutions and students (p 95). Institutions would risk losing students and even closure as no prevention of failure was guaranteed by the government. According to McCaig, the risks of exit and replacement, combined with access to new providers, were crucial in constructing a market. Student choice in combination with high tuition fees also increased risk for students, which again the TEF and the provision of detailed data on quality and outcomes would ameliorate.

On 30 May 2019, the Conservative government published a report from its post-18 review panel, presenting detailed proposals to reform higher and further education funding. Similar to the Browne Review, the 'Augar Review' offered a broad assessment of both the strengths and weaknesses of post-18 education in England. It identified many key problems, including further education and apprenticeships and the decline in part-time study and lifelong learning. Overall, it said more on FE than HE, proposing significant support for FE as well as lifelong learning. Yet it also provided answers on how to finance HE after a political backlash against the increase in fees (and Labour's flirting with the idea to abolish tuition fees). It argued that the student finance system should be altered to reduce the overall cost to the taxpayer of the student finance system. It somewhat moderated the financial pressure on students to study. It proposed lowering the annual cap on undergraduate fees from £9,000 to £7,500 per year, the reintroduction of maintenance grants and the removal of interest on loans. Yet it also made the student more responsible for the cost by proposing that any unpaid debts would not be cancelled until 40 years after graduating, rather than 25 years. Also, it argued that repayments should start at a lower point, when graduates earn £23,000 rather than £25,725. Although the report was clear in that the market cannot be left alone and government should play a role, it solidified the support for some market-based changes. There was a distinct concern about value for money that HE institutions are delivering. It problematised the increase of the costs of delivering traditionally lower-cost subjects. Subjects such as business, the creative arts and social studies create less value than others due to great numbers of students in these fields and cost far less than, for instance, science, technology, engineering and mathematics (STEM) courses. University funding would move away from those seen as 'low value' and targeted towards the high-cost subjects and priority areas in high demand. The Augar Review seemed to be wary of the downsides to increased competition for students. It argued that market competition had not evolved in the way intended, and there was 'extremely limited competition on price but intense competition for students through quality of offer, extensive marketing, and other inducements' (Augar, 2019, p 80). It did not fundamentally challenge marketisation and supported market competition under specific conditions offering choice and increased quality for students.

At the time of writing (March 2022), very little has changed in the HE policy landscape due to the political attention that the COVID-19 crisis, as well as Brexit, have taken up. It is unclear what the Augar Review's political influence will be. There are expectations that more government pressure for further marketisation is on the horizon (Fazackerley, 2020; Weale, 2020a).

Layout of the book

The argument this book presents unfolds itself as follows. The next chapter, Chapter 2, provides the context for the analysis. It further explains how marketisation has penetrated the modern HE system. It distinguishes three key dimensions of marketisation that are particularly relevant for the book. These are user-pay finance, managerialism and commodification. It demonstrates how these processes increased the role of markets, choice and competition in the provision of HE. It also elucidates the role of the state in marketisation.

The next three chapters deal with HE policy discourses that support HE marketisation in the English context. The chapters analyse key policy documents and illuminate how the discursive representation of work, skills and the labour market help construct the justification of marketisation. Chapter 3 focuses on how the role of education in the economy is understood. Here it outlines distinct assumptions on the importance of university graduates within the modern economy, inspired by the idea of the knowledge-based economy. It demonstrates that the ideological adherence to this ideal emphasises the need for HE expansion and later on the importance of inserting the right type of graduate skills in the labour market to achieve economic prosperity. A problematisation of whether HE was able to develop the right skills was salient to make a case for further marketisation

Chapter 4 examines how the role of education in work and the labour market is understood. It shows that the policy documents presume that the skills employers demand can be developed in HE. Yet universities are increasingly held to task to support the economy, adjusting to employer skills demand and ensuring the work-readiness of students. Employers, students and the state were thought to have a shared interest in making HE more attuned to the economy's needs. The importance of market competition to improve the quality of HE and the employability of its graduates was seen as desirable.

Chapter 5 demonstrates the reliance on Human Capital Theory (HCT) to understand the graduate labour market within HE policy discourse. The theory's expected relationship between education, skills and rewards justify marketisation in HE. The market for HE provision is seen as directly linked to labour market outcomes. The skills that employers need are closely aligned to the skills that universities teach. Marketisation makes sense if students are responsible for their labour market outcomes as well to ensure optimal human capital investment.

The next three chapters review the evidence concerning the assumptions made in the policy discourse, outlined in Chapters 3, 4 and 5. The chapters demonstrate that many of the labour market axioms in place to persuade audiences that more competition is needed in HE are overly simplistic or only partly true. Chapter 6 investigates how well the narrative of the knowledge-based society holds up. Here it finds that some key characteristics of contemporary Anglo-Saxon capitalism contradict how the knowledge-based economy was initially thought of. The greater use of technology may not necessarily reward graduate workers. Also, many so-called knowledge workers do not have strong labour market power as has often been assumed. As a result, graduate workers are misunderstood in terms of their expected status and earnings but also within their role in economic development.

Chapter 7 examines some of the evidence of the nature of modern graduate work. It will demonstrate that the role HE plays in skill development has been overstated. The employer demand for graduates is much wider than merely their human capital developed at HE. Many graduates face difficulties in capitalising on their skills and knowledge. This is reflected in the research on overqualification and skill utilisation. Also, the employer demand for degrees may substantially lie in the value of qualifications as a sifting mechanism within the graduate labour market.

Chapter 8 focuses on earnings. It highlights the unequal earning distribution within the graduate labour market and challenges the idea that earnings accurately reflect human capital investment or even perceived productivity. Here it expands on some non-educational factors that fundamentally shape earnings within the graduate labour market.

Chapter 9 reflects on why marketisation is so hard to reverse. It warns that one of the problems in changing the current drive for more marketisation is that many of the assumptions on graduate labour are shared by other policy and political projects. The chapter deals with three of them. These are: the idea of an education-based meritocracy; employability as means of individual empowerment and responsibility; and the reliance on HCT within economic, social and educational policies. The chapter demonstrates that each of them is problematic in their own right.

Finally, Chapter 10 concludes the book. It reflects on what resistance against marketisation in HE may look like and how this may shape how we imagine what the HE institutions are for. It ends with some thoughts on what the future may hold for HE in the UK and beyond.

2

Dimensions of marketisation

Marketisation has been widely acknowledged as a driving force in modern higher education (HE) systems (Lynch, 2006; Molesworth et al, 2011; Brown, 2013; McGettigan, 2013). This chapter explains how the role of competition and markets has transformed HE. It outlines three areas in which marketisation has manifested itself with the current HE landscape in England. These are: the rise of user-pay finance; increasing managerialism; and increasing commodification. Many other influences have been identified as salient impacts of marketisation, including growing within-institution differentiation, changing institutional identity, growing institutional instability, changing societal impact and commercialisation. The consequences covered here are the ones that can be most directly associated with the marketisation policy drive.

User-pay

The first key impact and at the same time a cause of marketisation of HE lies in how HE has been financed. Decisions around who should pay for it, in practice, are entwined by debates about whether the market should coordinate education provision. Once the cost of HE has been shifted to its users, rather than from public funds, it positions the institution and student differently in relation to each other. The market–consumer relationship provides a blueprint of how each of them should behave. As explained in the previous chapter, user-pay schemes are thought to lead to a system of financially motivated actors who are incentivised to pay more critical attention to their consumption and supply of HE. As Jongbloed (2003, p 114) explains: 'Marketisation policies try to push for self-steering and accountable entities that decide on the basis of reliable information. Through marketisation policies, students and colleges are encouraged to make their own cost-benefit analyses.'

In the English context, the perhaps most apparent change in HE provision is the rise in (undergraduate) tuition fees. Although state support for either student or institution has not always been a significant feature of the HE system, from the early 20th century this gradually changed as the state started funding its institutions. By the middle of the century, the state provided 90 per cent of university income (Newton et al, 2017, p 5). By 1962, there was free tuition for full-time domestic students, combined with maintenance grants and loans for students. The year 1998 saw the introduction of tuition fees paid by undergraduate students in England. The fees of up to £1,000 per year were to be paid up-front, but means-tested such that low-income students would still face no tuition fees. In 2006, tuition fees rose to £3,000 per year, and were no longer charged up-front but via an expansion of the income-contingent loan. Higher fees pleased Conservatives concerned at the rising contribution by the taxpayer. Labour also saw the increase in fees as a means to increase participation, aiding social mobility. Students from middle- and upper-class families were the beneficiaries of university, enjoying private returns from their publicly funded degrees. Charging tuition fees would bring in funds from those groups while offering opportunities to support low-income students (Murphy et al, 2019). In September 2012, HE institutions in England were permitted to triple their annual tuition fee from £3,000 to £9,000. The loans were still income-contingent, with a threshold for repayment of £21,000 per year with positive real interest rates applied. Teaching grants were cut radically, with lecture-based subjects receiving no government subsidies for teaching students. The intended competition on price between institutions never materialised as practically all institutions have opted to charge the maximum for the full-time undergraduate courses. The political aim of establishing an undergraduate market through the promotion of differentiation in tuition fees has not been lost, however (DBIS, 2015, 2016). Fee variation remains to be seen by many as the necessary mechanism for student consumers to be able to drive improvements in quality, affordability and differentiation effectively. Whether the fee increase has decreased the pressure on the public finances remains to be seen. Tuition fees are not paid up-front. Instead, students cover the cost of their degree through loans and only repay when they earn above an earnings threshold (currently £27,295 a year). How much the increase has lowered the burden on the taxpayer remains somewhat unclear. Furthermore, the sell-off of the loan book allows private capital to flow into HE finance and so this reliance on financial markets could increase the stability of the finance model (Hale, 2018).

What the increase in tuition fees undoubtedly achieved was to shift the purpose of HE towards a private good, and its benefits can be referenced against its potential future economic exchange value. The increase in tuition fees represented a massive transformation in the university income structure. Funding for universities has shifted towards fees (Bolton, 2021); the proportion from grants has fallen sharply while income from fees has risen. This has made universities financially dependent on the private market for students with around 80 per cent of universities' income derived from this market. The postgraduate market offers more opportunities to differentiate in fees. The cost of the average classroom-based postgraduate taught course for UK students was almost £9,500 in 2021–2, about £1,200 more than the year before (Baker, 2021).

Incentivised to invest in expanding their teaching operation to capture larger shares of the market as well as invest in buildings and facilities to help attract students, universities increasingly resort to private capital markets, that is, through private borrowing. Top-tier universities such as Oxford, Cambridge and Manchester have been able to sell public bond deals. For the vast majority, the private placement market is the only option, leading to large long-term debts (Gore, 2018) and reliance on financial markets. The pressures to raise private finance will lead to extra pressures to demonstrate financial health, shaping how the universities are run and how they behave. Through financialisation, universities will increasingly identify with and mimic for-profit corporations who find themselves facing similar pressures and incentives.

Revenue streams are highly correlated with the ability to attract students. Domestic student demand has been volatile since the removal of the student cap. Some elite Russell Group institutions, for example, have made a large increase in intake compared to some newer, post-1992 universities where the impact has been largely negative. Traditionally, the international student market provided a reliable income stream. Yet it remains highly competitive and open to shocks, as the COVID-19 crisis has shown. The latter also affected income from student housing tremendously, creating large financial risks for universities (Staton, 2021a). Universities have invested heavily in areas not directly related to teaching to attract students, such as new buildings and sports centres. The quality of facilities are thought to shape a student's choice of university. About 45 per cent of tuition fee income is spent on the direct costs of teaching (Hillman et al, 2018).

Value for money

A consequence of the fee regime is a heightened awareness or concern for the value for money that HE delivers to students. This traditionally was driven by concerns of the burden on the taxpayer. Yet with the rises in tuition fees, greater scrutiny is placed on the extent to which universities offer their students value for money. The recommendations of the 2010 Browne Review, and subsequent introduction of £9,000 fees, fundamentally changed the relationship between the student and their institution. The term 'value for money' has become embedded in policy discourse, expressing concerns over the quality of the product students are receiving as well as the labour market earnings they may expect from their investment. The drive for value for money is reflected in the efforts of the Office for Students (OfS). The market regulator states that assessing value for money is one of its core objectives:

> Students receive value for money when they experience the full benefits of higher education – both during their studies and afterwards – in exchange for the effort, time and money they invest. … Taxpayers receive

value for money when higher education providers use public money and students fees efficiently and effectively to deliver graduates, from all backgrounds, who contribute to society and the economy. (OfS, 2019, pp 3–4)

The quest to determine value for money for HE as a whole or through individual institutions or courses has been recently answered by a wide range of other institutions such as the National Audit Office (2017), Commons Education Committee (2017), House of Lords Economic Affairs Committee (2017), Higher Education Policy Institute (2018) and research by *The Times* (Hurst, 2019).

The Teaching Excellence and Student Outcomes Framework (TEF) administered by the OfS is a key tool to help evaluate and increase the value for money by improving the quality of teaching and incentivising universities to focus on graduate outcomes. Education minister Jo Johnson (2017b) noted that the TEF 'will tackle head-on the uncomfortable questions that many young people are starting to ask about their university; that many taxpayers are asking about the support they are providing for the system; and that many employers are asking about the supply of graduates entering the workforce'. The TEF assessment draws heavily on course satisfaction survey data but equally on the analysis of graduate outcomes, using the Longitudinal Educational Outcomes data set, which looks at employment and earnings of HE graduates at one, three and five years after graduation. It is thought that students want hard data on whether a particular course at a particular institution will lead to sustained graduate-level employment or the return in investment in terms of graduate wages.

The government has, over time, become more concerned by the alleged existence of 'low-value degrees' that do not offer student returns in the labour market. Increasingly, the government also applied this logic to courses that are seen as less important to the economy and society. For instance, in July 2021, the government announced that funding for arts courses would be reduced to target taxpayers' money towards subjects deemed more needed in the economy, such as science, technology, engineering and mathematics (STEM) subjects (Staton, 2021b). Early in 2022, the OfS set out regulations proposals to sanction institutions that were providing poor value for money to students (Adams, 2022). It outlined minimum acceptable outcomes for students with thresholds for drop-out rates, course completion and graduate employment. Institutions would have to pass these to avoid further investigation and penalties.

Managerialism

A second area in which marketisation has shaped HE relates to how institutions have been managed and organised, using new managerialist principles that mirror those used in the private sector. Universities are becoming business-like entities (Connell and Galasiński, 1998). According to Naidoo (2016, p 39), the incentive for marketisation is driven by the assumption that 'management principles derived from the public sector which monitor, measure, compare and judge professional activities will enhance higher education functioning'. HE institutions act as if they were part of a free market environment or according to corporate management standards. Universities use management principles derived from the private sector to monitor, measure and evaluate their processes and outputs. Managerialism represents the dominance of the interests of managers within the organisation and the supremacy of management ideas in how they should be run. Managerial principles are not only enacted by managers or management but also systematically embedded within the organisation as well as its culture. According to Shepherd (2018, p 1669), the main characteristics of managerialism include:

- the adoption of a more business-like approach and private sector practices;
- the establishment of a management culture;
- a rational approach to management (such as strategic planning and objective setting);
- a strengthening of the line management function (such as performance management);
- adoption of human resource management techniques to secure employee commitment;
- a shift from inputs and processes to outputs and outcomes;
- more measurement and quantification of outputs (such as performance indicators).

Over time, a sizeable body of literature has observed similar characteristics to be present in UK academia (Dill, 1997; Miller, 1998; Deem, 2001; Deem and Brehony, 2005; Deem et al, 2007). Already in 1997, Williams identified various management principles to be pertinent in British universities:

- radical reduction in the number of decisions made by committees;
- rigorous costing of all activities;
- attribution of overhead costs to all activities;
- pricing of contracts to cover full overhead costs;
- documentation of all aspects of teaching and student assessment;
- 'out-sourcing' of non-core activities;
- establishment of companies to handle income generating activities;
- creation of logos and other measures to stress corporate identity. (Williams, 1997, p 286)

It remains up for debate to what extent marketisation has created managerialism. They can be seen as two sides of the same coin. HE institutions mimic management approaches from the private sector as if their institution were in a free market in which profit motive and efficiencies are defined by market parameters called 'quasi-markets'. The development of these quasi-markets linked to managerialist frameworks in HE has altered relations within and between institutions, as well as the nature of rewards and sanctions in academic life (Dill, 1997; Williams, 1997; Deem, 2001; Naidoo et al, 2011).

Managerialism has infiltrated the job role of academics and their tasks, pursuits and incentives (Sang et al, 2015; Vican et al, 2020). It is sometimes juxtaposed against the interest of academics (and their freedom and autonomy), yet academics themselves now see it as the institutional logic of universities (Shields and Watermeyer, 2020). Academic work has changed due to managerial pressures. This includes many areas in which academia used to be fairly autonomous. As Middleton (2000, p 544) illustrates: 'Administrative and financial authority is decentralised through devolved budgeting and the use of income streams to determine course provision and individual workloads, but lower-level decision-makers are subject to stringent financial imperatives and market constraints.'

Part of managerialism in HE is the greater separation of academic work and management activities in both teaching and research. Managers have put increased control and regulation of the work of academics in particular through performance and productivity audit mechanisms. Their assessment has been treated as so-called 'market proxies', creating pseudo markets in the process (Ozga, 2009). The 'new managerialism' monitors employee performance (and encourages self-monitoring too). Ball (2003, 2012a, 2012b) gives much insight into the dominance of performativity in HE in which effort, values, purposes and self-understanding are all shaped according to measures and comparisons of output. This leads to a level and intensity of accountability that takes up most of the academic sense of personal worth and the worth of others, with academics being morally subjected to the performance system that constantly drives individuals to perform. Performativity cultures focus on measurement, leading to misrepresentation and devaluation of the meaning of academic work. Ball (2012b, p 30) notes that: 'the first-order effect of performativity is to reorient pedagogical and scholarly activities towards those which are likely to have a positive impact on measurable performance outcomes and are a deflection of attention away from aspects of social, emotional or moral development that have no immediate measurable performative value'.

The decline in autonomy can also be observed at the level of institutions (Enders et al, 2013). Increasingly, institutions have reduced opportunities to express their own purpose other than that dictated by the regulated market.

In contrast, historically, quality control in universities was heavily dependent upon self-regulation. Despite the influence of the market, state control has also increased (Shattock and Horvath, 2021). The audit demands of the state are often seen as part of a wider public service reform developed and maintained since Thatcher's administrations. For instance, the Education Reform Act of 1988 abolished University Grants committees. The New Public Management (NPM) concept is often used to capture the (neoliberal) policy doctrine applied in the UK public sector (and elsewhere). The term can mean many different things and represent a broad spectrum of changes in public sector reform approach (Gruening, 2001). Yet we can still have some heuristic value for our purposes here. In general, NPM strives to make government funding dependent on how well the public sector mirrors the free market to achieve value for money. According to Ferlie et al (2008, p 335), NPM relies on:

- markets (or quasi-markets) rather than planning;
- strong performance measurement, monitoring and management systems, with the growth of audit systems rather than tacit or self-regulation; and
- empowered and entrepreneurial management rather than collegial public sector professionals and administrators, seeking to produce a smaller, more efficient and more results-orientated public sector.

Similar to 'real' public sector organisations, universities have been subjected to a new public sector management approach in recent decades, reflecting a new relationship to the state and market (Deem, 2001; Deem and Brehony, 2005; By et al, 2008). NPM promoted performance management and customer choice in the UK HE sector, using market incentives and customer choice to increase efficiency and quality (Shattock, 2008). Key consequences were the decline in academic disciplines in governance and the enhanced flexibility of the academic workforce. In doing so, it shifts power from professionals to consumers and managers. For instance, Tolofari (2005) points out how vice-chancellors are acting in the manner of company chief executives.

Ranking

Another much-discussed element of managerialism in HE concerns the use of ranking mechanisms. Ranking becomes part of a wider managerial mode of governance where universities are aligned with market values and fixated on comparative performance and advantage. The ranking mechanism facilitates marketisation by introducing greater competition between and within HE institutions. Institutions' reputations are based on or supported by rankings. This directly impacts how well they can attract students, academic and other professional staff, research funders and partnerships. In particular, ranking has become a reputation-based market instrument to help attract students (David, 2016). Examples nationally are the *Sunday Times University Guide*, *The Times Good University Guide*, *The Guardian University Guide* and globally the *Shanghai Jiao Tong University Academic Ranking of World Universities* and *THES-QS World University Rankings*. Ranking competitions are likewise used to distribute funding and status such as the Research Excellence Framework (REF) and TEF.

The growing importance of ranking can be attributed to many factors outside a broader trend of marketisation. Globalisation and migration patterns have made HE a global marketplace that attracts students from all over the globe. A global benchmark for global consumers, therefore, perhaps would make sense. Yet within the drive by the government for greater marketisation and greater control to deliver outcomes for students, taxpayers, employers and the economy, performance indicators become necessary to monitor progress and produce improvements in quality efficiencies and responsiveness. Ranking mechanisms are thought to shape the incentives for universities and embed the logic of the market within organisational structures and processes. Anderson (cited in Palfreyman and Tapper, 2014, p 72) observes that the market in HE is 'partly a real one, in which change will be driven by student demand, and partly a proxy market in which the state pushes the universities in directions thought desirable by a variety of financial sticks and carrots, backed by audits and targets end performance indicators'.

The influence of ranking has frequently been criticised and seen as an instrument of new managerialism or as part of a neoliberal agenda in which market values suppress other aims of education (Gruber, 2014; Vican et al, 2020). The dominance of ranking has helped reconstitute an internal culture within universities driven by competition. It has shaped the minds of those working in academia towards greater instrumentality and shifted the perceived purposes of universities towards the fulfilment of measurable output. Lynch (2015, p 201) writes:

> One of the most serious implications of rankings is that they direct our attention into a different cognitive and normative order when evaluating higher education. Questions regarding the value, purpose and politics of higher education and rankings get swept aside in the bid to find the best 'method' of ranking. Social justice debates about access, participation and outcomes from higher education are side-lined.

Ranking also may negatively affect how students understand the status of HE institutions, aiding the commodification of HE, to which we will turn next. In 'Rankings and the reshaping of HE', Hazelkorn (2015) demonstrates with the use of institutional surveys how global rankings have reshaped the goals and behaviours of university managers and academic faculty. The book also shows that published league tables have a considerable impact on international student choice-making. Over time, university reputation has become an end in itself in capturing funding and talent acquisition. Global rankings also inform the policies of national governments and are accepted currencies of institutional quality. Hazelkorn notes that 'In many instances, governments have directly adopted or "folded-in" the indicators used by rankings into their own performance measures or used rankings to set targets for system restructuring' (2015, p 195).

Commodification

> We are deliberately thinking of higher education as a market, and as a market, it has a number of points of failure. Young people are taking out substantial loans to pay for courses without much effective help and advice, and the institutions concerned are under very little competitive pressure to provide best value. If this was a regulated financial market we would be raising the question of mis-selling. The Department is taking action to address some of these issues, but there is a lot that remains to be done.
>
> Amyas Morse, head of the National Audit Office
> (NAO, 2017)

> Unleashing the forces of consumerism is the best single way we've got of restoring high academic standards.
>
> David Willetts, Minister for Higher Education
> (quoted in Morgan, 2013)

The third and final area of change linked to marketisation is how universities become business-like entities in their objectives. Prime Minister Margaret Thatcher strongly believed universities should be run as private companies, reducing the control of academics and increasing the power of the customer. The Jarratt Report (Jarratt, 1985, p 22) even states 'universities are first and foremost corporate enterprises'. Likewise, the 1988 Education Reform Act firmly positioned universities as economic entities rather than state-funded service providers. Although British universities have always been private institutions, the spirit of the market was rather muted for a long time. They increasingly identify with market objectives, transforming into 'corporate universities' (Jarvis, 2013) or 'entrepreneurial universities' (Marginson and Considine, 2000). The idea that degrees must be treated as a product akin to other products in the service sector and traded on a marketplace for HE is accepted and integrated into how the university functions (Henkel, 1997; Bok, 2005; Dill, 2003; Steier, 2003; Komljenovic, 2020). As Lynch (2006, p 2) explains: 'Commercialisation is normalised and its operational values and purposes have been encoded in the systems of all types of universities.' Degrees are increasingly seen as products to be sold to consumers (that is, students) by providers (universities) (Naidoo and Jamieson, 2005). Growing recruitment of students overseas has added to these pressures.

A key characteristic of commodification is positioning students as consumers. Students are expected to behave like rational buyers, which drives the need for further transparency and greater information for students to make sound decisions in the marketplace. The change from the student being positioned as customers with preferences rather than a person with rights to education presents a massive shift in how all involved understand HE (Lolich, 2011). Commodification impacts the student experience and students' understanding of HE and themselves as learners (Nixon et al, 2018), although not for all (Tomlinson, 2017).

Market

The removal of caps on the number of undergraduate places in 2015 was a key step in creating a student market and has spurred significant commodification throughout the English sector. Within the policy framework, the expected result of this intensified competition is that successful courses will increase demand from students and courses below standard will be rejected by the consumer, lose revenue and be forced to improve or leave the market. This was thought to improve efficiency, quality and flexibility throughout the sector (Watts, 2017). We have seen that universities have removed degree programmes and departments that were recruiting or projected not to recruit enough students to profit (UCU, 2012). It is unclear whether it has improved the quality of HE programmes. What it has done is introduce a new level of uncertainty and instability into the sector. At the time of writing, there are labour disputes to avoid redundancies within under-recruiting departments at the University of Leicester, London South Bank University and the University of Liverpool (Weale et al, 2021). Similarly, termination of temporary contracts has been used to cut costs in underperforming institutions (Batty, 2020). Successful recruitment has become vital for most universities to survive. Some universities have increased the number of programmes on offer, and seeking growth in student numbers has been part of their business model. Especially during clearing, in which universities try to fill spaces on courses that are not yet full, universities pull out all the stops to attract students (Weale, 2019), giving potential customers more choice and power in the process (Hall, 2020).

As discussed before, the need for informed choice is a prerequisite for a well-functioning market. National Student Information data, and other performance indicators such as league tables, function as powerful incentives (Naidoo et al, 2011). The TEF is a key example of increasing competition and creating informed choice. Institutions are assessed using metrics on student satisfaction, graduate employment outcomes, continuation rates, staff-to-student contact time, employment data and institutional statements. These indicators, of course, represent a small set of indicators on what teaching quality may constitute in reality. Yet the framework shapes how those within HE define success (Tomlinson et al, 2020).

Reliance on international markets has incentivised commodification, as universities actively try to package and differentiate their (postgraduate) programmes to attract students in foreign markets and increase revenue (James-MacEachern, 2018). Higher levels of intake are financially incentivised. Nearly half of young people were given a place at university in 2019 with A-level grades lower than the advertised entry requirements (Sellgren, 2019a). The Augar Review (Augar, 2019, p 78) observes a trend in lowering entry requirements. This means that each year students with lower prior attainment, measured by A-level and BTEC grades, compared to previous years are entering HE. In addition, more prestigious universities are able to recruit more students, which leaves the institutions in the middle to recruit students who would traditionally enter lower-ranked institutions, and this leaves many universities scrambling for students or facing the grave financial consequences of these systematic failures (*The Economist*, 2018). The uncertainty of recruitment levels has created great anxiety among universities regarding their financial viability in the last few years (Fazackerley, 2018; Staton, 2021a).

Programme leaders need to think carefully about which niches or market segments they are aiming for. Some have predicted growing strategic differentiation both in research and education (Barber et al, 2013), although the evidence for the UK context is lacking. Teaching itself may come under greater scrutiny to align itself to the competitive pressures. McCowan (2017) observes an unbundling of the functions the university undertakes, which are being separated and conducted by distinct organisations. This applies to ancillary work within the university that has been outsourced, but there is also unbundling of taught courses and academic work in design, delivery and assessment of the course, which may be conducted by different institutions as well as a differentiation between the tasks of academics often along research and teaching lines (Macfarlane, 2011). The shifting relationship between academic and student also changed the work of academics with a greater need to improve student experience (that is, customer service). Research indicates that within marketised higher education contexts academics' affective experiences of 'customer' interaction can become psychologically straining (Ogbonna and Harris, 2004; Nixon and Scullion, 2021).

Competition between universities has grown more intense, leading to increased pressures to survive (Jack, 2019). An externality of increasing competition has increased institutional status competition. As tuition fees make up the majority of income for most English universities, we can see heightened value being attached to activities and investment that mainly benefit institutional reputation and institutional branding (Chapleo, 2010). Marketing has become of strategic importance to institutions and the cost of reaching the consumer has spiralled. The highest-spending universities are those in the lower and middle ranks of the UK league tables (Hall and Weale, 2019). For instance, the universities of Central Lancashire and the West of England spent £3.4 million each on marketing in 2017–18 (Jones, 2020).

Grade inflation

Although the relationship between commodification and grade inflation is sometimes disputed, there seems to be a market-related incentive for universities within the current HE landscape to offer higher grades. Currently, the proportion of students awarded first-class degrees in England has increased by almost 90 per cent between 2014 and 2020, with 80 per cent of graduates leaving HE with either a first or a 2:1 (Weale, 2020b). Research suggests that universities have actively changed 'degree algorithms' (which translate the marks achieved by students during their degree into a final classification) to improve the degree classifications (Richmond, 2018). The same research found that senior managers place pressure on academics to lower their standards.

It has become hard to deny that universities are incentivised to give out good grades to satisfy and attract students. Lambert (2019) reminds us that grade inflation is 'the rational outcome of the system under which universities operate'. Prospective students may look at institutional league tables, which often include the distribution of degree qualifications, and use this information to compare programmes. Likewise, students already within the course would be less likely to drop out and rate their degree better if given higher grades. Yet, there are major concerns about grade inflation, including from the government (Coughlan, 2020) and the OfS (OfS, 2020). The fear is that standards may be slipping and that an unfair race between institutions to give higher grades damages the sector's reputation.

Conclusion

This chapter has demonstrated how marketisation has penetrated the modern HE institution system. Marketisation is deeply intertwined with how HE is financed, how it is managed and the extent to which it identifies with the market. As a result, marketisation has shaped how we understand the role of university education, who can access it, and the rights and responsibilities of students, the state and HE institutions themselves. Table 2.1 explains how

Table 2.1: Dimensions of marketisation

Dimension of marketisation	Role of market	Role of choice	Role of competition
User-pay through tuition fees	Removal of recruitment cap. Students as market actors.	HE as investment, increased emphasis on informed choice.	Institutional competition. No real price competition between providers (yet).
Managerialism	Mimic market relations as if HE institutions were part of the private sector.	Audit mechanisms and accountability to aid market choice.	Institutional rankings and measurable performance outcomes.
Commodification	Students positioned as consumers; institutions as market providers.	Transparency and protection of quality controls (including OfS).	Ranking and student attraction.

the three areas covered in this chapter relate to marketisation's key elements of market, choice and competition.

In the previous chapter, we have seen that the state has been a clear driver of marketisation. Government interference has encouraged marketisation in its demand for accountability and the imposition of corporate styles of institutional governance. The powers of academics and bodies governed by them have weakened and managerialism has increased. Ironically, by injecting more market-led reforms into HE, the government has seized more control over the sector. This is what defines the role of a so-called neoliberal state. Other countries also run high participation systems, and other countries also have had public debates about how they can be financed (Cantwell et al, 2018). Yet in those systems, marketisation tends to be far less developed compared to England. There are undoubtedly many institutional and historical reasons for this. To capture some of these, we need to understand how HE policy in England has developed in the last 25 years and how it has persisted with further marketisation to address the HE sector's problems. The following three chapters will explore these issues.

3

Policymaking in higher education: understanding the economy

Introduction

> Our universities have a paramount place in an economy driven by knowledge and ideas. They generate the know-how and skills that fuel our growth.
>
> *Higher Education: Success as a Knowledge Economy*
> white paper (BIS, 2016, p 7)

> We live in a modern, knowledge economy, one which requires the advanced skills that university teaches.
>
> Chris Skidmore, Minister of State for Universities, Science,
> Research and Innovation (2019–2020) (Skidmore, 2019)

Government policy has played a key role in the marketisation of higher education (HE) in the English context. Some have explained in detail the role of the state in this process (for example, Watts, 2017). Some have stressed that the shift towards mass HE called for a political response on how to finance the HE system, which led to greater financial responsibility of the user, that is, the students (Palfrey and Tapper, 2014; Salter and Salter, 2014). Others have argued that a general neoliberal drive for market, competition and choice since the 1980s shaped HE, just as it has shaped the public sector (Saunders, 2010; Giroux, 2014; Maisuria and Cole, 2017; Vernon, 2018). They argue that the political motives for more marketisation are part of a hegemonic project to reinvent free-market capitalism, assisted by state governments who aim to inject neoliberal governance in all areas of life, including education. This chapter and the next two investigate what has helped drive the argumentation for greater marketisation in HE in the English context. Instead of assuming a blanket neoliberal force has taken hold of HE, we can be a lot more specific on how (quasi)neoliberal ideas present themselves in the marketisation movement. The chapters demonstrate that decision making around marketisation in HE does not necessarily rely *directly* on ideological commitments to markets and choice. Instead, we need to look at another feature of policy discourse; its depiction of the graduate labour market and work. In other words, to make marketisation desirable, HE policy relies on a specific narrative on the nature of graduate labour and the graduate labour market. This policy discourse makes distinct assumptions on the demand for skilled labour and graduate skills and the portrayal of HE degrees as financial investment in skills. In a nutshell, HE is expected to serve the needs of the economy as well as provide the basis for individual labour market success and subsequent prosperity and social mobility opportunities. Constructing policies to help achieve these goals relies on a very distinct economic discourse in which graduates and graduate workers play a crucial role.

Policy changes in HE

Very few policy areas in the UK have experienced so much change as HE. The Robbins Report, published in 1963, set in motion distinct growth in the size of the sector and HE participation. Since then, governments have continuously altered and tinkered with HE policy to fulfil some of the wider goals such as improving access, accountability and affordability, and improving standards. To what extent are these changes the result of coherent policy ideology and to what extent are they the outcomes of various political stakeholder interventions? Michael Shattock (2008) argues that HE policy in England has not been dominated by large overarching rationales but developed in piecemeal and pragmatic fashion. Changes are often the outcomes of haphazard decisions by policymakers lacking coherence and rationality (Shattock, 2012, p 2). He states that the UK HE policy has never been especially ideological but steered by the Treasury while influenced haphazardly through gentle politicking by policy networks. Policies in HE were also exogenously driven by stakeholders within the HE system responding to the growing demand for HE over time and measures applied in the public sector in general.

It is important to note that government policy such as HE policy is constructed, maintained and enacted on different levels. Changes in HE policy were also the outcomes of various government agencies, interest and pressure groups, funding councils, representative and public bodies, and so on, shaping policy from outside. But it is undeniable that the government itself changed, and the *perceived* needs of the country put explicit pressures on identifiable outcomes of the HE system. Relatedly, it is also important not to understand HE policies over the last decades as necessarily coherent narratives. They are a compilation of sometimes contradictory and contingently constructed texts, which makes finding any type of regularity challenging (Ball, 1993).

So how much can we read into these policy discourses? Policies matter and their impact on the world of HE and beyond is real in its consequences. They represent 'ways of representing, accounting for and legitimating political decisions; a means of classifying and regulating the spaces and subjects they hope to govern' (Brooks, 2018, p 746). So despite the limitations already outlined, I contend that HE policy documents express at the very minimum how policymakers think on the value and significance of HE and the direction it should be going. It exposes policymakers' and stakeholders' applied logic and assumptions that drive national policy in HE. Even though there are no overarching meta-narratives, we can find patterns in how policy documents 'understand' the world and justify policy directions. In this chapter and the next two, we will investigate ideas about the role of HE in the economy, the labour market, and graduates' labour market opportunities to rationalise and defend HE policy in general and marketisation specifically.

HE policy is of course frequently studied to understand changes in HE. Crucially, the idea that marketisation is anchored in government policy has been well established. Many have observed that the construction of markets has become a central aim within the discourses to restructure and reform HE (Newson and Buchbinder, 1988; Williams, 2004; Jessop et al., 2008; Shattock, 2008). The logic of the market underpins the political drive for marketisation (John and Fanghanel, 2015). Fairclough (1993) was one of the first to argue that the discursive practices of universities are being colonised by those of businesses. This is supported by later studies (Trowler, 2001; Askehave, 2007; Mautner, 2010; Morrish and Sauntson, 2013). Similarly, evidence of commodification can be found in HE policies (J. Williams, 2013). For instance, Kelly et al (2017) observe how UK policy discourse now conceives of undergraduate students as individual entrepreneurs, navigating themselves in a market-like field of education.

Before we turn to the policy domain, a few words on methodology. HE policy has been a rich area for discursive examination (Lester et al, 2017; Warriner and Anderson, 2017). Discourse here represents talk, text and action expressing narratives, sets of beliefs and ways of seeing the world. It is both socially shaped and socially shaping, or constitutive (Fairclough, 1993, p 134). Language is a socially and historically situated mode of action. Discourses use language to construct and justify rationalities of governance while constraining the ability to speak outside the structures that it creates. Motivated by political interests, power relations and ideologies, discourses can both reveal but also conceal power structures. In other words, discourses shape possibilities for thought and action through how words, positions and behaviours are managed to emphasise ideological politics and exert power. As such, they 'construct what can be said, thought, done, and also who can say what and with what authority by framing explicit intent, obscuring implicit intent, and/or garnering public support' (O'Neill, 2012, cited in Anderson and Holloway, 2020, p 202). Policy discourse can show how meanings within the policy framework are made and other meanings and rationales are excluded. As Ball argues, '[d]iscourse is not present in the object, but "enables it to appear". Discourse is the conditions under which certain statements are considered to be the truth' (Ball, 2015, p 311). Discourse analysis can open up taken-for-granted assumptions associated with educational policy rationalities exploring what it does, how it is constituted, and what it is understood to mean (Ball, 1993). Here I adopt what Anderson and Holloway (2020) distinguish as Type A in their typology of uses of discourses in the study of educational policy. Discourse within this approach is defined as a 'form of social practice that frames the ways in which policy can be understood. ... Accordingly, discourse is not seen as a representation of reality, but rather as constitutive of realities by making available certain ways of knowing and doing' (p 200).

This chapter and the next two will show how HE, as well as its finance and management, have become a policy 'problem' constructed and defined through a utilitarian economic perspective. They aim to uncover distinct assumptions about the need for HE to align its practices to the market or propose further development of market competition and choice in its educational programmes. The main aim here is not to problematise the power differences underlying the construction and normalisation of the discourse despite being of great importance. Instead, the chapters aim to outline how increasing marketisation has been underpinned by a distinct discourse on the nature of graduate labour and the needs of the economy.

An inductive document analysis was conducted on key HE policy documents for the English context published between 1997 and 2020, exploring how the relationship between education and work is constructed, represented and conceptualised. The policy texts discussed here do not necessarily represent how the discourse is used, adapted and applied within policy circles or how meaning is constructed within the layers of society, particularly within the HE system. However, these documents can illuminate how these discursive practices help construct policy and enactment of policies. They are very useful in understanding why marketisation has been a suitable or desired policy option. In the remainder of this chapter and the next two, I will highlight four aspects that are highly salient in the defence and justification of further marketisation. These are:

- how the role of education in the economy is understood (Chapter 3);
- how the role of education in work is understood (Chapter 4);
- how the graduate labour market is understood (Chapter 4);
- the reliance on human capital theories to understand the graduate labour market (Chapter 5).

How is the role of education in the economy understood?

The idea of the knowledge-based economy

Since the latter stages of the industrial revolution, HE has had a clear role in developing professional skills and expertise needed throughout the economy. For instance, the institutions created in the 19th century, classified as redbrick universities, were located in industrial centres to develop strong scientific and technical workforces needed to fulfil the local labour market demand. The post-war increase in demand for university education and the subsequent expansion of HE were accompanied by ideas on how university education could support a service-based economy driven by rapid technological change. One of the key ideas given prominence in the last decades is that of the knowledge-based economy (KBE). It was thought that the UK advanced economies had entered a new economic era that relied on the productive importance of knowledge and information, and its exploitation. To help the transformation into a so-called knowledge-based society, HE needed to be developed, expanded and financed (Brown et al, 2003). The concept of a knowledge society has a long history in different guises. From the 1960s onwards, scholars such as Peter Drucker, Daniel Bell and Alvin Toffler claimed that Western economies have entered a phase in economic history called the 'knowledge' or 'knowledge-based' era. In *The Coming of Post-Industrial Society*, Daniel Bell (1973) predicted that knowledge would replace capital as the critical factor of production as societies moved to post-industrialism. Knowledge would be used, created, acquired and transmitted throughout the whole economy and become a crucial element for producing goods and services and economic development. The creation, valorisation and application of knowledge would be the key driver of economic efficiency, competitiveness and profitability. The idea of the knowledge economy found new resonance in the 1990s, with the rise of the IT revolution and offered as a new economic paradigm for Western countries to pursue among growing economic competition (Reich, 1991; Blair and Schröder, 1999; Giddens, 2000). It was thought that Western countries would ultimately permanently lose routine and low-skilled work due to technological change and offshoring technology and globalisation. Britain and other developed economies should focus on competing for knowledge-intensive work. Building on their infrastructure and institutions and existing human capital in the workforce, they would have an advantage over competing low-cost economies such as China or India.

The idea of a KBE has underpinned the role universities needed to play within the economy and intrinsically linked HE policy with economic policy (OECD, 1996). It has successfully captured policymakers' imagination in most advanced countries, including the UK. The idea of a growing demand for graduates and graduate skills within the modern economy remains an axiom on which policymakers have demonstrated that a market for university education serves individuals, employers and the state. Further investment in education was also needed to maintain a comparative advantage over other nations (Sainsbury of Turville, 2006). A highly skilled workforce would lead to productivity gains and innovation in the workplace, leading to creating higher-value products and services in the process (Tholen, 2017a). It is important to note that within the UK context, expanding HE participation to improve the workforce's skill levels has become the default policy option to solve policy problems that go far beyond the needs of the KBE (Keep and Mayhew, 2010). According to Keep (2020), a key reason for this is reluctance by employers to invest in training, combined with a lack of pressure from governments to make them do so, or by sponsoring and encouraging the collective organisation of training. Successive governments have therefore fallen back on expanding the HE sector to boost skill levels.

Knowledge work

The advent of the KBE came with direct assumptions on the nature of modern work. Due to fast and far-reaching technological change, work has become more complex. Skilled workers who can transform knowledge and work with advanced technologies have been given a special status. In the knowledge economy, these knowledge workers who use and create value from knowledge and new technologies are the dominant force in productivity growth and innovation. They can capture, exploit and control knowledge, and are predicted to become increasingly powerful and influential, positioned as the new elites within the labour force. Due to the productivity gain they bring, knowledge workers are relatively more highly rewarded than other types of workers, leading to greater income inequality over time (Reich, 1991). Although not all graduates are necessarily knowledge workers, their advanced skills and expertise make them reap the rewards of the KBE. As Newfield (2011, p 9) describes, graduates were thought to be 'flexible, adaptable, innovative workers who could thrive in a rapidly changing market economy by constantly upgrading their skills and creating the new value that would give their companies the indispensable competitive edge'.

The KBE has created a vision of the social and economic future of society that has been persuasive within political and policy circles' imaginaries (Sum and Jessop, 2013). The OECD report *The Knowledge-Based Economy* (1996) begins with the declaration that in the KBE, 'innovation is driven by the interaction of producers and users in the exchange of both codified and tacit knowledge' (p 7) and highlights the forceful relationship among industry, government and academia in the development of science and technology:

> Government policies will need more stress on upgrading human capital through promoting access to a range of skills, and especially the capacity to learn; enhancing the knowledge distribution power of the economy through collaborative networks and the diffusion of technology; and providing the enabling conditions for organisational change at the firm level to maximise the benefits of technology for productivity. (p 7)

The idea that the role of government is to be an active facilitator for providing the knowledge infrastructure has since then become an economic policy pillar (Godin, 2006; World Bank, 2007; Moisio, 2018). O'Donovan (2020) recently argued that the influence of the KBE paradigm is on the wane. According to the author, the optimism attached to the KBE has been replaced by a more dystopian view of the role of technology in the economy. Automation and the rise of artificial intelligence may change the positive relationship between human capital investment and labour market opportunities. Unequal ownership of technology and knowledge shapes financial returns and the power of knowledge workers.

HE policy

In order to set the right conditions for a KBE, education and, in particular, HE needs to be promoted (for example, the Sainsbury of Turville, 2006; Browne, 2010). Investing in the development of human capital becomes economically imperative. Over the long run, innovation is the main source of productivity growth, which in turn drives improvements in prosperity and living standards. HE is positioned as a key location where innovation and technological advance can be located, particularly in its cooperation with the private sector. The authors of the Browne Review (2010) write that 'Higher education matters because it drives innovation and economic transformation. Higher education helps to produce economic growth, which in turn contributes to national prosperity' (p 14). Jessop (2017, p 854) argues that the KBE is 'not just a reflection of economic processes occurring in the background' but it is 'guiding the structural reform and strategic reorientation of higher education and research'. It means that HE needs to be more aligned to and in service of the needs of the economy and society. HE is the place where the skills of knowledge workers are developed. HE must play a more significant role in meeting the country's skills needs and preparing students for the so-called Fourth Industrial Revolution.

By widening access to education, opportunities become available to those who make educational investments. Educational improvements would equip more and more people to participate in knowledge-intensive work, encouraging innovative businesses to invest, which would lead to an ever-increasing number of knowledge-intensive jobs, with more and more people enjoying the higher incomes associated with those jobs (and thus improving social mobility). Policymakers have made increasing efforts to expand participation in education to increase the number of skilled individuals, often measured as the share of graduates in a cohort or (part of the) workforce. The HE system is evaluated on how well it can deliver on the perceived educational needs of the knowledge economy (Frank and Meyer, 2020).

Many successive governments have recognised the need for HE to support national economic success over the last century. For instance, Thatcher's government set out its proposals for changes in the structure and planning of HE to adapt to the economy in the white paper 'Higher education: Meeting the challenge' (DES, 1987). Yet the clearest examples of the influence of the KBE in HE policy came in the New Labour years, with the drive for greater HE participation. In 1999, Tony Blair famously put forward a target of 50 per cent of young people going into HE. The Third Way philosophy stated that active reflexive citizens can empower themselves by using knowledge and developing expertise to make decisions regarding careers, health, education, insurance and taking control of their lives (Delanty, 2003, p 76). Through market competition, it aimed to achieve better outcomes for citizens in their engagement with the welfare and educational provision with the active goal of improving equity and social justice in society. The KBE sets out conditions for all individuals to improve their lives economically, improve social mobility and reduce poverty. A globalised market for skilled work would give a greater number of people opportunities for prosperity by becoming knowledge workers (Brown and Lauder, 2006). Yet a competitive edge in the global market could only be achieved if the workforce actively transformed through workers investing in their own human capital. The KBE imagery produced an excellent vehicle to produce equity, social justice and prosperity by letting individuals make their own choices in terms of their education. The seeds of promoting the position of students as consumers were sown.

In the Dearing Report, the New Labour optimism shines through; there is a feeling that the KBE provides distinct possibilities in improving the economy through HE. It reports on how HE has become of national economic importance and that its place in the national economy will grow (NCIHE, 1997, p 348). Similarly, the 2003 white paper aimed to improve the economic contribution that universities and colleges make through innovation, improving the skills of the nation and stimulating new businesses in an increasingly competitive world (DfES, 2003, p 92). It makes an explicit case for expansion of HE based on the predicted demand of a more highly skilled workforce with 80 per cent of new jobs over the next decade to be graduate jobs (DfES, 2003, p 16). Throughout the New Labour years we see how HE is assumed directly to contribute to the development of the higher-level skills needed by the knowledge economy (see DfES, 2003; DIUS, 2008). It is important not to exaggerate or essentialise New Labour's vision for universities. The Secretary of State for Business, Innovation and Skills, Peter Mandelson (2009), stressed that universities have multiple societal aims and are 'not factories for producing workers'. He also emphasised that knowledge for its own sake as well as historical awareness and critical thinking are vital. The economic role of a university is nonetheless posed as absolutely essential as opposed to beneficial:

The sectors in which British firms have potential comparative advantage in the next decade – low carbon, digital communications, life science, the creative industries: these are all absolutely reliant on high levels of knowledge, of skill and innovation. They will also draw heavily on our capacity for research and our ability to commercialise it. So our universities are inescapably central to our economic future. (Mandelson, 2009)

This message was echoed by the Minister of State for Higher Education and Intellectual Property, David Lammy, who not only regarded universities as being central to Labour's efforts to build a strong economy, but posed the alternative as an economic disaster (Lammy, 2009). The doom scenario is often described as a low skills equilibrium in which the UK economy would be stuck in a vicious circle of low value-added, low skills and low wages leading to weak economic performance. The idea has been around since the late 1980s in academic debate (Finegold and Soskice, 1988) but its usage in policy circles has often been less coherent (Sisson, 2021). In policy documents, it is often used rather rhetorically to enforce change. 'Without further expansion of HE skills there is the danger of a low skills equilibrium which would reduce levels of productivity and lower growth relative to the UK's international competitors, and hence lower levels of prosperity' (Browne, 2010, p 17).

A clear aspect of the idea of a knowledge-based society is the direct relationship between HE and the penetration of knowledge within the economic system. This is thought to be achieved through the development and spread of new technologies as well as the growing pool of highly educated knowledge workers. Research is conducted in HE and contributes directly to the nation's wealth-creating capacity as it becomes a crucial resource to industry, and for public services and commerce to flourish. There is an assumed synergy between the private sector and knowledge produced at universities as creators of knowledge: 'In a knowledge-based economy both our economic competitiveness and improvements in our quality of life depend on the effectiveness of knowledge sharing between business and higher education' (DfES, 2003, p 60). Not much effort is made to understand how exactly the knowledge universities produce will enhance the needs of corporations. Policy documents are often rather vague on how exactly universities need to contribute to the KBE's proliferation of knowledge. Yet, universities are portrayed as key agents in the transformation of individuals:

Knowledge is advancing so rapidly that a modern competitive economy depends on its ability to generate that knowledge, engage with it and use it to effect ... above all, this new economic order will place a premium on knowledge. Institutions are well-placed to capitalise on higher education's long-standing purpose of developing knowledge and understanding. But to do so, they need to recognise more consistently that individuals need to be equipped in their initial higher education with the knowledge, skills and understanding which they can use as a basis to secure further knowledge and skills. (NCIHE, 1997, p 55)

Likewise, the details on the mechanism through which a skilled labour force would lead to a high skilled, high waged economic route is often far from clear. Universities supposedly supply skilled workers and the private sector makes use of them to grow and to innovate:

The exchange of knowledge, including through a growing supply of graduates and postgraduates, and through the development of the skills of those already in the workplace, must underpin a future of high value business strategies based on innovation. We need more knowledge intensive, innovating organisations, and they in turn need more highly skilled, adaptable people. (DIUS, 2008, p 8)

As businesses and other employers shift up the value chain they increase their capacity to use and benefit from knowledge and high level skills. High level skills supply makes high value added strategies sustainable. Together, they help to position Britain as a key knowledge economy at the forefront of 21st century innovation and enterprise. (DIUS, 2008, p 10)

International competition

The general orientation of New Labour's education policy was strongly focused on the global competitiveness of the economy. The UK's comparative advantage in the future would be defined by high-performing, high value-added sectors. It actively positioned HE to contribute to Britain's competitive edge in the global market by producing and disseminating economically productive knowledge. The expansion of HE is seen as directly related to strategies to improve the UK's global competitiveness (Leitch Review of Skills, 2006).

As we have seen before, HE is positioned as a key contributor to Britain's competitive advantage in the global market. Universities are expected to contribute to each country's competitive standing in the global marketplace by producing and disseminating economically productive knowledge (Moutsios, 2010) and creating a labour force that will help investment and demand for high skilled goods and services. The supply of human capital becomes the competitive advantage in itself. In the KBE narrative, national economies compete on human capital to attract foreign investment for their knowledge-intensive industries. National governments can create favourable circumstances for investment in and subsequent growth of knowledge-intensive industries and sectors, such as the high-quality infrastructure, robust regulatory and legal frameworks, and the HE sector's size and quality. Universities are the engines of knowledge and their graduates are necessarily bundles of human capital, performing knowledge work and innovating.

The Dearing Report emphasises that the rising value of HE in economic terms can only be understood within a global context, raising the stakes to deliver the right skills: 'With the global approach to production and service provision, the factors which will determine the economic future of the UK will be the quality, relevance, scale, and cost-effectiveness of its education and training, and the commitment of its population to lifelong education and training' (NCIHE, 1997, p 55). The report explains how within the global economy, successful HE policy helps in attracting investment from multinational corporations (leading to a so-called magnet economy [Brown and Lauder, 2006]):

> In a global economy, the manufacturers of goods and providers of services can locate or relocate their operations wherever in the world gives them greatest competitive advantage. Competitive pressures are reinforced by the swift pace of innovation and the immediate availability of information through communications technology. When capital, manufacturing processes and service bases can be transferred internationally, the only stable source of competitive advantage (other than natural resources) is a nation's people. Education and training must enable people in an advanced society to compete with the best in the world ... high quality, relevant higher education provision will be a key factor in attracting and anchoring the operations of global corporations because of the research capability of its institutions, and the skills and knowledge it can develop in the local workforce. (NCIHE, 1997, p 9)

The report identifies the ability to both attract as well as lose high-value economic opportunities and investment as other many international competitors are similarly aiming to improve the contribution of their HE systems to aid economic performance. The investment in HE must be seen in a relative light as its effectiveness depends on how it compares with other countries. The report warns us that the 'UK cannot afford to lag behind its competitors in investing in the intellect and skills of its people' (NCIHE, 1997, p 9). The 2003 white paper observes with worry how the proportion of the labour force educated to degree level in the UK is 17 per cent compared to 28 per cent in the US (DfES, 2003, p 16). It warns:

> The challenges are clear. Many of our economic competitors invest more in higher education institutions than we do. France, Germany,

the Netherlands and the USA all contribute 1 per cent of GDP in public funding to higher education institutions, and Japan is planning to increase public investment from 0.4 per cent to 1 per cent. This compares to 0.8 per cent in the UK, rising to approximately 0.9 per cent by 2005 because of our generous spending review settlement. Our competitors see – as we should – that the developing knowledge economy means the need for more, better trained people in the workforce. (DfES, 2003, p 10)

Concerns about the UK competitiveness by directly benchmarking HE data can also be seen in the Browne Review. Referring to an OECD survey the authors stress that:

[O]n the numbers of people who have the skills provided by higher education, the UK ranks 15th among the 30 OECD countries. For younger workers (25–34 year olds), the UK ranks 19th, down from 14th five years ago, so its relative position is worse for younger people that it is for older people, and both are in decline ... countries – such as Korea, Japan, Ireland, Belgium, France and Spain – that have historically lower levels of participation than the UK have now moved ahead of us and their participation rates among young people are higher than ours. The OECD average shows a sharper increase than the UK as well. (Browne, 2010, p 16)

Direct action to correct the slipping of educational outputs is deemed crucial to secure economic competitiveness. We can see that taking on the competition on human capital is the only way to a realistic road to prosperity:

In a fast-changing and increasingly competitive world, the role of higher education in equipping the labour force with appropriate and relevant skills, in stimulating innovation and supporting productivity and in enriching the quality of life is central. The benefits of an excellent higher education system are far-reaching; the risk of decline is one that *we cannot accept*. (DfES, 2003, p 8; emphasis added)

And to compete in the increasingly competitive world of the future we will need a higher proportion of people with high level skills. It is no coincidence that most of the world's developed countries, and many of its developing countries, are increasing the numbers of their people who reach higher education. They share our basic analysis; that in the world of the future there will be increasing demand for well-educated, imaginative and adaptable people to enable businesses and services to innovate and thrive. High level skills help form a sustainable knowledge economy in which ideas inform and improve practice. *This is an economic imperative.* (DIUS, 2008, p 9; emphasis added)

The erstwhile optimism has been traded in for a fear of lagging behind. Consider for instance Prime Minister David Cameron's use of words to describe this sense of urgency:

We simply cannot allow our universities to continue to fall behind their international rivals. Just look at what's happening in India and China. In the last three years, India has built eight new Institutes of Technology, twelve universities and seven new Institutes of Management. And in the next fifteen years, the number of graduates from Chinese universities is expected to grow five-fold. This is the competition we face. (Cameron, 2010)

We've got to be ambitious if we want to compete in the world. When China is going through an educational renaissance, when India is churning out science graduates any complacency now would be fatal for our prosperity. (Cameron, 2011)

Ball (2017) notes that Cameron's narrative of educational reform along with the demands of the global economy is expressed as 'comparative, necessary and urgent' (p 20).

The labour market needs more graduates

The growing demand for advanced skills and pressures of the global economic competition drive a perceived need for growing numbers of graduates within the policy discourse. Dearing argues that 'proliferation of knowledge, technological advances and the information revolution mean that labour market demand for those with higher level education and training is growing' (NCIHE, 1997, p 4). This has led to direct growth of the HE sector to accommodate both individual and national needs: 'Our overriding priority is to ensure that as we expand higher education places, we ensure that the expansion is of an appropriate quality and type to meet the demands of employers and the needs of the economy and students' (DfES, 2003, p 3).

The 'Leitch Review of Skills', commissioned due to concerns over the skill levels and gaps in some sections of the workforce, echoes this message but provides more nuance. It advocated skill upgrading across all levels as well as placing greater emphasis on employer engagement and workforce development to get the right skills: 'A highly-skilled workforce drives innovation, leadership and management, enabling businesses to compete in the global economy. Ensuring that high skills are of world class quality and relevance to the economy is just as important as determining the quantity of people that should be qualified to these levels' (Leitch Review of Skills, 2006, p 21). Although the report very much proposes a supply-led skill strategy, a key message in the Leitch Review is that not only the quantity but also the quality of skills matter (see also Rammell, 2007). Yet in later education policy documents, this nuance is lost again:

> We know that, if we are to match the aims of other countries – for example, to achieve skill levels equivalent to the best OECD countries – then scraping over 40% by 2020 will not be enough. Others will have done better. (DIUS, 2008, p 5)

> Graduates are central to our prosperity and success as a knowledge economy, and higher education is a key export sector. Research indicates that a 1% increase in the share of the workforce with a university degree raises long-run productivity by between 0.2% and 0.5%; and around 20% of UK economic growth between 1982 and 2005 came as a direct result of increased graduate skills accumulation. (DBIS, 2016, pp 8–9)

Over time we also see the concept of the 'employable' graduate appear, suggesting that not all additional graduates would benefit the economy. This crucial shift from a rather generic strategy of skill upgrade to a market-led one is seen in the *Students at the Heart of the System* report from 2011. The demand for HE is now also being explicitly linked to market demand. While not denying that more graduates constitute a greater asset to the economy, it moves away from a centralised economic policy to improve the skill base of the workforce. Instead, it highlights that ultimately it will be demand and supply forces that will determine how many graduates are needed:

> We have no target for the 'right' size of the higher education system but believe it should evolve in response to demand from students and employers, reflecting particularly the wider needs of the economy. ... Employers will continue to demand graduates and higher-level skills. ... To enable the sector to respond to student demand, both in relation to choice of institution, and expansion to meet volume of demand, we want to introduce ways to free up student number controls, while ensuring that overall costs are managed. (DBIS, 2011, p 49)

The assumption being made here is that the *market* for HE can ultimately indicate the perceived needs of the economy. This implies that a market in HE can adequately offer a signal of demand as well as supply. Competition and choice for the student will ultimately lead to greater and relevant human capital development. It will fine-tune both the quantity and quality of skills employers so badly need. Yet without a sufficient mechanism of choice and market information, a market cannot function. This is why Minister for Universities and Science, David Willetts, argued that marketisation changes are ultimately in the universities' own interest. Commenting on the proposed changes within the Browne Review, he argues:

> The more important point, though, is that, despite the risks associated with any change, the reforms we undertake will improve higher education in the long run. Those institutions which attract more students and pull in businesses seeking to boost the skills of their employees will be able to grow. They will reap the rewards of good teaching that students and employers recognise and value. They will be able to innovate, to make the most of greater autonomy, to pursue their institutional missions, including research. (Willetts, 2010)

The strategic economic significance of HE as a developer of skills is expressed through its demand and supply within the labour market. Students' choices reflect the monetary payoff and earning premium to the market. Growing marketisation is actively aligned with the needs of the KBE. Consider the report 'Success as a Knowledge Economy' DBIS (2016), in which it is argued that competition will demonstrate HE institution economic utility in relation to the needs of the economy, arguing for greater competition between institutions. Market signals and market demand will fulfil the educational conditions of the KBE. Also, greater competition between institutions will ultimately support the needs of the KBE as it drives up the quality and quantity of the graduates needed: 'There are strong arguments to encourage greater competition between high quality new and existing providers in the HE sector. Graduates are central to our prosperity and success as a knowledge economy, and higher education is a key export sector' (DBIS, 2016, p 8).

We can see the first signs that marketisation is positioned as a prerequisite for creating an HE system that can deliver for the KBE. Ultimately, the interests of employers, students and the economy come together through the competition mechanism. HE's value to the economy is expressed in relation to the market between employers and future workers. Chapter 4 will investigate how the graduate labour market is understood in HE policy.

4

Policymaking in higher education: understanding work and the labour market

We cannot build the workforce the country needs to thrive in the new economy without a significant contribution from universities. Our HE sector can provide both the general, transferable skills demanded by jobs in the knowledge economy, but also the specific, vocational skills demanded by many jobs from nursing to video game design.

Minister Sam Gyimah, Minister of State for Universities, Science, Research and Innovation 2018 (Gyimah, 2018)

This chapter expands the analysis of policy discourse into the narratives on work and the labour market. We have seen in the previous chapter that many key assumptions on the knowledge-based economy (KBE) to this day underpin the rationales of higher education (HE) reform. Yet the narratives on the economy within HE policy are intertwined with more specific assumptions on the nature of modern graduate work and the graduate labour force. These, likewise, become highly salient if we want to understand the justification for marketisation in HE.

Chapter 3 demonstrated that the idea of the KBE helped promote the idea that expansion of HE is needed as the demand for it has increased due to the nature of the modern economy. The growth of the graduate workforce will sustain the new economy and directly lead to productivity improvements. Assumptions on the nature of white-collar jobs accompanied these notions. Let us start again with the Dearing Report, whose authors observe that work itself is changing radically:

Labour market requirements for those with higher education qualifications are changing dramatically. Many of the employer organisations which gave evidence to us support this view. This will affect overall demand. The Confederation of British Industry told us: 'as the economy and organisations change, the areas in which graduate skill and qualities add value will multiply ... large numbers of graduates are adding value not just in expanding numbers of traditional graduate jobs but also in a widening range of previously non-graduate roles'. ... It would indeed be surprising if the labour market did not need time to respond fully to the increased supply of those with higher level qualifications. We are persuaded that jobs are being progressively redefined to utilise graduate skills. (NCIHE, 1997, p 89)

We can see two assumptions here:

- Graduates add value to existing roles.
- Work is being upskilled as the supply of graduates grows.

In other words, graduates themselves upskill their jobs and use their advanced skills to improve and develop the work process. This even applies to roles where university education may not strictly be deemed necessary: 'Increasingly, graduates will enter jobs not traditionally filled by graduates, causing their jobs to be redefined and reducing the number of layers needed in the organisation' (NCIHE, 1997, p 56). There is an acknowledgement that the skills we traditionally associate with HE may not fully overlap with those needed in modern high-skilled work. HE should be transformed to allow graduates to be better prepared for work: 'Institutions will need to be more flexible in the way they organise their resources and in their organisational structure. Programmes will need to give students the opportunities and skills to work across disciplines and to develop generic or transferable skills which are valuable in many contexts' (NCIHE, 1997, p 59).

The Dearing Report points out that the nature of graduate work is defined by technological change and, because of the speed of this change, skill demands are changing fast. HE will be challenged but is ultimately able to keep up. Graduates are trained for the work of the future as they are best positioned to deal with the knowledge-intensive and technological content of graduate work. It, therefore, offers mainly opportunities for HE in providing the skills that are needed: 'The role of higher education in an advanced economy is not just to develop a senior echelon although it must continue to do that: it is increasingly involved in developing the capabilities of people in a whole range of activities' (NCIHE, 1997, p 77).

The responsibility falls to HE to be responsive to changes in work and change their teaching accordingly (in partnership with industry). The 2003 white paper repeats the expectation of growth in the number of graduate jobs that normally recruit those with higher education qualifications (DfES, 2003, p 16), calling for further expansion of HE. In addition, universities have a significant contribution to make in closing the productivity gap as well as creating a basis for economic growth, presuming a direct relationship between productivity and skills gap.

There is compelling evidence that education increases productivity, and moreover that higher education is the most important phase of education for economic growth in developed countries, with increases in HE found to be positively and significantly related to per capita income growth. (DfES, 2003, p 58)

If we want to close the productivity gap we must close the skills gap, and that in part means boosting higher education. (DfES, 2003, p 16)

The report praises the development of technical and vocational skills in HE but warns that employers will not necessarily value vocational tracks. It furthermore emphasises the need for intensive cooperation between the private and public sector to develop the right technical skills. The concept of 'employability skills' (Mason et al, 2009; Suleman, 2018) also features prominently within the report. These skills are conceptualised as a mix of social and communication skills that are transferable between employers:

As well as improving vocational skills, we need to ensure that all graduates, including those who study traditional academic disciplines, have the right skills to equip them for a lifetime in a fast changing work environment. Therefore, we will continue to sponsor work already under way by HEFCE to integrate the skills and attributes which employers need, such as communication, enterprise and working with others, into higher education courses, on a subject–by–subject basis. (DfES, 2003, p 42)

All these skills are thought to be developed at HE, and form the basis of long-term employability. Tentatively, the importance of market forces to coordinate the skill demand of the modern economy comes to the fore in the report. Yet predominantly the document signals a dual national skill strategy based on 'raising the skills of the workforce at all levels, and ensuring that the education and training system responds effectively to demand from employers' (DfES, 2003, p 58). The importance of the market mechanism in determining the demand and supply of 'graduate skills' (Tholen et al, 2016) is made more explicit in the Leitch Report published three years later in 2006, in which the authors emphasise the necessity of shared responsibility of employers, individuals and government for investment in training and education. Employers and individuals should contribute most to training as they reap the rewards of the 'private' benefits.

The general upskilling strategy in order to keep up with the skill demand in modern work is echoed in the consultation paper by the Department of Innovation, Universities and Skills, *Higher Education at Work: High Skills, High Value* (2008). Responding to the Leitch Report, it outlines a high skills supply strategy aiming for more employable graduates, in particular science, technology, engineering and mathematics (STEM) graduates. The argumentation rests on a particular view of the work that graduates do as highly skilled, innovative and high value. It equates skills developed at HE as high skills, and contributing to innovation and raised productivity. The barriers that are stopping HE institutions from developing the skills needed by employers seem technical, all within the reach of universities to solve:

> So the evidence suggests that what employers want from graduates is generally what they get. But concerns remain that:
>
> - in some sectors there is a mismatch between the needs of business and the courses provided by higher education institutions;
> - graduate employability needs to improve, particularly in terms of business awareness, where 48% of CBI members are dissatisfied;
> - there are not enough graduates who combine high-level maths and science knowledge with the capacity to work effectively in industry. (DfES, 2003, p 14)

The need for greater so-called employability skills must be incorporated in the degree programmes to prepare students for work. This presents merely an adjustment to make sure that these can be covered in the curriculum. It not only is possible to prepare fully for these changes in work, but universities have also become *responsible* for doing so: 'We want to see all universities treating student employability as a core part of their mission. So we believe it is reasonable to expect universities to take responsibility for how their students are prepared for the world of work' (*DfES, 2003*, p 14). The idea that HE has a direct role in providing the skills needed for skilled work became widely accepted and part of a wider skill strategy focused on the supply-side of the labour market (Keep and Mayhew, 2010). The expectation that universities can deliver the skills needed by employers becomes more explicit after that point in policy document. Universities were imagined as de facto agile skill factories responding to employer demand. Consider this statement by Mandelson (2009):

> We need employers to communicate clearly and constructively to universities the skills they need so that courses can adapt and evolve – something that businesses have not always done effectively. Perhaps they have been shy or felt that they would not receive a hearing? We need universities to communicate to students the career trajectories from different subject choices, and the likely market demand for their skills.

The shared interest between students and employers is stressed in *Higher Ambitions: The Future of Universities in a Knowledge Economy* (DBIS, 2009) (as well as the 2011 white paper *Students at the Heart of the System* [DBIS, 2011]). It highlights the need for universities to promote both employability and answer to employers' skills demands. University education no longer on its own will lead prosperity but has to be understood in relation to how well it can adjust to the skills demanded by both employers and prospective students. HE's value is reflected in the employers' valuation of its graduates:

> Higher education has become better attuned to the needs of employers over the past decade … employers continue to report skills shortages, particularly in science, technology, engineering, mathematics and other key skills that underwrite some of our most competitive sectors. They also report a lack of 'employability' skills in graduates such as business awareness and self-management. Both of these deficits are holding back our economic prospects. (DBIS, 2009, p 41)

The report underscores again that the cooperation between industry and HE is needed for the effective development of skillsets: 'The capacity of the higher education system to equip people for the modern world of work depends on this relationship being productive and based on mutual understanding. We expect universities and businesses to work together to anticipate, shape, and respond to demand for skills in the economy' (DBIS, 2009, p 46). There are undertones present of a Germanic skills system in which relatively extensive cooperation exists between HE institutions and employers (Ertl and Sloane, 2004; Baethge and Wolter, 2015). Yet currently, the English system is very far removed from such a system (Mason, 2020), despite some intentions to create meaningful connection between industry and HE such as degree-level apprenticeships (Augar, 2019). It is important to note here that the pressure on universities to deliver on the needs of employers was not just coming from the government. In 2011 the National Union of Students (NUS) and the Confederation of British Business (CBI) published a joint policy paper calling for HE institutions to adapt their curricula according to labour market needs so that they 'can help students achieve a return on their investment by securing good jobs' (Confederation of British Industry and National Union of Students, 2011, p 5).

How the current tuition fee regime works with the need for more coordination is outlined in the green paper *Fulfilling our Potential: Teaching Excellence, Social Mobility and Student Choice* (DBIS, 2015) and the white paper *Success as a Knowledge Economy: Teaching Excellence, Social Mobility and Student Choice* (DBIS, 2016). Both documents explicitly position the HE consumer market to coordinate the skills developed by HE and the skills demanded by employers. A competitive market in HE will offer students sufficient information to select those courses. Employers will be able to benefit from more employable students and improved market signals in recruitment:

We expect higher education to deliver well designed courses, robust standards, support for students, career readiness and an environment that develops the 'soft skills' that employers consistently say they need. These include capacity for critical thinking, analysis and teamwork, along with the vital development of a student's ability to learn. (DBIS, 2016, p 43)

Properly regulated, a competitive higher education market will create stronger, higher quality providers, that will further enhance the global reputation of the sector, and will serve students, employers and taxpayers better. (DBIS, 2016, p 23)

By promoting choice and competition and ensuring minimum standards of quality, it protects the interests of students, employers and taxpayers as well as the reputation of the sector both at home and abroad. (DBIS, 2016, p 62)

The Augar Review (2019), which gives a lot of attention to skill demand, stresses that the workforce needs to be agile to respond to skill change. It acknowledges that skills mismatch is a significant problem as graduates cannot use the skills they have acquired during HE. Also, skill gaps are hurting the economy. A better mix of skills, in particular STEM skills, is needed to alleviate the UK's skills problem. Refreshingly, it also strongly calls for developing degree-level apprenticeships instead of a continuous focus on traditional HE degrees. Even the problem of overqualification is acknowledged. The report states that it is a 'hotly contested territory' (p 27) and reviews some of the evidence: 'The panel is in no position to provide a definitive estimate, but notes that the UK is an outlier internationally in terms of the proportions of graduates in non-graduate employment' (Augar, 2019, p 27).

The discussion of the skill mismatch and overqualification provides a much broader and nuanced discussion of what a KBE may require. Yet the underlying assumption on the role of the university remains more or less unchanged. HE should and can deliver skills demanded by employers. There is a direct, albeit imperfect, relationship between what skills are developed in HE and how well companies can perform, reflected in the overall productivity performance. Recent reports draw on econometric research to claim that no less than 20 per cent of UK economic growth and at least one third of the increase in UK labour productivity between 1982 and 2005 came as a direct result of increased graduate skills accumulation (Holland et al, 2013). HE is therefore seen as a key instrument to address skills deficit in order to raise productivity:

In terms of productivity the UK lags behind most of its counterparts, with workers in the UK producing less in each hour they work than those in the US, Germany or France. According to the Office for National Statistics (ONS) 'compared with the rest of the G7, the UK had below average real productivity growth in both output per hour and output per worker terms in 2016'. This failure to match its competitors is in part caused by persistent skills shortages. (House of Commons Education Committee, 2018a, p 16)

Our higher education system needs to have a much sharper focus on developing skills. This could make an important contribution to filling the nation's skills gaps and solving the UK's productivity puzzle. (House of Commons Education Committee, 2018b)

So, within HE policy, the universities are increasingly held responsible to support the economy, adjusting to employer skills demand and ensuring the work-readiness of students (Brooks, 2018).

The role of universities remains at the forefront of the UK's economic strategy as understood within the educational policy domain. Yet the mechanism through which the right skills for the economy are developed has become the market. Graduates have been strategically positioned as both subjects of economic opportunity as well as great assets whose skills are of high value to employers and the economy. These assumptions are aligned with the view of the graduate labour market, to which we will turn now.

How is the graduate labour market understood?

Graduate work is often identified as high-status, professional/managerial, high-skilled, knowledge-intense, complex, autonomous and high-waged and distinct from non-graduate work (Tholen, 2017a). As a result, the graduate labour market is also associated with these characteristics. For graduates, their degrees are deemed badges of suitability for professional and managerial jobs and signals of merit within recruitment. This idealised version profoundly shapes how policymakers and the media talk about the role of HE in economic, educational and social policies. We can see this in HE reform proposals. Graduates have become a distinct type of worker with special advanced skills that employers highly value. They are also often equated with high-skilled workers:

Highly skilled workers are quicker to adapt to new tasks and technologies and are themselves a direct source of innovation. A one percentage point increase in the proportion of the workforce with a degree, instead of just A level or equivalent qualifications, led to an increase in productivity of 0.5%. The value that employers place on graduates, demonstrated by the financial returns for graduates, is amongst the highest in the developed world. Therefore, convenient and accessible higher education is an important asset for a community in raising the skills of its people. (DBIS, 2008, p 6)

Graduates are also thought more likely to bring innovation into the workplace. Growing numbers of graduates in the workforce would benefit the whole economy:

Employing graduates creates innovation, enabling firms to identify and make more effective use of knowledge, ideas and technologies. Internationally successful businesses employ high levels of graduates, and 'innovative active enterprises' have roughly twice the share of employees educated at degree level than those that are not active in innovation. (Browne, 2010, p 14)

This special status of graduates within the labour market can be found throughout recent HE policy. The Dearing Report stresses that the labour market has fundamentally transformed itself with the advent of the KBE. It includes the rise in the proportion of professional and skilled jobs and a decrease in the proportion of unskilled jobs as well as the growing number of graduates in the workforce. Dearing emphasises that graduates will have increasing opportunities in the labour market and their HE will have given them the higher skills to succeed. Dearing observes an organisational and occupation change that will benefit graduates if they can adapt to change careers various times in the course of a working life and develop 'new sets of skills, to work across conventional boundaries and see connections between processes, functions and disciplines and, in particular, to manage the learning which will support their careers' (NCIHE, 1997, p 57). HE needs to equip graduates with the skills and attributes required to be effective in a changing world of work and upon which to found and manage several careers. Graduates need to take more responsibility in their learning and adapt their own skill development according to the quickly changing demands of the labour market and commit to lifelong learning. HE is understood to be able to support workplace learning in terms of developing skills throughout their lives, including flexible access and short courses and flexible qualifications. University graduates are expected to be all-round analytically skilled workers as well as specialists.

Employers emphasised to us in their evidence the importance of high level analytical skills. The development of such skills characterises higher education, and should continue to be one of its primary purposes. Indeed, many employers are seeking individuals with highly specialised knowledge and skills, with the medical and veterinary fields as the most obvious examples. But employers are also concerned about the general capabilities and potential of those with higher education qualifications, not just about the subject they have studied. The recruitment patterns of employers demonstrate that they are often looking for rounded but adaptable people who can successfully tackle a range of tasks and be effective members of a team. (NCIHE, 1997, p 130)

It acknowledges that employers want graduates to have a wide range of skills, including personal, and communication and practical skills. It highlights a range of skills that HE could contribute towards, including willingness to learn, self-management and motivation, interpersonal skills, team working and communication. Dearing states that the future of HE institutions depends on how well they can take the opportunity to educate skilled workers for modern work. Again we see that HE is held responsible for developing the skills employers demand in the labour market. In later government documents, the set of graduate skills and capabilities demanded by employers has even widened and the task of HE institutions to provide them ostensibly Herculean:

Employers particularly value broad 'employability' skills, such as communication, motivation, independence, analysis, confidence and problem solving. This is one of the strongest messages from employers to government. And students tell us that they share certain concerns with employers – particularly about employability and the quality and availability of information, advice and guidance (IAG). (DIUS, 2008, p 6)

Students and employers are thought to have a joint interest in an HE provider focused on the provision of a wide array of skills. The government once more holds HE accountable to develop the skills demanded and rewarded in the graduate labour market. Likewise, the *Fulfilling Our Potential* report (DBIS, 2015) gives universities a vital role in closing the perceived skills gap within the labour market. This is different from previous policy iterations because the lack of relevant skills and knowledge developed is now framed as more actively from those 'investing' in HE education. The skill gaps caused by HE's failure to teach the right skills is presented as evidence of suboptimal market outcomes for students:

Higher education providers need to provide degrees with lasting value to their recipients. This will mean providers being open to involving employers and learned societies representing professions in curriculum design. It will also mean teaching students the transferrable work readiness skills that businesses need, including collaborative teamwork and the development of a positive work ethic, so that they can contribute more effectively to our efforts to boost the productivity of the UK economy. (DBIS, 2015, p 12)

In other words, the expectation that HE is delivering the skills needed to succeed for individuals, and to succeed in the KBE, has a distinct market, or as some would have it, neoliberal solution: competition and greater opportunity for market choice to change the curriculum according to the employer demands. It is here that the Teaching Excellence Framework (TEF) makes sense:

That is why we are developing a new Teaching Excellence Framework. It will identify and incentivise the highest quality teaching to drive up standards in higher education, deliver better quality for students and employers and better value for taxpayers. Our aim is to ... help employers to identify and recruit graduates with the skills they require by providing better and clearer information about courses and degree outcomes. (DBIS, 2015, p 18)

TEF scores are partly based on labour market destination data such as employment in skilled work (using Destinations of Leavers from Higher Education (DLHE) data). The TEF becomes a meaningful instrument to measure the labour market value of a degree predicated on the idea that it is HE teaching that determines labour market outcomes:

The aim is to improve the teaching that students receive, which in turn should increase their productivity and help them secure better jobs and careers. It should enable employers to make more informed choices about the graduates they recruit, providing better understanding of the range of skills and knowledge they bring from their course, and deliver graduates who are more work ready following an active engagement in their studies. (DBIS, 2015, p 21)

Based on the data available, students can now ascertain the quality of the teaching and the labour market outcomes they can expect concerning their course of choice. Marketisation is needed to insert equity and efficiency for students as they are now in a position to maximise their employability through their HE choices:

For the first time we will link higher education and tax data together to chart the transition of graduates from higher education into the workplace better. This rich new data source will give students the information about the rewards that could be available at the end of their learning, alongside the costs. This innovation is at the heart of delivering our reform agenda ambitions: improving choice, competition and outcomes for students, the taxpayer and the economy success as a knowledge society. (DBIS, 2016, p 14)

Conclusion

This chapter, along with Chapter 3, demonstrate how HE has a clear purpose for the labour market and the economy within the policy discourse. How work and the labour market are understood is driven by wider ideological ideas on economic development. The HE policy discourse relies on the ideal of the knowledge society to understand the role of education in work and the economy. It then positions HE to deliver the skills and knowledge needed to flourish and improve productivity. HE is expected to fulfil the skill needs of employers and prepare young people to reap the benefits of the modern economy, which is thought to be driven by knowledge-intense technological change. Participation growth is paramount to the economy's needs to compete internationally and provide opportunity to all through human capital investment (improving social mobility through a firm commitment to widening participation and greater social inclusion in the process).

Employers and workers have a shared interest in educational upgrading as university education is crucial in delivering the skills needed by employers, leading to greater requirements for qualifications. The Dearing Report sets out a key framework on the role of HE in the economy and the opportunities attached to students, on which subsequent policies build. Over time, notions that university education provides a crucial condition in our economic development, and the future of knowledge work depends on the skills developed at HE, have reified.

From Dearing onwards, marketisation has slowly crept into the discourse on the role of HE in the knowledge economy as a means to achieve greater coordination between the needs of employers, students and the state. The policy discourse initially emphasised a general upskilling of the workforce, led by an assumption that the growth of skilled jobs could grow almost unlimited within a globalised economy. Over time, the narrative of the KBE stayed strong but without the striking optimism characterised in the debates in the 1990s. Later on, the success of the economy is still deemed highly dependent on the skills delivered by HE. However, with concerns about the actual skills that employers need, HE came under more pressure to deliver the right skills and knowledge. It was the market mechanism that was deemed to provide information on which skills were demanded and which educational programmes to invest in to realise labour market returns to their HE investment. As Newfield (2011, p 9) writes about financing universities in the KBE ideology:

> Students were to focus on the developing the knowledge base for tomorrow's jobs. If they were constantly having to pay more and more for their education, this was not necessarily bad: they were buying a private good that would arm them to create the higher incomes for themselves that would also benefit society as a whole. Their rising incomes would allow them to repay their rising tuition.

After the 2008 economic crisis, the UK government's view on the economy became far more strategic. Playing on the UK's strengths to improve the basis for long-term growth, its outputs needed to be more tailored to support an economic recovery. In tandem with the ongoing concerns about the costs of HE for the taxpayer, the confidence in market competition to improve HE in relation to both the quality of its education and the employability of its graduates grew. The increase of tuition fees thus made sense from that perspective, as did the commodification and the type of managerialism observed in Chapter 2.

The expectation of increased earnings linked to individual HE investment also became more prominent in the justification for further marketisation. Chapter 5 will further investigate how (future) earnings are understood to relate to university education. For this, we need to assess the influence of human capital theory and how policymakers have interpreted it.

5

Policymaking in higher education: human capital

The influence of economics shapes our world arguably more than ever before (Roscoe, 2014; Aldred, 2019). One of the most influential economic paradigms in the last 60 years has been Human Capital Theory (or Theories) (HCT). HCT has become the dominant economic theory to not only to lead Western countries' economic policies but also educational and social policies (Spring, 2015; Brown et al, 2020). This chapter demonstrates that the fundamentals of HCT underpin many of the supportive arguments for marketisation in higher education (HE). Like the assumptions on the economy and work discussed in the previous chapters, the HCT foundation matters. As we will see in the next three chapters, this matters as there are good reasons to question or even reject some key assumptions of this theoretical framework in its application in the marketisation debate. The chapter will briefly introduce the key characteristics of HCT before outlining how it has shaped policy thinking on marketisation of HE.

HCT has a long history and intellectually in its early form can be traced back to Adam Smith and Alfred Marshall. It did not grow to real prominence until the 1960s (Brown et al, 2020). Core contributions were made by Chicago school economists Jacob Mincer and Theodore Shultz at the turn of the 1960s (Mincer, 1958; Schultz, 1959, 1960, 1961), as well Gary Becker (1964) who developed the theory in new directions. The concept of human capital is used to highlight the classic insight that productive wealth is embodied in labour, skills and knowledge (OECD, 2001). Any stock of knowledge or characteristics the worker has (either innate or acquired) that contributes to his or her economic 'productivity' can be included (Garibaldi, 2006; Acemoglu and Autor, 2011). Human capital investments are 'activities that influence future monetary and psychic income by increasing the resources in people' and 'include schooling, on-the-job training, medical care, migration, and searching for information about prices and incomes' (Becker, 1994, p 11). The individuals thus make investments in themselves and as such become objects of investment, of inputs and outputs.

Marketable skills that workers possess are regarded as a key form of capital. Workers improve their skills through training or education which are 'the most important investments in human capital' (Becker, 1994, p 17). Education drives the marginal productivity of labour and marginal productivity drives earnings. Human capital acquired through on-the-job training or formal education tends to increase a person's productivity in the workplace, leading to increased earnings. Wages are based not on the characteristics of jobs, but on the productivity of workers. The lifetime earnings of educated labour, therefore, define the value of investment in education.

HCT has become a foundational theory within modern labour and education economics and beyond, and is used and empirically tested throughout the social sciences. It also became the cornerstone of educational policies in most developed nations. The idea that a country's prosperity is seen as directly linked to the cognitive skills of its workforce is now very much accepted (Hanushek and Woessmann, 2015). Post-war growth in participation in education contributed towards levels of rising national economic growth experienced in many countries. Education thus became a powerful tool to improve economic growth. It explains the increased earnings associated with all additional levels of education (Psacharopoulos, 1994; Keeley, 2007). The growth of human capital within the workforce reinforces the stimulation of economic growth. Companies will modify or improve their production processes to adapt to the growth in the supply of skilled labour available to them.

HCT does not deny that a wide range of factors including socioeconomic advantage could shape the earnings of workers, but human capital investment continues to be the key explaining factor of graduate earnings within the modern economy. Earnings reflect private rates of return for individuals and express how employers value certain types of human capital. Likewise, proponents acknowledge that there are non-monetary contributions and benefits of education to the individual and society (including its value as consumption). But these can be hard to calculate and are therefore often left as positive externalities. As posited by neoclassical economics, rationality is assumed for workers and employers. Individuals make rational investment decisions about how much and what type of education or training to purchase. People would invest in education up to the point where the private benefits from education are equal to the private costs. Employers act rationally and with self-interest in understanding degrees as proof of productive skills and knowledge that warrant this premium and would not pay this premium if they did not see a return.

Human capital has dominated our thinking in how to understand the role of schooling in our society as well as foundational in our thinking about the role of HE in developing work-related skills. This may have to do with its simplicity in explaining why those more educated on average earn more. Marginson (2019) has argued that a key reason why HCT has become influential is that it has become 'a widely understood metaphor for relations between work and education, that is grounded in the foundational narrative of a linear continuum between education, work, productivity and earnings' (p 289).

This chapter demonstrates how HCT has been critical in theoretically underpinning policy for HE marketisation. The direct relationship between education, skills, productivity, jobs and earnings has provided a crucial part of the justification of why more market and competition were needed to improve its functionality and maintain its affordability for the taxpayer.

Private economic benefits of higher education

From a human capital perspective, the economic returns are of the most significant importance to measure the value of an educational programme and have the benefit of being directly observable. Education is foremost an investment in human capital, not a form of consumption (Schultz, 1971). Although no policymaker would deny that university education has a wide range of aims, including personal development, the economic benefits of HE have received a lot more attention than the non-economic ones. Equally important, the value of degrees has been over time directly linked to the average wage premium of its graduates.

The economic benefits of investing in HE are delineated in the Dearing Report. Two of the most significant were increased employment rates and pay levels relative to those without HE credentials. The demand for HE places was expected to rise, primarily linked to the growing individual financial benefits of HE. The labour market outcomes represent 'strong positive incentive for individuals to commit themselves to a programme of higher education' (NCIHE, 1997, p 286). The 'learning is earning' adage remained an essential supposition in subsequent policy documents, often supported by empirical evidence:

> Graduates derive substantial benefits from having gained a degree, including wider career opportunities and the financial benefits that generally follow. On average those with a higher education qualification earn around 50% more than non-graduates. (DfES, 2003, p 81)

> Higher education leads to a better chance of being employed, and an average net lifetime earnings premium comfortably over £100,000 compared to holding 2 or more A Levels. (DBIS, 2016, p 42)

With each additional increase in tuition fees, greater emphasis was placed on understanding HE as an investment good in which students invest while emphasising the shared interest of employers and students in greater and better human capital development. The debate on how to prepare students with the skills of tomorrow has become closely entwined with debates on who should pay for HE. The assumed direct relationship between education and productivity became a strong defence for making HE education a private good, assuming that the graduate premium is caused by the skills and knowledge HE imparts. The employer demand for skills is reflected in the graduate premium:

> Higher education qualifications are more than a signal to the labour market – they bring real skills benefits which employers are prepared to pay a significant premium for. The fact that studying different subjects brings different labour market benefits (which can't be explained by the qualifications the students began the course with) argues strongly that employers are responding to real and significant skills and qualities resulting from higher education qualifications. (DfES, 2003, p 58)

The university system plays a critical role in equipping people with the skills they need to prosper (2009, p 40). In the knowledge-based economy (KBE), there is a premium on sophisticated skills, intellectual confidence and employability, so these 'had to be' among the key returns from HE.

Informed choice and labour market tailoring

As an economic theory, HCT conceives of individuals as economic agents that act as so-called *homo economicus* basing their choices on cost–benefit analysis (Becker, 1996). Gary Becker did not contend that these choices are necessarily driven by self-interest. They could be driven by a wider set of values, motives and preferences but actors do try to maximise personally conceived welfare. According to Teixeira (2014, p 1), Becker's economic approach to human behaviour is based on 'simplified assumptions regarding human behaviour, a result of individual choices characterised by utility maximisation, a forward-looking stance, consistent rationality, and stable and persistent preferences'.

Students as economic market actors anticipate the future consequences of present actions. Therefore, investments in education are planned according to the calculated return in relation to individuals' utility functions. It does not have to be the maximisation of future earnings but this has just received all the attention. The positioning of students as economic actors looking to make the right human capital investment emphasises the need for informed choice. One of the barriers that hamper a (free) market is the lack of transparency and information for market actors (supply and demand) to make optimal choices. The need for greater information to make decisions becomes a driving factor in policy reform towards greater marketisation. The Dearing Report identified that students need 'clear information and guidance' to make 'well-informed decisions about courses' (NCIHE, 1997, p 109). Highlighting the market between students and employers, the authors also include the need for employers to have detailed information about educational programmes: 'Those who participate in higher education should receive an experience of assured quality and the users of higher education – both students and employers – should have access to enough information about what is on offer, its standards, quality, costs and intended outcomes, to enable them to make informed choices' (NCIHE, 1997, p 86). The 2003 white paper elaborates on the need for more information:

> To become intelligent customers of an increasingly diverse provision, and to meet their own increasing diverse needs, students need accessible information. … Students decide which HEIs to apply to, and employers decide which to recruit from, based on a wide range of different factors. Choices are bound to be complex; but we believe that the quality of the institution's teaching should be a very important consideration. Neither students nor employers should have to base their decisions on perceptions of relative prestige which may be outdated or unreliable, but should be able to draw on up to date and robust assessments of the quality of learning and teaching. (DfES, 2003, p 48)

Students and employers would need similar data on the quality of teaching or skill development, implying that what matters here is that quality of teaching is purely expressed labour market utility (in line with HCT). It can be directly measured and should be transparent to all involved. The solution lies in information in which both types of stakeholders can ascertain whether their investment is able to be translated into favourable labour market outcomes. This is even more explicit in the Browne Review: 'Prospective students also need good information so they can reflect on how different learning choices will affect their career prospects' (Browne, 2010, p 40).

The 2011 white paper repeats this instrumentalism and consolidates the notion that HE provision of skills and knowledge should be transparent and tailored to the customer. Also the direct relationship is noted between students' investment and sufficient information: 'As graduates are asked to contribute more than they do at present, the higher education sector should be more responsive to their choices and continuously improve the design and content of courses and the quality of their academic experience' (DBIS, 2011, p 14).

Greater competition to make the investment, identification and promotion of human capital improvement remain the key threads throughout the document: 'Enabling greater competition, while removing unnecessary regulations, is an important theme of this White Paper, because of the benefits for all users of higher education. We want to ensure that the new student finance regime supports student choice, and that in turn student choice drives competition, including on price' (DBIS, 2011, p 19). Again, the benefits mentioned in this quote refer to human capital benefits. Of course, the proposed idea for HE institutions to decide what tuition fees to charge failed to create real competition as soon as practically all HE institutions chose to charge the maximum tuition fees. In the *Higher Ambitions* report (DBIS, 2009), employers are also involved in both offering information as well as coordinating the skills universities provide with their needs:

> It is increasingly important that they [students] consider how their programme of study will affect their long-term employment prospects. Employers need to do more to help potential students understand the importance for their own future prospects of acquiring high-level skills. As recommended by Alan Milburn's report, they should offer prospective students information about what sorts of jobs and future opportunities are available in a particular sector, the skills needed to get those jobs, and how those skills might be gained. (DBIS, 2009, p 42)

Here, we see HCT's direct relationship between education, skills and labour market opportunities. The *Fulfilling Our Potential* green paper (DBIS, 2015) noted that the transparency in key information, including labour market prospects for students, is not merely useful but critical for the student to make any HE decision:

> Since reforms to the higher education sector in 2012, student choice has become a key driver of change. But imperfect information about teaching quality, course content and graduate outcomes makes it hard for prospective students to make decisions on which courses to take or where to study. ... We know that information about what they can expect from university is crucial to young people making life changing decisions. We recognise that higher education is not the only option for young people, so it is essential that they have the best information and support available to be able to make these huge decisions. To be able to make the best choices about where and what to study, individuals need access to robust, timely and objective information regarding the quality of teaching they are likely to experience and what this is likely to mean for their future employment. (DBIS, 2015, p 11)

By referring to those who decided not to attend HE, it emphasises in line with HCT, that if the expected financial returns to a particular course of programme are lower than the investment costs, the investment will unlikely be made. A rational actor can only make a cost–benefit analysis if there is transparency in the market. The same applies for employers who are assumed to use detailed course-specific information on skill development to successfully recruit graduates: 'The absence of information about the quality of courses, subjects covered and skills gained makes it difficult for employers to identify and recruit graduates with the right level of skills and harder for providers to know how to develop and improve their courses' (DBIS, 2015, p 19). The quote also shows the utilitarian view of HE in which the value and quality of educational promises is a direct function of its role as developer of work skills. *Success as a Knowledge Society* (DBIS, 2016) repeats the call for more transparency for both student and employer to make informed choices and also suggests that better information could have prevented disappointing labour market outcomes: 'However the outcomes that we observe from English higher education are not consistently strong. This starts when students cannot make informed choices. ... This leads to dissatisfaction and poor outcomes' (DBIS, 2016, p 42). It also directly aligns the call for greater marketisation with the need for better information as part of the government's HE reform:

> Give students the information about the rewards that could be available at the end of their learning, alongside the costs. This innovation is at the heart of delivering our reform agenda ambitions: improving choice, competition and outcomes for students, the taxpayer and the economy. (DBIS, 2016, p 58)

> Information, particularly on price and quality, is critical if the higher education market is to perform properly. Without it, providers cannot fully and accurately advertise their offerings, and students cannot make informed decisions. (DBIS, 2016, p 11)

In all of this, we see that the labour market outcomes are boldly interpreted to be caused by university teaching. In offering data on labour market outcomes, students will be provided with valid information about the strength of the teaching, that is, human capital development, to improve the market coordination between the demand and supply in an HE market.

The role of skills

From a HTC perspective, not every investment in human capital created through HE may be a good investment due to substandard teaching or the lack of demand in the labour market for the skills developed. Similarly, on a national level, state investment in HE may not be the right investment, even within the high skill demand of the knowledge economy. Education will not always necessarily deliver the skills needed in the economy. For individuals, the graduate premium is a reflection of the value of certain types of human capital within the labour market. This leads to the circular argument that when a university education does not yield sufficient earnings returns, the relevant educational programme must not have developed the right skills. The Browne Review unequivocally states that graduate skills are the basis of the graduate premium. Teaching quality as labour market preparation is directly related to labour market outcomes. Between–institutional employment outcomes differences for graduates who studied the subject reflect differences in teaching qualities. The value of a course is directly linked to how well it can achieve employability:

> It is sometimes suggested that a number of popular subjects are of little value. Stereotypes about what courses offer the best employment prospects are often wrong. Graduates in some subjects, popularly thought to confer poor employment prospects, are actually found to have good rates of employability. ... Furthermore, the data on employment and further study outcomes at six months show a spectrum of performance in each of the university mission groups, with new universities such as Edge Hill (95 per cent) and Nottingham Trent (93 per cent) demonstrating that excellence is not the preserve of a select group of institutions. (DBIS, 2009, p 43)

HCT underpins much of this thinking. The assumption is that HE provides students with skills that employers reward with jobs and higher wages. Suppose graduates are not finding (suitable) jobs or are not paid premium wages. In that case, there must be something wrong with what and how they are taught at university which has caused their investment to fail to deliver the expected returns.

Another area in which we can observe the reliance on HE to deliver individual labour market success and national economic growth is how policy discourse deals with labour market skills mismatch. In the media and political circles there are growing concerns about labour market mismatch, including graduate unemployment and underemployment in particular after the 2008 economic crisis (Tholen, 2014). The authors of the Dearing Report seem aware that the expanding graduate labour force has caused some graduatisation of the labour market but this seems to be a rather natural phenomenon with limited consequences on the role of HE within the labour market. In the last decade, however, overqualification has become too widespread to ignore. In *Fulfilling Our Potential* (DBIS, 2015), we see that both vertical and horizontal mismatches are deemed policy issues. Yet both types are deemed to be caused not by a lack of demand or a rapid rise of the supply as a result of the rise of mass HE, but failures in skill formation in HE:

> While employers report strong demand for graduate talent, they continue to raise concerns about the skills and job readiness of too many in the graduate labour pool. Recent indications that the graduate earnings gap is in decline, and that significant numbers of graduates are going into non-graduate jobs, reinforce the need for action. (DBIS, 2015, p 8)

Ultimately, degrees are thought to be valued because of the skill developed within an educational programme, and their value on the labour market is a reflection of it. Once this is accepted, any type of labour market issue for graduates can be linked to their HE experience. Take the phenomenon of degree inflation. Jo Johnson (2017b), at the time Minister of State for Universities, Science, Research and Innovation, discusses the idea that the growing demand for higher levels of education is a result of employers' response to the growing supply of graduates in the labour force. Individuals would need more and more educational credentials to distinguish themselves from other candidates irrespective of the job content (based on the so-called signalling function of education, which we will be addressed in Chapter 7). Johnson thinks this idea is absurd. He tells his audience:

> A range of evidence suggests the pessimists are wrong, and that economies with more university graduates enjoy higher rates of economic growth overall. These productivity uplifts are a sign that university degrees provide a real economic benefit, not just a prestigious credential. … The idea that higher education provides real and significant benefits is consistent with what we hear from employers across the country: that the economy of the future will continue to require graduates, and lots of them. The steady rise in the level of formal qualifications held by those in employment does not simply reflect qualification inflation caused by large increases in the supply of graduates, as pessimists maintain. It is happening as a result of more fundamental changes in the occupational structure of the UK as a knowledge economy. Some 1.8 million new jobs will be created between 2014 and 2024, and 70% of them will be in the occupations most likely to employ graduates. (Johnson, 2017b)

Johnson here demonstrates a strong HCT view that the knowledge-based economy has made the skills that graduates have developed in HE of ever greater value. He then uses this stance to admit that there are a minority of courses which deliver poor or questionable outcomes, as indicated by the findings of a student survey that more students in England believed they have received poor value than good value. Johnson suggests that lower employment outcomes and customer dissatisfaction are both indicators of poor value for money in HE. This highlights how far HCT, as well as consumerism, have penetrated policymakers' understanding of HE.

How does the influence of Human Capital Theory lead to marketisation?

HCT relies on the importance of the market mechanism in the labour market. Workers supply their human capital and employers offer labour market opportunities and wages according to their needs. The market mechanism also extends to the market in education and training providers in connecting employers and labour market candidates. Once education is regarded as an investment (cost plus effort) students (and their families) will become market actors in the education market and this applies most for non-compulsory education. Although policymakers do not refer to the theory explicitly, its influence supports arguments for further marketisation in HE. In the Dearing Report, the justification for introducing tuition fees rests on the now accepted idea that the graduate premium to a large extent represents the investments made by those attending HE. Based on a fairness principle, they should shoulder at least some of the costs of HE:

> There is overwhelming evidence that those with higher education qualifications are the main beneficiaries from higher education in the form of improved employment prospects and pay. Individuals who benefit in this way are not drawn proportionately from the socio-economic groups that currently fund higher education through general taxation. We conclude, therefore, that graduates in employment should make a greater contribution to the costs of higher education in the future. (NCIHE, 1997, pp 288–289)

The focus on the (economic) beneficiaries of HE seems in line with mainstream economists' approach to how to pay for what is, in a strict sense, not a public good. Graduates are thus held responsible for contributing to the costs of their learning. The report locates responsibility for funding HE between the government, students and employers. The funding arrangements should, as a reflection of the various beneficiaries of HE, share its costs while maintaining equitability so that individuals are not denied access to HE due to lack of financial means. The report draws on the idea that within the KBE, human capital development requires investment, that is, market choice that leads to optimal economic outcomes for the three key stakeholders (state, student and employer), stating: 'If our vision of a learning society is to be realised, students will have … to make a greater investment in their own futures' (NCIHE, 1997, p 304).

For Dearing, the role of a market to coordinate the interests of the state, employers and students was still modest. This interconnection becomes explicit in later policy documents. For instance, the *Success as a Knowledge Economy* (DBIS, 2016) report continues to not only position students as consumers but equates their interests with those of employers – which is the development of skills rewarded in the labour market. It observes that many problems that students have with HE can be solved by greater choice and competition:

Many students are dissatisfied with the provision they receive, with over 60% of students feeling that all or some elements of their course are worse than expected and a third of these attributing this to concerns with teaching quality. Employers are suffering skills shortages, especially in high skilled STEM areas; at the same time around 20% of employed graduates are in non-professional roles three and a half years after graduating. While the graduate premium has remained substantial, even as student numbers have expanded rapidly in recent decades, recent research suggests there is large variation in graduate outcomes across both providers and subjects, and even for those that studied the same subject within the same provider. ... By introducing more competition and informed choice into higher education, we will deliver better outcomes and value for students, employers and the taxpayers who underwrite the system. (DBIS, 2016, p 8)

The solution is to create a *competitive market between providers* which 'incentivises them to raise their game, offering consumers a greater choice of more innovative and better quality products and services at lower cost' (DBIS, 2016, p 11). This need for increased competition is directly linked to the need for students to make optimal human capital investments that ultimately will serve all parties: 'But there is currently little pressure on providers to differentiate themselves in this way. This is a cause for concern as poor decisions by the student as to which course and institution to attend can prove costly not just for them but for the broader economy and the taxpayer' (DBIS, 2016, p 11).

Apart from further choice, the need for value for money and institutional accountability is required to drive up quality. In cases where labour market outcomes are comparatively low, institutions may have underperformed as skill providers. HE reform, therefore, needs to be based on providing greater choice and transparency to allow a drive to improve the right skill development. Again, only a quasi-market can achieve this. The education-as-investment approach inspired by HCT makes marketisation and choice crucial requirements for a well-functioning HE system. By creating market condition (despite it not being a pure free market), learning, student satisfaction and economic returns will be optimised:

We need to ensure that our higher education system continues to provide the best possible outcomes. These come from informed choice and competition. We must provide incentives for all institutions to improve and to focus on what matters to students, society and the economy. By removing student number controls and making it easier for new providers to enter, we will create the conditions that will allow choice and competition to flourish. But what is also needed is the information to allow students to determine where the best teaching can be found. (DBIS, 2016, p 43)

The direct association between what university teaches and labour market outcomes is echoed in the Augar Review (Augar, 2019). It proposes a wider range of HE and further education (FE) reforms to avoid university students being left stranded with poor earnings and escalating debts. HE should be reformed to minimise these cases. The report optimistically concludes that 'lifting all the boats would bring significant benefits for students, taxpayers and employers alike' (Augar, 2019, p 65). The solution to the lack of benefits to some degrees remains more market solutions in the form of greater understanding of the financial returns to a student's investment in identifying courses deemed low value for money. The search to create value for money remains a central mode in thinking about the structuration of HE. The report also emphasises the role of better market information, including earnings returns to graduates *studying specific subjects at specific institutions*. Yet, it does offer a much more nuanced view of the role for HE influence on graduate wages when it states:

> Earnings are largely a product of the labour market for particular skills and qualifications and should not be regarded as a measure of teaching quality. They also vary according to location: a graduate working in an economic cold spot is likely to earn less than her or his counterpart working in a hot spot. However, if analysed with care, the data provide an insight into the early career financial consequences of degree study and will be a useful source of information for students, government and HEIs alike. (Augar, 2019, p 87)

It also emphasises that HE serves a wider set of values to society. Yet it recommends that it is in the interest of the state to hold HE institutions to account if their graduates do not see financial returns to their investments.

The *Value for Money* report (DfE, 2018), published by parliament's education committee, is, as the title suggests, dedicated to how the student can become an autonomous consumer who can make informed choices within HE according to their preferences, most importantly investment returns.

> Students increasingly want to know where their money is going, the quality of the product they will receive and what they should expect in return. (DfE, 2018, p 4)

Value for money in higher education has been defined in a variety of ways throughout the inquiry. These can be broadly divided into value to the economy, and value to the individual both in a non-monetary and monetary sense. (DfE, 2018, p 4)

Although it acknowledges the non-monetary benefits for the individual, the report does not elaborate on these substantially. Key arguments revolve around the variability of returns to education in terms of degree and institution, which may not always be known to the consumer, leading to suboptimal outcomes for the student, employer and taxpayer. The report, again, calls for better information on teaching quality defined as labour market outcomes: 'Higher education institutions must be more transparent about the labour market returns of their courses. This is not simply a measure of graduate earnings but of appropriate professional graduate-level and skilled employment destinations' (DfE, 2018, p 32).

Once more, the value of HE courses lies in how well they provide labour market returns. This has been positioned as the key leading principle that should drive the sector. Marketisation is the logical step to improve the value of HE. The Office for Students (OfS), the market regulator, is the guarantor that competition, choice and student interest will be central in how HE institutions are managed. Using predominantly satisfaction data, continuation figures and employment data, the Teaching Excellence Framework (TEF) exercise was thought to offer robust judgement on poor quality, 'bearing down on provision of dubious value' (Augar, 2019, p 98). Here low-earning graduates are also deemed a taxpayer issue as they are unlikely to pay back (entirely) their student loans:

With higher returns, more graduates will be able to pay back more of their loans, reducing the amount that needs to be subsidised by the taxpayer in the longer term. This is on top of the benefits to taxpayers from having a stronger economy powered by a higher skilled workforce. (DBIS, 2015, p 21)

Conclusion

Human capital in the HE policy discourse is expressed in:

- *The increasing importance of the economic benefit of HE*: HE is understood through an instrumental economic lens and functions primarily as a key developer of productive work skills. Other understandings are acknowledged yet receive little attention or recommendations.
- *The positioning of students as investors in human capital*: students are assumed to access HE for career-related reasons predominantly. They will use HE not only as a means of labour market preparation but of labour market maximisation. They need detailed information on employment outcomes

to help reveal differences in teaching quality – allowing them to make informed choices in the HE market.

- *The market for HE provision is directly linked to labour market outcomes*: skills developed at HE, and demanded by employers, become a key reason why HE participation leads to labour market outcomes such as the graduate premium. The graduate premium is a reflection of the productive differences between graduates and non-graduates. Labour market outcomes constitute information signals on the investments students and the state have made.

- *The understanding that the skills employers need are closely aligned to the skills that universities teach*: participation in HE should lead to skill development based on what employers demand to maximise returns for students. This is thought to be in the interest of employers and the taxpayer. It is assumed that the teaching quality, course content, that is, what is taught and how it is taught, directly leads to labour market outcomes such as salary, employment rate and share in graduate employment. Students (should) examine this information if they want to make the best investment choice.

HCT has led to a focus on the supply-side of labour within the KBE, as opposed to, for instance, consumer demand or the cost of raw materials (Brown et al, 2020). Improving the skills and knowledge of the workforce would benefit all. As McCaig (2018) has demonstrated, national human capital arguments have been made in educational policy documents to support the continued expansion of participation in HE. Yet over time, the utilitarian view of HE as a skill provider has pushed away other meanings, although they can still be found albeit often in the margins.

This chapter has demonstrated that HCT underpins the assumed relationship between education, skills and rewards, and has justified driving marketisation in HE. As market actors, students (and their families) are regarded to be in the best position to make decisions on the level and type of educational investment according to preferences and academic abilities. Individuals become capitalists, expressing themselves in HE choices in which their human capital is a private possession to be invested. There is a close match between the rewards one reaps in the labour market and individual productivity. So, any investment in education that increases productivity to the individual will, under normal circumstances, result in greater financial returns. Educational choices are reduced to a trade-off between (monetary) costs and benefits. The clearest costs are tuition fees, study costs and foregone earnings (opportunity costs). The clearest benefits are labour market-related, including expected or future earnings. People are competent to evaluate their 'attributes properly in determining whether it is worthwhile to act, and if it is worthwhile, people respond by reallocating their resources' (Schultz, 1975, p 834). In theory, the market mechanism would prevent overinvestment in education as low returns to certain degrees would stop most prospective students from choosing them. Individuals will need market signals to respond to economic demand for different types of skills, the cost of education and the changes in earnings (Schultz, 1975, p 840). Yet in order for the student to make investment decisions the following are necessary: competition in producing educational services along with efficient prices of these services; students acquiring optimal information; and an efficient capital market serving students (Schultz, 1971, pp 181–182). The graduate premium and other more specific information on the earnings of graduates of particular courses show prospective graduates whether their educational choices are sound financial investments. They also signal whether, on average at least, there are significant financial rewards over a lifetime. Any investment in education that offers increased productivity to the individual will, under normal circumstances, result in positive financial returns.

The student as a market actor that can optimise its choices in HE, benefiting themselves, employers, and the wider economy as a whole. For HCT, education is however not necessarily a private good. The state has a vested interest in quality education. The assumed benefits in productivity and labour market outcomes have become the driving principles in determining the value of HE to society while supporting the widening participation agenda and efforts to improve social mobility.

HCT positions the student as a market actor that maximises its utility through market choices. In other words, to make students responsible for their labour market outcomes, we *need* to assume a close correspondence between the advanced knowledge and skills acquired in HE qualifications and those demanded, used and most of all rewarded in (high-skilled) work. The lifting of the fee caps, the entrance of the market for new providers, and competitive audit mechanisms to inform student choices all lead to competition intensification justified by the need to improve the market position of graduates.

6

Graduate work in modern capitalism

Introduction

It has become increasingly challenging to make generalisations for those workers with university degrees. In 2017, as many as 42 per cent of individuals aged 21 to 64 were university graduates (ONS, 2021). Graduate workers work in a wide variety of jobs, occupations and sectors under diverse conditions (Tholen, 2017a). The surge of graduates in the labour force has led to debates about whether there are too many graduates. The answer, of course, depends on one's view of what higher education (HE) is for. Even those who take a more economic-utilitarian approach can take an optimistic view in which an increase in skills supply upskills the whole economy (as we have seen in Chapter 3). Companies adjust their product market and competitive strategies to take advantage of this highly educated workforce while moving up the value and quality chain. This lifts the whole national economy. Increasingly more attention is paid to the type of skills graduate labour market entrants possess. Whether there are too many graduates then also depends on one's view on overeducation; how do we define it, and to what extent does it matters (Trow, 1973; Marginson, 2016).

This chapter will look at graduate work and evaluate the assumptions on work and employment outlined in the previous three chapters assessing the role of graduates in the economy, the demand for their skills, the work that graduates do and how it relates to HE. Five key axioms of the HE policy discourse are:

- The knowledge-based economy requires graduates and their skills and knowledge.
- Knowledge workers and their unique skills and status drive the modern economy.
- The graduate labour market is sustained by growing demand for skills associated with HE.
- Employers are predominantly interested in graduates because of their university education.
- The graduate premium reflects the demand for graduates and their skills.

It is important to note that the policy discourse on marketisation is not alone in portraying the work that graduates do this way. It is supported by various government policies and media portrayals (Tholen, 2014).

By reviewing some of the empirical evidence on the nature of modern capitalism, the graduate labour market and graduate work, it will become clear that the argumentation for further marketisation is built on an unrealistic representation of graduate work. It is important to note that I do not claim to offer an overview of *all* the evidence that supports or contradicts these substantial and often broad assumptions. My aim is modest; I will show that the relationship between education, skill, jobs and earning is much more complex than assumed. This makes many of the policy documents' assumptions highly uncertain and partly true at best. I demonstrate that graduate work, the graduate labour market and the role of university education is idealised in HE policy. The simplification of the role of HE in work makes the argumentation around marketisation unsustainable.

This chapter and the following two chapters work in tandem. This chapter will example the nature of capitalism, including the role of knowledge. I then turn to the evidence on graduates' work, the skills they use and the labour market they find themselves in (Chapter 7). Chapter 8 focuses on earnings, and at the end of the chapter, I will assess what a renewed view of graduate work means for the call for further marketisation in the UK context.

Capitalism

The policy rationales around marketisation in HE draw on a particular view on the nature of modern capitalism. As explained in Chapter 3, the concept of the knowledge-based economy is adhered to and utilised to support the idea that individuals can reap the benefits of the growing premium on human capital investment. The demand for skilled workers is thought to be driven by technological developments that favour skilled over unskilled labour by increasing its relative productivity and, therefore, its relative demand (Bound and Johnson, 1992; Berman et al, 1998; Acemoglu, 1998, 2002; Conte and Vivarelli, 2011). According to the skill-biased technological change (SBTC) theory, new technologies (in particular computers) increase the demand for higher skills, and the human capital available in the labour force are the basis for economic growth (Romer, 1990). These technologies are complementary to skilled (educated) workers and a substitute for the unskilled. At the same level of human capital, productivity is much higher when (computer) technology is used for those with advanced skills (Autor et al, 1998). The unskilled also face a greater danger of the destruction of their jobs through automation. As these technologies become more widespread, the relative demand for the higher educated leads to greater earnings inequality between educational groups (Katz and Murphy, 1992; Levy and Murnane, 1992; Acemoglu and Autor, 2012).

A related but somewhat contrasting thesis is that the growing demand for skilled workers has to do with the substitutability of tasks with the new technologies. 'Routine-Biased Technical Change' (Autor and Dorn, 2013; Goos et al, 2014) explains that repetitive tasks that are easily codified can increasingly be performed by computers (for example, through algorithms). As routine tasks are more likely to be found in jobs with middling skill levels, there will be a polarisation in skill demand rather than a general upgrading as predicted by SBTC.

The supply of skills within the labour force leads to greater demand for skills within the mainstream economic view. So growth in the supply of advanced skills as expressed through the participation in HE becomes a major asset for further economic development. Growth in the demand for more-educated workers from SBTC may even outgrow the relative supply of more-educated workers, leading to growing inequalities between the skilled and unskilled. Goldin and Katz (2009) famously depict a race between education and technology. They explain that rapid educational growth kept skill differentials in check during the mid-20th century. However, from 1980 to 2005, a slowdown in relative education supply growth contributed to a rising premium in the earnings of university graduates. According to the authors, if the education system fails to keep pace with technological innovation and the rising demand for higher-level skills, rising income inequality will follow.

It is true, of course, that technological change has significantly altered the economy and nature of work. Yet there is much more to the story. Capitalism developed in ways in which labour loses out to capital, and economic success is not linked to human capital. What is called technoscientific capitalism is increasingly underpinned by rentiership or the appropriation of value through ownership and control rights, for example, intellectual property and monopoly conditions (Birch, 2020, p 3). The capitalist logic of accumulation of this data-driven economy seems to be based on the concentration of knowledge and power by large corporations (Zuboff, 2019; see also Frase, 2016; Christophers, 2020). There seems little evidence to suggest that this will benefit the labour power of the growing number of so-called knowledge workers in our society apart from a small group of elite workers at the top.

Take the emergence of the sharing economy (or access economy, Eckhardt and Bardhi, 2015), which is based on economic activities that rely on digital platforms that connect consumers to a service or commodity through the use of a mobile application or website enabled platforms (Cockayne, 2016, p 73). One study estimates that in 2017 there were around 1.1 million gig workers in Britain (Balaram et al, 2017). The majority of what we call the sharing economy is on-demand employment which includes gig employment (using digital platforms on which to offer services) and cloud working. The latter involves online job markets in which companies make requests online for tasks or services they need, which includes many high-skilled activities such as computer programming, design, translation, administrative or accounting tasks, etc. They have created a growing number of freelancing contracting professionals (particularly within the US context), where platforms such as Fiverr, Upwork and TaskRabbit create platforms on which these workers sell their skill, knowledge and expertise. Although platform workers could be engaged in any kind of employment relationship, it is clear that many are in a very insecure one which is often not in the interest of workers, and has been linked to driving down the wages, security and employment benefits (Kalleberg, 2013; Codagnone et al, 2016; Scholz, 2016; Ravenelle, 2019). Firms are constantly trying to find new business models and cheaper ways of producing goods and services. This has resulted in increased use of non-standard employment arrangements, on-demand business models, outsourcing, self-employment and a shift of the costs, risks and responsibilities from employers onto workers. Technology has further promoted this trend by facilitating the outsourcing not only of jobs, but also of individual tasks, as it has significantly lowered the transaction costs involved in doing so and made it possible even for small and medium enterprises to outsource. This has all been enabled by technology (Hill, 2017). An estimated third (33 per cent) of platform workers were educated to degree level in 2017 (Rahim et al, 2017, p 15). Others estimate the share of gig workers with degrees to be 44 per cent (Balaram et al, 2017, p 18). We can associate the emergence of platform working with the broader trend of self-employment. Between 2001 and 2016, the growth in self-employment was driven mainly by those who have a degree (or equivalent) (ONS, 2018). For firms, business models based on outsourcing work to self-employed workers generally means more flexibility to adjust the workforce in light of changing and sometimes unpredictable economic conditions, as well as significant cost savings. Non-standard employment results in lower investment in training (OECD, 2014). While self-employment may mean increased flexibility for workers, they are unlikely to reap the benefits if they have little bargaining power over those who employ them. It leaves workers not only in poor working conditions but also underpaid. Because of the diversification of employment relationships, the returns to workers' skills are increasingly unevenly distributed, enabling technology firms to capture increasing shares of profits. The market power of groups of skilled workers has been eroded fast within the technology sector. A small number of companies have monopolies, and its workers (both skilled and unskilled) lose ground in wage development (Eeckhout, 2020).

Fleming (2017) argues that it is in fact Human Capital Theory (HCT), discussed in Chapter 5, that has enabled the individualisation of the workforce, including the rise of zero-hours contracts and precarious employment structures. In HCT, each person is already their own means of production. Human capitalists become entirely responsible for their economic fate through their own investment choices, with training and education as a key self-investment opportunities. The worker becomes individualised and treated as a self-contained enterprise. HCT sees this as empowering. Yet the worker needs to take all responsibility for all the costs and benefits associated with being an economic actor. This *radical responsibilisation* invites an individualistic contract-based business model, as it 'reimagines employees as competitive, self-interested agents that are somehow *external to the firm*, rather than an internal core resource that requires company investment, training and stewardship' (p 695, emphasis in original). Yet for most workers, the reality means increasing insecurity and pressure to accept bad working conditions (including overwork, unpaid work). Instead of becoming freer, wealthier and autonomous, workers suffer from what Fleming describes as the 'uberisation' of work, even those with advanced skills.

Another defining feature of the modern economy is how companies (are allowed to) operate and manage their workforce. According to the blueprint of the knowledge-based economy, knowledge workers would take an increasing share of the wealth created. In liberal market economies such as the UK, stock markets play a central role in the economy and financial systems are centred on the financial markets (Hall and Soskice, 2001). The focus on shareholder profits is in sharp contrast with the interest of knowledge workers. Inequalities based on the *ownership* of knowledge and data and the monopolies created by large tech giants define the economy more than the ability to transform knowledge by individual workers. Ownership of companies tends to be widely dispersed among individuals and institutions; corporate governance is characterised by the prioritisation of stockholders' interest, which will define how companies operate and affect how they organise and reward work. As Hutton (2015) explains:

> No reimagining of contemporary British capitalism is possible without the reimagination of how companies are owned. Companies are, after all, the central economic actors in the market economy – the investors, the innovators and employers. They give any capitalism its particular character and dynamic. Britain's increasingly divided society and the character of its labour market, with the emergence of so many contingent low-wage jobs, is inextricably intertwined with how its companies behave.

Some see the UK as a particularly irresponsible, dysfunctional and extreme type of capitalism whose benefits do not reach wider society (Mayer, 2019). It remains solidly invested in an economy in which labour is unlikely to become the dominant factor. Schram (2015, p 15) calls this a 'neoliberal economy', which involves 'growing reliance on automated production, increased outsourcing to foreign countries, declining negotiating power for labor with decreasing union membership, and other relevant factors weakening the position of ordinary workers conspired to decouple their wages from economic growth'. The lack of labour power has helped a system in which labour has become commodified. Larry Elliott (2018) explains:

> Britain's flexible labour market has resulted in the development of a particular sort of economy over the past decade: low productivity, low investment and low wage. Since the turn of the millennium, business investment has grown by about 1% a year on average because companies have substituted cheap workers for capital. Labour has become a commodity to be bought as cheaply as possible.

In contrast to the knowledge-based economy narrative, the labour power of the skilled worker does not always depend on their human capital but how well they can protect themselves from commodifying forces. Even skilled workers could be subject to insecurity and low rewards due to downsizing, delayering and the influence of global labour markets. These forces greatly affect the graduate labour market (Harvey, 2000). Without legal or state-related constraints, companies have greater opportunities to use and exploit knowledge to increase profits and reduce costs. In their book *The Global Auction* (2012), Phillip Brown, Hugh Lauder and David Ashton examined skill-formation strategies of 30 leading companies operating across seven countries. To corporate competitive advantage the role of skills and human resources become increasingly important. Unlike the idea that only Western nations would specialise in high-skilled high-valued goods and services, non-Western countries also compete globally for these types of investment. High-skilled work that used to be exclusively performed in Western economies can now be performed all over the globe. The quality and productivity gap between developing and developed economies is closing due to the increasing supply of highly educated workers in the global labour market, especially in China and India. As a result, greater movement of other high-end work to lower-cost locations has occurred, which has continued since the book's publication (Brown et al, 2020).

Technology

Western advanced economies rely increasingly on innovation to generate wealth and jobs in the knowledge-based economy narrative. The value of corporations is now derived primarily from their intangible assets – such as their workers' human and social capital and the intellectual property that they create. Consequently, a country's long-run productivity and economic growth are seen to depend heavily on the education, training and skills possessed by its labour force, a good ICT infrastructure, a favourable economic and institutional regime, and an efficient innovation system (World Bank, 2007).

There is no doubt that the modern economy continues to change with increasing speed with the emergence of new technologies. This has shaped the economy's outputs towards more technology-intensive goods and services and fundamentally shaped work itself. Technical advances since the 1980s have been the main driver in helping workers become more productive. It is not unreasonable to think that these technologies are biased towards those with the skills to adapt and use new technology. Nevertheless, this remains a rather general trend. There are many caveats to this story and the future of the influence of technology on work is also somewhat uncertain.

The current digital transformation of the economy is affecting business, public services and the wider society. A whole set of new technologies and unprecedented computer power is transforming advances in data analytics, artificial intelligence (AI), the use of Big Data, the connectedness of workers and firms, robotics, and the Internet of Things (IoT). What the influence on work will be is a point of debate. Some have argued that the influence of digital transformation on work is fundamentally different to anything we have experienced in human history (McAfee and Brynjolfsson, 2012; Frey and Osborne, 2013), while others are less convinced (Mokyr et al, 2015). The tasks associated with each job will continue to change (Spitz-Oener, 2006; Bessen, 2016).

Technological progress and innovation will trigger changes in the labour markets. Some tasks and occupations will be substituted in the same way as many other tasks and occupations have been since the industrial revolution. The demand for some high-skilled labour will increase, particularly for those workers who have skills that complement the digital economy. One key technological change often mentioned is automation, technology applications where human input is minimised and replaced by self-governing systems often driven by computer power such as monitoring devices, drones, robots and automated vehicles. There is currently no consensus on the impact of automation (see Schlogler and Sumner [2020] for an overview of some key studies that estimate and predict the effect of automation on employment). They range from highly pessimistic predictions of mass unemployment (for example PWC, 2017), to those who expect far less disruption or far less net job loss (for example WEF, 2020). Others have emphasised that automation is likely to alter jobs rather than eliminate them (Dellot and Wallace-Stevens, 2017). Acemoglu and Restrepo (2018) emphasise that with new technologies, new occupations are emerging. These new occupations account for a large percentage of employment growth. Therefore, technological change may support both employment growth and decline (see also Atkinson and Wu, 2017; Lane and Saint-Martin, 2021). There is limited certainty on the feasibility of many labour-saving automation technologies. The degree of adoption will ultimately depend on many factors, including the economic risks and returns given capital and labour costs. Great uncertainty is also present around the kind of tasks that machines could do. Again we see a variety of views on this but in general there is an agreement that routine and repetitive tasks will be automated. McKinsey Global Institute (2017) predicts that, overall, 49 per cent of the paid activities undertaken in the global economy have the potential to be automated. In particular, in data collection, robots may replace roles that involve data processing and predictable physical activities. The pace and extent of automation will be shaped by occupations, and wage and skill levels, however: 'Essentially all occupations, whether high skill or low skill, have some technical automation potential, including CEOs; we estimate about 25 percent of their work could potentially be automated, primarily such tasks as analyzing reports and data to inform decisions, reviewing status reports, preparing staff assignments, and so on' (McKinsey Global Institute, 2017, p 8).

There is evidence to suggest that automation may serve the interests of skilled workers. Within services, automation could reduce the mundane and routine in favour of more intellectually stimulating tasks, making roles more interesting and overall more skilled (Lacity and Willocks, 2016). Others emphasise that many existing high-skilled jobs will be complemented by new technologies (Autor, 2015; Brynjolfsson and Mitchell, 2017). Levy (2018) notes that tasks which require unstructured cognitive activity and unstructured social interaction are difficult to replace by robots. Many jobs will have tasks that AI can immediately replace, although most changes will be slow (Wilson et al, 2017; Wright, 2019). Based on an occupational analysis, the ONS has analysed the jobs of 20 million people in England in 2017, and has found that 7.4 per cent are at high risk of automation. Professional, managerial and associate and technical occupations tend to be relatively more protected (ONS, 2019). Currently, the occupations with the highest risk of being automated are predominantly low-waged but also the young are relatively at risk (Roberts et al, 2019). There remains a firm conviction among economists and policymakers that the replacement caused by automation targets the low-skilled and lower educated hardest. This prediction is supported by the idea that technology drives the demand for skilled workers. Therefore, it seems correct to assume that occupations that require advanced education tend to be less at risk for automation (Frey and Osborne, 2013). Yet degrees may not shield the risk if the jobs graduates enter are susceptible to automation. It is also important to realise that automation is not intrinsically good or bad for skilled workers. As the co-author on a report of the impact of automation notes, 'new technologies could just as easily be used to deskill jobs, strip workers of their bargaining power, put downward pressure on wages, amplify monitoring and standardisation of work, and bake biases into recruitment' (Dellot, 2017). Corporations are actively reshaping knowledge work. Brown et al (2012) explain that through digitalisation, standardisation and fragmentation many types of knowledge work can be more easily performed and managed in work locations around the world, as standardising knowledge makes it possible for complex tasks to be broken into smaller components. Technology offers the opportunity to maximise efficiency, standardising and routinising, just as occurred in manufacturing in industrial Taylorism (see also Head, 2014). The fragmentation of jobs is again made possible by flexible labour relationships, in which knowledge workers are increasingly dispensable and interchangeable. Only a small share of high-skilled, highly paid creative positions will be highly valued and regarded as crucial talent with generous remuneration. Many knowledge workers see their power, work conditions, wages and work autonomy diminish through the very same technological change that is thought to empower them. Similarly to Brown et al (2020), economist Richard Baldwin (2019) observes how globalisation combined with new technologies such as AI makes it easier to outsource services jobs. Middle-class occupations will have to compete with software and robots. Some developing nations will benefit, but Baldwin predicts a sharp fall in professional jobs in Western countries. The stark differences within the knowledge workforce are also recently observed by Burrell and Fourcade (2021), who see the bifurcation within the digital economy. A new but small occupational class of software developers, tech CEOs, investors, and computer science and engineering professors has emerged, which they call the coding elite. It consolidates power by holding and controlling the digital means of production such as the data and software. The cybertariat are the enormous army of IT professionals who for very little 'must produce, refine, and work the data that feed or train the algorithms, sometimes to the point of automating their own jobs and making themselves redundant' (p 25). They face precarity, surveillance and unstable wages for their work.

The nature of knowledge work

Another issue with the knowledge-based economy narrative is its understanding of knowledge work. The nature of knowledge work has been idealised as creative and autonomous, exerting greater power against management. The idealised view of knowledge work has been criticised within employment studies as unrealistic (Burris, 1993; Frenkel et al, 1995; Alvesson, 2001, 2004; Warhurst and Thompson, 2006; Jian, 2008; Tholen, 2017a). For example, Vanderburg (2004) observes that so-called knowledge work increasingly mirrors standardised low-skilled work. The labour process fragments and standardises any creative potential: 'The knowledge worker adds and transforms information in a manner almost entirely prescribed by the system, which, in turn, takes this information to the next work station and so on' (p 331). Knowledge work might not be that different from other types of work. According to Felstead et al (2020), not just knowledge workers but the jobs of a wide range of employees show innovative aspects such as coming up with ideas about improving the work processes they use, the products they make and the services they provide. Job discretion for high-skilled occupations has not increased overall in OECD countries (Holman and Rafferty, 2018), including the UK (Gallie et al, 2018). Studies on knowledge-intensive occupations show that knowledge work can be performed with low levels of control and autonomy, including research and development engineers (Gleadle et al, 2012), management consultants (Donnelly, 2006) and software engineers (Marks and Scholarios, 2008). Their job quality often depends on the work process and practices in the companies they work in, not their human capital. The idea that the knowledge economy would have brought greater autonomy to knowledge workers seems too optimistic, particularly in the UK context. As deregulation grew within the skilled labour markets, so did the control over workers through thicker and more rigid management structures, according to a study by Kleinknecht et al (2016). The authors observe that organisations employing high shares of flexible workers have higher shares of managers in their personnel. They argue that flexibility in labour markets (that is, easier firing and higher labour turnover) requires more management and control and damages trust, loyalty and commitment (Kleinknecht et al, 2016, p 1137).

Another issue for the knowledge-based economy narrative is the reliance on SBTC. This theoretical perspective has come under increasing criticism in recent years. One key flaw of SBTC identified is that it does not set out in much detail how technology exactly interacts with work and productivity. It does not specify how skills are deployed in work; the impact of technology on labour and production is somewhat of a black box (Adams, 2018). It cannot deal well with any unobserved skills in economic analysis (such as interpersonal skills). The wide variance in the returns to HE makes this point even more important. The observed polarisation between the skilled and unskilled labour market is likely caused by a range of developments other than technological change. Fernández-Macías and Hurley (2017), for instance, question whether technology is indeed the main culprit for growing wage inequality and argue that too much focus has been placed on technology. Mishel et al (2013) found for the US that SBTC cannot adequately explain the wage trends of the last three decades. Hunt and Nunn (2019) also found that computerisation and automation have not caused rising wage inequality and occupation-based employment polarisation in the US. Others point at other factors such as workplace specialisation not driven by replacement by machines (Cortes and Salvatori, 2019).

Knowledge and technology unmistakably play a central role in capitalist societies. Yet the assumptions linked to the knowledge-based economy are deeply ideological. Policymakers have used them to support their own vision of society, including policies on work, education and social mobility. A fundamental axiom is that the value of human capital increases over time as societies become more technologically advanced (Brown et al, 2020). Investment in education would give individuals the opportunity to become high-waged, high-skilled knowledge workers. Education can barely keep up with the demands of technological change in the economy and the workplace. Technology has helped increased high-skill employment but under the conditions set by our current capitalist system. Educated groups as a whole may have done well relative to less-educated counterparts. But the role of human capital and, in particular, that related to formal education is far from straightforward. To demonstrate this, we will in the next chapter turn to the graduate labour market to assess the extent to which, and why, employers value degrees.

7

The graduate labour market

The graduate labour market has seen significant changes in recent decades. It is regularly the cause of great concern within the media and policy circles (Tholen, 2014), especially during economic downturns and other economic disruptions. The COVID-19 pandemic has severely affected the opportunities of those leaving higher education (HE). During this period job opportunities were well below pre-pandemic levels, with a sharp decline in graduate roles advertised, leading to intense competition (Conboye and Warwick-Ching, 2021). The graduate labour market has recovered in most sectors. Yet some structural features of the graduate labour market compromise the idea that all individuals can be economically successful with the right HE investment.

Demand for graduates

In Chapters 3 and 4 it was shown that many endorse the idea that our economy requires more higher qualified workers. It is assumed that employers increasingly need skills developed at university. As technological change accelerates, work becomes more knowledge-intensive and complex, and more university-trained workers are required. The reality is that the competition for skilled jobs is increasingly competitive. The stakes are incredibly high for those leaving university with severe challenges in finding routes to high-skilled or well-paid jobs. Some of these barriers can be directly linked to the wider UK economic environment. Bailey and Harrop (2018) identify three work trends for the UK economy. The first is low productivity leading to stagnant pay: 'Far from the pace of innovation and technological change being too fast, as many have predicted, the UK's record on productivity suggests that it is actually far too slow' (p 334). The second is high wage inequality, which we will turn to in the next chapter. The third is a changing labour market defined by the growth of insecure work, underemployment and part-time work. Graduate workers are part of the wider economy and a significant share is subject to stagnant and low wages, and insecure work. The general increase in uncertainty affects jobs that, in the past, facilitated wage growth and training for young workers (O'Reilly et al, 2019). Careers have become less predictable and structured for young people (Benko et al, 2011). A 2016 report from Barclays bank found that 24 per cent of workers under the age of 34 have already worked in four industries, compared to 59 per cent of workers over 65, who spent time in just three industries for their entire career. Those who continue on this path will have seven times as many job roles as their parents (Dizik, 2017). Yet this all may matter very little if the demand for graduates in the labour market remains strong.

Finding out the demand for graduates is not straightforward and not well captured in the employment rates for these groups. Some have examined the share of job openings demanding a university degree over time, looking at how often employers formally demand university qualifications (Jackson, 2007; Dörfler and van de Werfhorst, 2009). For instance, using detailed job vacancy data to estimate the change in employer skill demands in the US since 2007, Blair and Deming (2020) observed a sharp rise in the share of online job vacancies requiring a bachelor's degree (from 23 per cent in 2007 to 37 per cent in 2019). The authors infer that the skill demand has increased substantially in this period. Confirming the skill-biased technological change (SBTC) theory, the authors found an increase in demand in qualifications across all labour markets, inferring that a rise in demand for qualifications is caused by a rise in the demand for graduate skills. Many policy analyses come to the same conclusion and find no oversupply of graduates (for example Wilson et al, 2014; Universities UK, 2015), feeding into a long-standing academic debate as to whether HE supply is outpacing demand (Schomburg and Teichler, 2006; Figueiredo et al, 2015). There is considerable evidence that suggests that the demand for graduates has grown. A recent study examines patterns of occupational change between 1992 and 2015 for Germany, Spain, Sweden and the UK (Oesch and Piccitto, 2019). It shows that job growth was strongest, in all four countries, in the top-quintile occupations and the highest-earning occupations. There was growth in the lowest-earning occupations as well. When quintiles were rank-ordered based on mean education, there was strong growth in the highest educated quintile. In the UK, by far the strongest growth occurred in managerial occupations and associate managerial occupations such as business professionals and financial managers, but no change in socio-cultural (semi-)professionals such as teachers, medical professionals and modest growth in (semi-)technical professionals (p 459). So the demand might be highly unevenly distributed. Other evidence suggest that routine-biased technical change has had very limited effect on the demand for UK graduates. Based on econometric analysis Montresor (2019) found that between 1993 and 2014 expected technology-skill complementarity effects at the top of the job distribution are counterbalanced by growing number of graduates within the UK labour force, leading to intensifying job competition. The author suggests that 'the growing pool of graduates may have out-weighed the demand for skills' (p 188). Henseke et al (2018) found an increase in the share of UK jobs requiring degrees between 1986 and 2012 and no significant change between 2012 and 2017. Learning and training time have decreased since 2006, suggesting a slowdown in the demand of skills (see also Winterbotham et al [2020] for evidence of the drop in training provided by UK employers). This brings us to the question of why employers demand graduates and are willing to pay a premium.

Overqualification

The evidence on overqualification also helps to moderate the general upskilling assumption made by both the knowledge-based economy narrative and that of SBTC. Overqualification is generally defined as when a job-holder has a qualification above what would currently be required for someone to get the job (rather than to perform the job). So for graduate overqualification, it would be measured as the workforce that hold a university degree but work in a job that does not require one (Chevalier, 2003). There are various challenges to conceptualising and measuring attainments, requirements and mismatches scrutinised in prior literature (for example, Desjardins and Rubenson, 2011; McGuinness et al, 2017). Also the idea that overqualification is an involuntary state has been challenged (Steffy, 2017).

A growing body of work indicates that in the UK, overqualification is a significant and permanent feature of the UK graduate labour market (Di Stasio et al, 2016; Di Stasio, 2017). Estimates of graduate overqualification do vary according to methodology, at between 30 per cent and 50 per cent. Recently, Delaney et al (2020) estimate that about half of UK graduates up to 29 years old in 2016 were overeducated. The ONS (2019) observes that in 2017, the average overeducation rate for graduates with a first degree or equivalent qualification was 30.9 per cent. The overeducation rates for non-recent and recent graduates with first degree or equivalent were 29.2 per cent and 38.6 per cent respectively. The study suggests that the incidence of overeducation has increased over time.

Studies report some degree of graduate overeducation in all countries, but also suggest that the prevalence and severity of overeducation tend to vary across national contexts (Barone and Ortiz, 2011; Reisel, 2013). McGuinness et al (2018) examined 98 studies of overeducation, covering approximately 40 mainly high-income countries. They report an average overeducation rate, across all studies, of 24 per cent. Overqualification in the UK is relatively high compared to other countries. The UK is among the top ten European countries with the highest percentage of individuals with tertiary education (Verhaest and Van der Velden, 2013). Overqualification for the UK graduate labour market seems like a structural problem with serious consequences. For those affected, it can lead to pay penalties (Green and Zhu, 2010), long-term scarring in employment opportunities (Nunley et al, 2017) and lower job satisfaction (Wu et al, 2015).

Skill utilisation

The discussion on overqualification leads to a wider question about which skills are in demand. Does overqualification mean that these graduates' skills are not in demand? Does it matter if graduates enter jobs in which degrees are not required as long as they use their skills? The importance of qualifications in *getting* a job is not the same as the necessity of skills in *performing* a job. In other words, overqualification may not lead to underutilisation of skills if the job allows a wider set of skills to be used. Green and Zhu (2010) distinguish 'formal' and 'real' overqualification. They found that a significant share of workers are in jobs that do not require degrees to access but are using skills developed in HE (formal overqualification). A minority find themselves in jobs with both educational and skill mismatches (real overqualification) (see also Flisi et al, 2017). The incidence of skill underutilisation seems extraordinarily high throughout the UK labour market (Brinkley et al, 2009). Between 1997 and 2017, the use of high-level literacy and numeracy skills has fallen and social skills and self-planning skills have stagnated after a period of steady expansion until 2012. Complex problem-solving skills have become more critical (Henseke et al, 2018). Again, the consequences of skill underutilisation are real in terms of pay penalty as well as career progression (Green and Zhu, 2010; Summerfield and Theodossiou, 2017). Okay-Somerville and Scholarios (2013) found that British graduates working in associate professional and technical occupations had a lower incidence of skill utilisation, job control, opportunities for skills development, job security and pay than those in traditional graduate occupations.

Research suggests that a growing number of graduates are not using advanced skills at work. Beaudry et al (2016) found that individuals with university degrees are increasingly placed into lower-skilled jobs. Since 2000, the demand for those who can perform cognitive tasks often associated with high educational skills has declined in the US. Horowitz (2018) also observes a decline in the utilisation of skills (verbal, quantitative and analytic skills) for graduates. He found, again for the US context, that HE expansion erodes the value of a university degree, as it increases the risk for underemployment in less cognitively demanding occupations. In other words, when overall education increases, graduate workers are more likely to accept low-skilled work and *not* move into more skilled work.

What is a graduate job?

Another issue with the dominant narrative on the role of graduates in the economy is that it lacks a solid justification of how it defines a graduate job (Tholen, 2017a). Most occupations deemed graduate occupations are constituted of both graduate and non-graduate workers, particularly in managerial and semi-professional types of roles. Existing proxies of high-skilled work (occupational classification, educational backgrounds, income) do not map very well onto the work that graduates perform. Graduates use a wide variety of skills and a wide variety of skill intensity. Therefore, it is hard to define what is 'suitable', 'appropriate' or 'matching' work for university graduates. The concept of a graduate occupation is very fluid. There is a growing overlap in the employment distribution between graduates and non-graduates (Brynin, 2013; Gardiner and Corlett, 2015). In many graduate occupations that were traditionally non-graduate occupations, graduates are preferred not because of the academic skills they may possess but because of non-academic skills or social characteristics (Purcell and Elias, 2004; Tholen et al, 2016). Humburg et al (2013) found that interpersonal skills (communication skills, teamwork skills) are almost as important as professional expertise for employers recruiting graduates.

Professions under fire

Graduate work has often been presented as the gold standard of employment within policy and media circles (Tholen, 2014). Yet even those graduates that end up in the established professional occupations characterised traditionally by high levels of trust, autonomy, control and expertise (for example medicine, law, engineering and so on) experience adverse changes in their work conditions. In the last decades, a general deterioration of influence has been an increasing challenge to the professions' authority, discretion and autonomy (Malin, 2000; Noordegraaf, 2016; Ponnert and Svensson, 2016; Livingstone et al, 2021). Their protected positions seem particularly under strain due to the market forces that expect higher quality professional services at lower prices, through increased competition and the introduction of performance incentives (Leicht and Fennell, 2011). Market forces challenge their independent, autonomous position as well as their self-contained area of knowledge. Some have observed that professional trust has been replaced by organisational and bureaucratic values (Evetts, 2009). Professional identities may also shift to become more suited to managerialism (Du Gay, 1995; Halford and Leonard, 1998; Nixon et al, 2001). Technological change may also be undermining the position of the professional. Susskind and Susskind (2015) argue that professionals' expertise will be democratised through new information systems. In many cases, the monopolies on expertise that professionals rely on will no longer be tenable.

I have previously argued that it has become more difficult for graduate occupations to professionalise due to the growth in educational credentials (Tholen, 2017b). As labour market precarity continues to spread within expert and professional fields, educational programmes also adapt and focus less on abstract knowledge and professional identity and more on skills that improve employability (Besbris and Petre, 2020). It is perhaps unclear whether we have entered a period of de-professionalisation in which professionals slowly lose the ability to influence and the power to define the contents and forms of their own work. But we can observe that even graduates in the most protected occupations experience changes that challenge the idea that the advantages graduates have within the economy is stable and based on their skillsets.

Signalling and credentialism

Within the policy discourse outlined in the previous chapter, employers need HE institutions to train workers for high-skilled work. Investment in HE makes these individuals suitable for professional and managerial work. Their advanced productivity is subsequently rewarded through higher wages. But there are alternative theoretical explanations why employers value education and are willing to pay a premium for graduates. Key ideas related to why degrees may be linked to a favourable labour market is signalling (Spence, 1973) and screening (Stiglitz, 1975) theories. As such, they have been accepted by many economists and sociologists alike as a viable alternative to Human Capital Theory (HCT). Signalling theory assumes that workers who earn a degree are able to signal their desirable qualities to potential employers better. Potential employees use educational qualifications as a way to demonstrate their abilities to potential employers. These abilities include skills used in the performance of the job and their work ethic, ability to follow instructions, and dedication to complete (new) tasks. Screening theory focuses on the employers' role. In the absence of concrete knowledge about an applicant's future productivity, education completion may signal the capacity to learn. HE employers are using the possession of a certain educational qualification to screen that an individual possesses the necessary capabilities. In both signalling and screening theories, the value of education is attributed to its role in reducing uncertainty in the labour market rather than developing productive skills. Educational attainment signals to employers that a job-seeker is desirable (Spence, 1973).

In line with signalling theory, economist Bryan Caplan (2018) has argued, in fact, that most of the benefits of HE education come from signalling. Most degree programmes only marginally increase students' productive skills (some basic literacy or numeracy) (see Arum and Roksa, 2010). The primary function degrees seem to have is as a 'signal' to desirable underlying characteristics, intelligence, conscientiousness and conformity. It has only a small effect on improving human capital. According to Caplan, HE's enormous costs make it a very inefficient allocation.

Both signalling and screening theories show that education has a positional role in allocating jobs and workers (Thurow, 1975; Hirsch, 1976). The desirability of candidates can be understood as a queue in which labour market participants are ordered from most qualified to least desirable. The signal helps applicants distinguish themselves from others and moves them further towards the front of the labour market queue. Education is a proxy for desirable traits such as trainability in the labour queue. Those who gain more education may move forward in the line and become employable. The need for additional years of education is thus at least partly driven by the action of other potential applicants rather than the skill requirements of jobs. In other words, the value of educational credentials is relative to the amount and type of education held by others. An HE degree is largely a positional good: the more people who have one, the less it is worth. This means that the value of a degree depreciates as it becomes more common in the labour market, if the demand for skilled workers does not increase as fast. To create an advantage over others in the labour market, prospective workers in later cohorts must distinguish themselves with more education, creating a feedback loop where each cohort of workers needs to attain more education to secure their place in the labour market queue (Freeman, 1976; Hirsch, 1976; Thurow, 1975; Collins, 1979; van de Werfhorst and Andersen, 2005). In other words, a generation ago lower level qualifications would have provided the same signal (Goldthorpe, 2014; Di Stasio, 2017).

After HE expansion, educational credentials may offer less informative signals to employers. As a result, they may raise the educational requirements to screen for better-qualified applicants (often called 'credential inflation'). This educational race has served mainly as a (wasteful) competition rather than economic development of growing employability of the workforce. The evidence on underutilisation and overqualification covered earlier suggest that there are not enough jobs to 'absorb' all of the well-educated workers in the population. Of course, this depends on one's view of what the purpose is of HE. Irrespectively, many have observed the devaluation of an HE degree in the labour market by employers (Battu et al, 2000; Figueiredo et al, 2013; Bol, 2015; Mok and Neubauer, 2016). As a result of the weaker signals that degrees provide (in particular undergraduate ones), non-educational signals such as personal capital including personal characteristics may have become more critical (Brown and Hesketh, 2004; Anderson and Tomlinson, 2021). Alternatively, degrees or certain types of degrees are merely minimum standards (or hiring floors) employers would consider (Di Stasio, 2017). There is some evidence that employers use a tick-box system to filter candidates based on the league table position of their universities (Richardson, 2019).

Comparative research between the UK and the Netherlands examined how Dutch and British students socially construct the positional competition for jobs within their educational and labour market contexts (Tholen, 2013). The findings illustrated two contrasting approaches to employability. The

Dutch students understood the competition for jobs was based on absolute performance, a clear relationship between skills and the labour market, and human capital development in areas of experiences, skills and abilities. For the British students, it is based on relative performance, ranking of candidates and the importance of signals. This is echoed in Di Stasio and van de Werfhorst (2016) who found, based on a vignette study with employers, that English employers primarily sort applicants based on relative signals of merit such as grades, in line with queuing theory. Dutch employers instead base their ratings on fields of study and occupation-specific degrees.

Skills developed at universities are often of far less importance in the UK context. There is a relatively weak relationship between the HE system and employers compared to other national contexts in which there is a lot more coordination between these parties. Recently, Araki (2020) found, based on OECD data for 26 countries, that both educational attainment and skills lead to occupational and monetary rewards. Yet, unlike what the HCT predicts, the premium for educational attainment alone far outweighs that for skills. The devaluation of high credentials happens due to educational expansion (credential inflation). However, this depreciation might also be linked to skills diffusion. The effect of credentials in the labour market is shaped by the societal level of educational expansion as well as how scarce skills are in the workforce.

The idea that educational qualifications such as HE degrees, irrespective of the skills attached to them, offer advantage is an established position within sociology. The social closure tradition is based on the work of Max Weber (1978) (and after him Collins [1979] and Parkin [1979]) and argues that educational credentials are mainly cultural rather than technical and are used for exclusionary purposes rather than to increase productivity (Brown, 2001). Credentials are socially sanctioned criteria for allocating labour market outcomes to individuals who possess such qualifications, while excluding less-educated people regardless of their actual skills. The increase in educational requirements for jobs is therefore not the result of an increasing demand for skills. Instead, employers select candidates according to their cultural or professional preferences as participation in HE increases in the general workforce. The possession of a certain level of education closes off opportunities from less-educated people, leading to increased economic rewards (Smyth and McCoy, 2011; Bol, 2015). Education becomes a means of exclusion. It allows the educated elite to perpetuate class advantage by limiting access to desirable jobs (Dore, 1976; Collins, 1979). Middle-class employers seek workers whose cultural training and background matches their own.

In this line of thought, with the expansion of education, more credentials are needed to maintain class position, leading, again, to rising educational attainment to enter high-status occupations and positions as well as raising educational requirements by employers. If everyone has the same qualifications, employers will insist on higher-prestige or more advanced degrees to maintain the same selectivity. The reason for the durable inequalities is that educational credentials lead to economic benefits by excluding others (less-educated people) from taking part in the select community where rewards are allocated (Hirsch, 1976; Collins, 1979; Murphy, 1988). Simply holding a degree becomes less important as a signal of merit in itself than the specific discipline studied and the institution at which it was granted (Lucas, 2001; Boliver, 2011; Sullivan et al, 2014; Bukodi and Goldthorpe, 2016).

Previous work on software engineers, financial analysts, lab-based scientists and press officers demonstrated that deliberate social closure is still relevant in the graduate labour market (Tholen, 2017a; see also van de Werfhorst [2011] and Ruggera and Barone [2017] for other evidence). Other studies found that within the elite labour market, a distinguished education degree from a high prestige university provides a direct advantage, irrespective of skills (Rivera, 2015; Posselt and Grodsky, 2017). It is often said that selective institutions recruit the most talented individuals as well as provide them with the best education. This would explain their success in the labour market. Yet, the cultural background linked to their educational trajectory is the basis for cultural matching with the assessors' social background, which shapes the recruitment process in elite firms (Rivera, 2012). Morley and Aynsley (2007) show that English employers distinguish between traditional universities and the so-called new universities (former polytechnics); graduates from traditional universities are believed to be more competent than others. Isopahkala-Bouret (2015) shows how credentials need interpretation by employers and others in the field, demonstrating the perceived status inequalities were justified and experienced by graduates within the dual system of Finnish HE. The graduates with an academic master's degree argued that new, professional master's degrees should have lower status because of the competitiveness, length, quality and reputation of their own studies. An unequal status was attached to these professional degrees, irrespective of the technical skills and experiential credentials of the degree-holders.

Conclusion

This chapter and Chapter 6 show that the basic tenets of the knowledge economy are at best partly observed in how work and the labour market are organised in the UK. There are some fundamental contradictions between the ideal of the knowledge-based economy and how capitalism and technology shape work, knowledge, power and opportunity in society. The evidence on the graduate labour market highlights the difficulties in assuming that the demand for graduates is related to workers' educational human capital. The role of HE is often more modest than assumed and other organisational, occupational and cultural factors shape how jobs are allocated and work conditions are implemented.

The marketisation discourse, driven by HCT, stipulates that degrees are proof of learning and demonstrate that graduates have developed skills and knowledge that employers want in a knowledge-based economy. For the debate on the marketisation of HE it is crucial whether the demand for graduate workers is driven by the skills developed at HE. We know that the demand for graduates is highly unevenly dispersed. We also know that employers are looking for a wide range of skills that are not developed at HE. Many graduates work in roles where HE plays a minor role in skill development (and not as a producer of credentials). The role of university education within graduate work and the labour market is much more complex than HCT portrays it as. It remains an arena where various groups and individuals have different resources to influence outcomes. A wider socioeconomic field in which forces of labour market demand and the expanding supply of graduates create opportunities for some but also leaves many behind. The marketisation discourse is unable to deal with this complexity. It relies on an individualised perspective on labour market competition.

HE's signalling and credentialing role in the labour market is largely ignored in the policy discourse. Yet employers have increasingly turned to degrees as a sifting mechanism within the graduate labour market. The greater availability of HE credentials in the labour force could, under certain circumstances, mean that educational credentials provide less of a signal in the competition for jobs. The value of credentials depends on many factors, some are institutional (see Vogtenhuber, 2018) and some will depend on the positional competition for jobs. So why does it matter if degrees are credentials or signalling devices? Does it not associate rewards to individual investment? Should the individual, therefore, still not be held responsible for its costs and demand transparency and value for money from HE? The next chapter will look into these questions by examining the role of HE in how rewards are distributed.

8

Earnings

Within the dominant view, the solid and, on average, relatively high returns to higher education (HE) have become proof of the demand for skills and knowledge imparted by HE institutions. Drawing on Human Capital Theory (HCT), it shows that differences in earning between graduates and non-graduates and the relationship between HE courses and earning potentials are primarily based on the demand for skills of employers, reflected in the skill premiums. There remains a substantial premium for graduates as a group compared to the non-graduates (Walker and Zhu, 2013; Britton et al, 2020). Yet, there is more to the story. There is no consensus that the graduate premium is holding up (see Abel et al, 2016). Also pay *on average* has remained flat for most graduates over the last decades (Donovan and Bradley, 2018). Holmes and Mayhew (2012) show that between 1994 and 2007, the UK graduate premium had fallen for all except those in the top 20 per cent. The authors observe that: '[T]hose outside the top 20 percent now more closely resemble those working in mid-range occupations rather than those in top jobs' (p 1). Also, not all graduates see a great payoff to university education. The differences in earnings within the graduate population are substantial. Research by the Department for Education (2019) examined median earnings one, three, five and ten years after graduation. Across graduate cohorts, graduate earnings (in nominal terms) have been increasing. After adjusting for inflation, these increases largely disappear. Five years after graduation, male earnings increase more over time than female earnings. Earnings for the lowest quarter of earners was only £19,000 per year ten years after graduation (compared to £42,500 for the top quarter). As one would expect, the subject studied was a major factor with those studying medicine and economics earning much more than humanities and liberal art graduates, and creative arts and design graduates, after ten years (respectively, £53,300 and £49,800, £22,800 and £23,300). Green and Henseke (2016) found that the returns to HE have become more dispersed, with those at the upper quartile of the residual distribution increasing while those at the lowest quartile have fallen. There is also considerable difference within some fields. For the tax year 2018/2019, gross annual earnings for business and management graduates ranged from £19,000 to £70,800 five years after graduation (law, economics and computing also show wide variation) (gov. uk, 2021). In general, earnings diverse enormously around subject choice and institution choice (Belfield et al, 2018; Borgen and Mastekaasa, 2018;

Sullivan et al, 2018a; Bol et al, 2019). The backgrounds of the students continue to have a powerful effect (Kernohan, 2022).

The question is what caused these differences in graduate returns. Differences in graduate earnings are not an issue for the dominant discourse. They are a reflection of the demand and supply of specific graduate skills. Different subjects develop different skills. Different institutions will offer different quality programmes which shape skill development and consequently earnings. Selective recruitment into HE may also recruit more able/skilful or intelligent individuals, but these individual differences receive far less attention in policy documents. There are, of course, differences in academic abilities before people attend university. These differences will impact labour market outcomes and thus earnings. Belfield et al (2018) estimate that the average impact of attending HE on earnings at age 29 is much lower (26 per cent for women and 6 per cent for men as opposed to 50 per cent and 25 per cent) once controlled for differences in pre-university characteristics such as family background and prior attainment (see also Caplan [2018] for US evidence).

The question remains what the studies on skill premiums tell us about the relationship between HE attainment and wages. For instance, how meaningful are the categories of graduates and non-graduates given the heterogeneity within these groups? There are also severe interpretive issues with associating educational experiences with earning outcomes. Most fundamentally, we cannot isolate the role of education in workers' earnings. Very few of us think that all work skills are exclusively developed in formal education. We know that many skills are developed in a wide range of situations (Tholen et al, 2016). The workplace remains a place of developing work skills and abilities valued by employers (and in line with HCT). Yet we need to know more about why and which skills are rewarded. Many skills developed at HE are used at work, and employers are interested in recruiting and rewarding those who have these skills. The clearest examples are fields such as medicine, law and engineering. We can observe that HE directly prepares students for working in these fields. Many courses indeed have vocational aspects. Yet we know that graduates enter the labour market with a wide range of skills and knowledge, some of which are not demanded or utilised or, in fact, rewarded. Liu and Grusky (2013) found a growing demand for most types of skills but not all of them translate into a rising payoff. The authors empirically examined the relationship between workplace skills and skill premiums between 1979 and 2010, using occupational ratings from the Occupational Information Network (O*NET) and US current population surveys. The authors separated analytical, verbal, quantitative, creative, science and engineering, computer, managerial and nurturing skills. Only for analytic skills was there a stark rise in returns and a modest growth of the returns to managerial and nurturing skills. Social skills, not the skills associated with HE, are increasingly rewarded in the labour market (Cunningham and Villaseñor, 2016; Deming, 2017).

It remains incredibly challenging to isolate the experience of HE because many factors play a role in how wages are set, many of which cannot be neatly expressed in variables or no data is available. Because of these methodological problems, skill premium estimates are rather crude. In reality, the relation between earnings and skills is ambiguous and depends on many economic and organisational factors. Moreover, earnings are shaped by many factors not, or not only, indirectly related to either education or skill. The remainder of the chapter will cover some key structural sociological and economic forces that have heavily influenced wage setting in the UK and beyond.

Economic context

The type of capitalism a country adheres to shapes how the returns to economic activity are distributed. In liberal market economies such as the UK, market forces fundamentally compromise the idea that workers' earnings reflect their contribution to the goods and services produced. Assessing the findings of a new McKinsey Global Institute white paper, Foroohar observes (2021):

> The losses suffered by labour relative to capital are even more extreme than previously thought. While productivity gains since the mid-1990s amounted to 25 per cent in real terms, wages grew only 11 per cent. Meanwhile, capital income increased by two-thirds. If there is any doubt that the link between productivity and wages has broken down, this should put it to rest.

Institutional factors, often expressed on the national level, drive wages. A key example are labour market institutions. Kristal and Cohen (2017) estimate the decline in unions and the fall in the real value of the minimum wage explain about half of the US's rising inequality. Other studies have comparable findings (Western and Rosenfeld, 2011; Jacobs and Myers, 2014; Dromey, 2018). Government policies affect earnings through taxation policies with a greater share of income going to a smaller share of earners (Volscho and Kelly, 2012; Jacobs and Dirlam, 2016). Governments create and maintain regulatory environments for high-income workers, particularly in sectors that disproportionately take up earnings. In the UK and US, the deregulation of the financial industry has led to dramatic income increases in the white-collar financial sector, creating significant inequalities in wealth and income (Tomaskovic-Devey and Lin, 2011; Volscho and Kelly, 2012; Lin and Tomaskovic-Devey, 2013).

Occupations and organisations

We also have to acknowledge the influence of workplaces and sectors in the setting of earnings. Some organisations can remunerate work more than others irrespective of the skills involved. Rosenfeld (2021) shows that our earnings often do not reflect our market value or work performance. Employers restrict labour market mobility and obscure workers' value. Many workers cannot make successful claims over the share of the organisation revenue they should receive. Individual performance is in addition often difficult to measure in modern work. Particularly within skilled labour markets, within-occupational inequality has become more expressed (Brown et al, 2012). Xie et al (2016) found that for scientists, engineers, computer scientists, teachers, social scientists, medical doctors and lawyers between 1960 and 2007, the between-occupation inequality increased but there was also growing divergence within the same occupation controlling for sex, age, work hours and education. Tang et al (2020) found for highly educated workers in the US, 90 per cent of wage inequality remains if controlled for job characteristics such as industry, occupation and location. This implies that wage inequality is primarily driven by within-industry/occupation inequality. Mouw and Kalleberg (2010) found that earnings increases within certain occupations, such as managers and computer systems analysts, disproportionately drives US wage inequality. The effect of education had not changed since 1992. Sakamoto and Wang (2017) found for the US that wage inequality among college-educated workers is now more directly affected by employee bargaining power and employer rents than by occupation. Also in the UK, wage inequality is strongly driven by within-occupation inequality (M. Williams, 2013; Bol and Weeden, 2015). Avent-Holt et al (2020) find that for five countries (Denmark, Finland, Germany, Japan and South Korea), establishments representing workplaces and jobs explain more of the variance in wages than do occupations. They argue that earnings are closely tied to organisations in particular in so-called job-centred labour markets (found in liberal market economies). In these, wages are mainly established at the individual or workplace level. Firms and workers differ in their market power. These inequalities produce high levels of earnings inequalities at the individual level. The role of the skills use is salient but only within an organisational context. As the authors state: 'It is not just what skills and general tasks one performs (e.g. occupation) that matters, but where and with whom we work as well' (Avent-Holt et al, 2020, p 10).

Social factors

Social factors influence earnings in various ways, and often indirectly. I will focus here on gender and ethnicity before turning to class, acknowledging the prominence of age, sexuality, location and others. There is a gender pay gap for UK graduates and this seems to be widening. This gender gap in earnings for female graduates compared to male graduates is firm even controlling for all other relevant variables such as age, occupation, firm size, field of study and all kinds of job characteristics (Lažetić, 2020). This has been explained by the fact that men are more likely to be found in highly skilled employment and less likely to be in part-time employment. Some have argued that these differences can be partly explained by individual factors such as job-searching behaviour and greater confidence levels (Cornell et al, 2020). Yet it is clear that these differences cannot be reduced to performance or skill level. Men begin earning on average 10 per cent more than women 15 months after they leave university (Adams, 2019a). Occupations dominated by females or those experiencing a significant inflow of female workers tend to be devalued in status and pay (Busch, 2018).

We can see similar inequalities for ethnic groups with different mechanisms at play. There remain persistent wage inequalities for minority workers, for both graduates and non-graduates (Henehan and Rose, 2018), even controlling for other relevant variables (Britton et al, 2021). Ethnic minority graduates face more difficulties in finding (graduate-level) work (Lessard-Phillips et al, 2018). Zwysen and Longhi (2018) found that British ethnic minority graduates are between 5 per cent and 15 per cent less likely to be employed than their White British peers six months after graduation. These differences cannot be fully explained by parental background, local area characteristics and university career. Various studies have emphasised the structural inequality in opportunity and outcomes for certain minority groups of graduates (Ashley and Empson, 2013; Kim, 2015).

Class inequality

The influence of social class on earnings will be dealt with in more detail, as the available evidence demonstrates most clearly how social inequalities in society continue to undermine the tenets of the education-based meritocracy that defines the policy discourse (see Chapter 9). Class inequalities still drive earning inequalities in graduate work. Studies into the returns to HE have shown that the individual returns to education are significantly determined by class background (Bukodi and Goldthorpe, 2011; Crawford and van der Erve, 2015; Jacob et al, 2015; Crawford et al, 2016; Gugushvili et al, 2017; Duta et al, 2021). Class remains a key determinant of the graduate premium even if many other factors are controlled for (Kernohan, 2020b). Britton et al (2016, p 55) estimate that controlling for different student characteristics, degree subject and institution attended, the gap between graduates from higher- and lower-income households is around 10 per cent at the median.

The role of social background mediates both education and labour market outcomes. There is a vast literature on the relationship between educational attainment and class destination and what this means for social mobility. There remains much disagreement over the role of education in explaining social mobility patterns. For some, educational attainment fully explains the link between social origins and class destinations (Sullivan et al, 2018b; Jacob and Klein, 2019). Yet for many others family background plays an independent role. Witteveen and Attewell (2020), for instance, find for the US that parental education and parental income are associated with substantially higher post-college incomes. The individual's own attainment only partially mediates this association.

There are a variety of reasons that, even if participation in HE increases for all groups, class differences remain consistent and hard to eradicate. Parents' economic and cultural resources exert an influence on their offspring's labour market outcomes. There are numerous processes involved. Sociologists point at different forms of capital developed through family background and transmitted to children (Bourdieu, 1986; Coleman, 1988). Those who are the first in their family to attend HE have significant lower educational and labour market outcomes than those who are not, over and above other sources of disadvantage (Adamecz-Völgyi et al, 2020). Family origin shapes the type of educational institutions attended on all levels of education. We know that HE institution attended matters in labour market outcomes. The class make-up of different institutions is heavily skewed in the UK context, with the most prestigious universities having the highest share of students from privileged backgrounds (Boliver, 2013). Financial resources can finance advanced levels of education (such as postgraduate degrees), pay for tuition and living costs, and support unpaid internships or volunteering. Through support and access to valuable networks, (affluent) parents can help their children in the transition from university to their first job while they seek jobs, facilitating job search or residential mobility. Parents' social networks may provide access to information about vacancies or potential employers. University-educated parents may have experience in making these transitions themselves. A recent survey found that graduates from professional backgrounds were 47 per cent more likely to use family connections to find their first job and twice as likely to receive financial support during the job-hunting process (Hall, 2021).

Cultural capital and social skill development significantly occur within the family, in particular in the early years (Karlson and Birkelund, 2019). Both are considered beneficial in the recruitment process and benefit those from advantaged backgrounds (Rivera, 2015). Those from advantaged backgrounds are more likely to have the relevant cultural knowledge of how to deal with different institutions and employers, how to negotiate with gatekeepers, and, again, they have the social networks to facilitate access to critical information and contacts.

Wealth remains a key factor in explaining who enters high-earning occupations. Borgen (2015) reports that those with privileged backgrounds at the top end of the wage distribution, who are already more likely to attend high-quality (selective) universities, seem to benefit most from attending selective universities in the labour market than those from less affluent backgrounds. In other words, their returns to attending 'high-quality' university are much higher. It is well known that a small top share of families and individuals (the so-called 1 per cent) take up a large share of the growth in earnings (Dorling, 2019). These are predominantly graduates and these high earners also skew the graduate returns to education. This leads us to the role of privilege within the discussion of rising wealth inequality (Piketty, 2014; Savage, 2021). Next to the divide between the 1 per cent (or 0.1 per cent or 0.01 per cent) and the rest, we can also see a divide between the top professional-managerial class and all other classes. Mitnik et al (2016) observe a growing advantage of the professional-managerial class relative to all other classes. In *The Meritocracy Trap*, Daniel Markovits (2019) explains that parenting practices and the education system are set up to reproduce these elites' status. Life chances are stacked in favour of these elites. Parents can prepare their children for success through admission to a top preschool and a private secondary school and elite HE institutions monopolise elite education for each successive generation. Elite graduates then monopolise the best jobs. Markovits is commenting on the US context but there are indeed significant labour market advantages associated with private schooling and elite HE in the UK as well (Green and Kynaston, 2019). They are largely caused by selective sorting mechanisms that place certain graduates in high-paid industries and sectors (Rivera, 2015; Green et al, 2017), whereas the effect of elite education on productivity or skills development remains unclear (Ogg et al, 2009; Klein, 2021). We know that elite employers recruiting for high-paid career trajectories tend to select elite institutions. Donnelly and Gamsu (2019) found that although elite employers recruit from a wider range of universities than the authors expected, the highest-paid graduates are still predominantly recruited from older elite institutions, suggesting a two-tier recruitment process. Brown et al (2012) found that many multinational corporations adhere to an ideology of 'talent' that favours the recruitment of students from elite universities. These students are the ones that are more likely to move into the relatively small number of highly compensated managerial jobs.

Great equaliser?

For a considerable time there was a reasonable consensus among sociologists that educational attainment has an equalising effect within society. It increases mobility by moderating other avenues of intergenerational status transmission. As a result, intergenerational mobility is higher among college graduates than among people with lower levels of education. Indeed, studies have found that undergraduate degrees, in particular, serve as 'equalisers' for labour market outcomes. They found that once a degree is attained, social origin has no or little effect on, for instance, occupational prestige (Breen et al, 2009, 2010; Torche, 2011; Pfeffer and Hertel, 2015; Karlson, 2019). Falcon and Bataille (2018) found that the equalising effect only holds for undergraduate degrees and inequality increases sharply for more advanced degrees.

Yet in recent years, US research in particular has begun to contradict the undergraduate-degree-as-equaliser thesis. Fiel (2020) does not find any significant differences in mobility across education levels. Witteveen and Attewell (2020) find that the parental transmission of advantage occurred for graduates with a bachelor's degree, as well as those with advanced degrees. University has an equalising effect, but social background continues to heavily shape earning potential. Zhou (2019) finds that selection processes have inflated the effect of undergraduate degrees on social mobility. Suppose university graduates from low- and moderate-income families are more likely to be selected on attributes such as ability and motivation than those from high-income families. In that case, the higher mobility effects simply reflect varying degrees of selectivity of graduates from different family backgrounds. The author found that once this is adjusted for, intergenerational income mobility among college graduates is very close to that among non-graduates.

The Effectively Maintained Inequality (EMI) hypothesis (Lucas, 2001) states that despite growing participation in HE, children from privileged families will find ways to 'outperform' others through educational means such as completing the most prestigious education tracks. Bloome et al (2018) found for the US that the expansion of HE in itself reduced income inequality, yet growing educational inequality and rising educational returns work the other way. Consistent with EMI, college students from high-income families are more likely than their low-income peers to attend selective schools. We know that the children of the wealthy are more likely to become wealthy themselves through the use of their parents' wealth, even controlling for biological factors. Wealthy parents are using their wealth to work for them (Black et al, 2020). The advantage of children from privileged families can be explained by the costly and financially rewarding advanced degrees they obtain and the selective institutions they attend (Oh and Kim, 2020). Even without the educational system, family wealth can offer strong advantages in the labour market, particularly in Britain and the US (Gregg et al, 2017). Laurison and Friedman (2016) found that workers from working-class backgrounds in high-status occupations earn 17 per cent less, on average, than individuals from privileged backgrounds.

Conclusion

Economists have demonstrated that increased outputs in the HE sectors do not necessarily lead to increased productivity or economic growth (Chang, 2011; Holmes, 2013). Which skills matter and under which circumstances to create individual and national prosperity is a difficult question. Modern capitalism does necessarily reward the skills and knowledge of graduates. The idea that HE can become an investment good has led to a simplification in the relationship between education, skill, jobs and rewards. Instead, what is on offer is an attractive narrative, built on the idea that capitalism now provides the conditions for university graduates to flourish as the skills and knowledge they have developed at university will have given them the tools to succeed in the new economy. In the proclaimed knowledge-based economy, technological change and globalised competition were thought to increase the demand for HE and likewise the payoff for it. HE was considered the great route to high-skilled and high-paid employment. A cornerstone of the drive for greater marketisation has been based on the evidence on the graduate premium. The graduate premium is deemed a reflection of graduates' skill demanded by employers.

The evidence presented in this chapter demonstrates that it is not necessarily learning that leads to earnings. Bol (2015) finds that increases in education have eroded the absolute earning power of university degrees in industrialised nations. The advantage that graduates from privileged backgrounds have is also not likely to end. Graduates' earnings are also highly uneven. And although the returns to education have increased, a more comprehensive set of conditions helped achieve this. Earnings depend on far more factors than individual skill development at university, many not covered here (Marginson, 2015).

The obsession with the graduate premium drives the rhetoric of making individuals more financially responsible for HE choices. It is based on a strong belief that the market can optimise the returns to their investment in HE. With the help of more data and information, graduates can select the course which will improve their human capital to then capitalise on its value in the labour market. Yet of course, these promises are largely false as labour market outcomes are the product of much larger forces. In addition, the graduate premium is not stable or necessarily increasing in the future. As Cappelli (2020, p 41) reminds us:

> and the farther out the guess, the less valid and useful guesses will be. Whether the college premium remains high or whether it continues its decline, which occupations and therefore which college majors will be highly paid, and so forth, will be difficult to know. The rollercoaster

up-and-down of the college wage premium over the last 50 years suggests as much.

Yet despite this, the policy discourse is fundamentally build on HCT and unable to change its position in how HE contributes to earnings, exemplifying how intransigent and uncritical the HE policy discourse on marketisation can be. The next chapter will explore this unwillingness to adjust its labour market assumptions.

9

The misinterpretation of graduate work

The dominant economic discourse that supports the rationale for marketisation in higher education (HE) has misrepresented the nature of graduate work and overstated the role of HE within the economy. It strengthens the rationale for market forces to dominate HE institutions, despite the continued resistance against further marketisation. This misunderstanding of the graduate labour market outlined in the previous three chapters is however widespread within policy, media and academic circles (Tholen, 2014). Thus, its appearance within the marketisation debate is far from coincidental or unique. It is important to stress that a range of forces and arguments has driven marketisation as a policy choice. Political concerns about growing public costs would undoubtedly be one of them. So in avoiding an oversimplified approach to understanding HE marketisation in the English context, this chapter outlines a wider policy climate in which these misunderstandings of graduate work are sustained and actively used. In other words, looking at some of these debates and policy stances will contextualise the continuous misunderstanding of graduate work. This chapter explains how dominant positions in three related policy debates/ areas, adhered to by both the political right and centre-left, rely on and support the spurious understanding of the graduate labour market. All three represent central axioms of modern policymaking in the UK and beyond. These are: the idea of an education-based meritocracy; employability as means of individual empowerment and responsibility; and the reliance on Human Capital Theory (HCT) within economic, social and educational policies. The chapter demonstrates that all these share an understanding of the relationship between work and education with the policy discourse on marketisation in HE. It helps explain why changing some of these assumptions is a challenge as they are tied up with many other political dogmas and positions. Equally important, the chapter will show that all three are in themselves problematic by highlighting some of the key criticisms posed against them.

Meritocracy

> Over the coming weeks and months the government will set out an ambitious programme of economic and social reform

that will help us make this change and build a true meritocracy in our country. But there is no more important place to start than education.

Prime Minister Theresa May (2016)

But today I want to send a strong message – that social mobility isn't about getting more people into university. For decades we have been recruiting too many young people on to courses that do nothing to improve their life chances or help with their career goals. True social mobility is about getting people to choose the path that will lead to their desired destination and enabling them to complete that path. True social mobility is when we put students and their needs and career ambitions first, be that in HE, FE or apprenticeships.

University Minister, Michelle Donelan (2020)

There has been a long-standing commitment to improving social mobility in Western nations and in the UK in particular (Payne, 2017; see Cabinet Office, 2009, 2011 for policy examples). Educational policy has played a fundamental role in supporting this aim. There is a strong belief in the idea that the role of the influence of social background and other ascribed characteristics on life chances is in decline (the so-called modernisation thesis). In other words, society is becoming 'meritocratic' in character (Jonsson, 1992). Within a post-industrial society, employers will increasingly select people based on their talent, abilities and educational credentials (as opposed to ascribed characteristics) as technological and economic advances require full use of human resources available in the workforce (Blau and Duncan, 1967; Bell, 1972, 1973). Economic efficiency makes education the dominant criterion of selection in labour markets and educational credentials thus become the most important currencies. Over time, the association between individuals' educational attainment and their eventual class destinations strengthens.

The commitment to improving social mobility remains fundamental to creating a fair society. The notion of equality of opportunity is central to meritocracy as an ideology of social justice. Equality in opportunity in education is therefore also a prerequisite. Here the promotion of education as a fundamental cornerstone of meritocracy is pronounced. The association between individuals' class origins and their educational attainment weakens due to the growing demand for it in modern societies. Young (1958) observed that merit was directly associated with educational attainment and qualifications obtained through the formal educational system become the core mechanism through which social mobility would need to be achieved. Widening educational attainment between different groups is taken as the leading indicator of meritocratic progress. For many decades governments have tried to reduce the influence of social background on educational outcomes. Through increasing access and participation in all levels of education, the influence of social class in people's labour market destinations was expected to decline.

The ideal of an education-based meritocracy has fully penetrated government thinking in the UK context for a very long time (Themelis, 2008). Traditionally, for those on the right an education-based meritocracy would justift unequal labour market outcomes as a result of a fair competition. Those on the left see the great potential to allow greater social mobility and equal opportunity for all, in particular working-class children. Goldthorpe and Jackson (2006, p 95) note that it seemed 'an highly attractive "progressive" goal to which centre-left parties can commit themselves, while entailing no radically redistributive measures of a kind that might threaten the "median voter" electoral strategies on which these parties typically rely' (see also Bloodworth, 2016). It is therefore not difficult to see how the support for university participation has become a key policy tool to improve social mobility (Tholen, 2014). As we have seen in the previous chapter, the idea that HE could be a great equaliser is not only politically salient but has also been supported by research. Authors such as Saunders (1997, 2000) have aimed to demonstrate that education works meritocratically in the UK. Those who reach the highest positions in society generally do best in education. Growing participation in HE would reduce or minimise class-based inequalities in opportunity. It would allow those from working-class backgrounds to enter well-paid professional jobs. Due to the growing demand for skilled workers, the economic returns to HE have been substantial and stable. In addition, improving social mobility through education seemed more straightforward and desirable than other options that would alter the capitalist economic system that drives economic inequality. As a result, the HE system has been given a vital role in the allocation of jobs and life opportunities. Here we can see that, similar to the policy discourse outlined in Chapters 3, 4 and 5, this educational meritocratic drive relied on a tight relationship between HE participation and labour market success. Degrees were deemed to be badges of proven ability, which employers recognise and use in a fair way to allocate jobs. Whether the UK is a meritocracy is a rather philosophical question, yet it is important that the idea of education-based meritocracy has persistently been criticised for various reasons (for example, Hayes, 2013; Bloodworth, 2016; Appiah, 2018; Markovits, 2019; Sandel, 2020; see Wooldridge, 2021 for a contrasting argument to revitalise education-based meritocracy). I will distinguish three key areas of critique posed against it to highlight its problematic nature in its own right.

Meritocracy is not possible through educational policy

Some argue that trying to achieve meritocracy through government educational policies is misguided. What is needed in unequal societies such as the UK is egalitarianism. We need to reduce class-based inequalities, focusing on outcomes instead of improving opportunities for the less advantaged. Instead of aiming for elevating a few talented working-class children into high-status occupations, there is a need to improve the life conditions of all. Yet, the obsession with meritocracy has replaced or perhaps devalued redistributive policies (Bloodworth, 2016; Reay, 2017). Education may have contributed to absolute social mobility, whether adults tend to have higher occupational positions or income than their parents did, but it has a mixed record in improving relative social mobility, that is, the chances of those from different class backgrounds achieving different class destinations (Mandler, 2020).

The persistent role of class in educational outcomes has led to scepticism that an education-based meritocracy has been even remotely achieved, often pointing at the reproduction of inequality through education. As Diane Reay (2017, p 123) tells us, 'meritocracy has become the educational equivalent of the emperor with no clothes, all ideological bluff and no substance'. A large sociological literature shows that social class has a significant effect on educational attainment, often controlling for ability (Bukodi and Goldthorpe, 2013; Bukodi et al, 2021); hardened social-class inequalities, to be found in the unequal distribution of resources and the education system, favour the most advantaged. In other words, the social structure of British society seems to prevent merit from driving intergenerational social mobility despite all the policy efforts. A key critic in this debate is sociologist John Goldthorpe. He has not observed any indication that increasing participation has negated the class effect on class destinations over time. With colleagues he has produced a large body of work demonstrating that the role of education in mobility processes has been decreasing in importance over time along with the declining significance of merit (Goldthorpe, 1996; Goldthorpe and Jackson, 2008; Bukodi et al, 2016; Bukodi and Goldthorpe, 2018; Bukodi et al, 2021).

This literature is supplemented by sociological contributions that stress how family background shapes life opportunities (Bourdieu and Passeron, 1977). Meritocracy would require that the labour market be mainly based on educational qualifications. Yet, in reality, employers look at a wide range of abilities, skills, dispositions and traits within hiring and promotion processes, many of them non-educational and non-meritocratic (Moss and Tilly, 2003; Jackson, 2001, 2006; Acker, 2006; Laurison and Friedman, 2016; Fiel, 2020; Zwysen et al, 2021). Because of the direct effect of social origin on labour outcomes that cannot be explained by education, there are distinct limits to how education can sustain a meritocracy. Others have argued that the educational system is not a meritocratic institution to begin with (for example, Mijs, 2016).

Unjust legitimisation of inequality

A more general criticism is that meritocracy falsely legitimises inequalities of power and privilege. Inequalities become necessary and legitimate (Jost et al, 2003; Alesina and Angeletos, 2005; Frank, 2016; Heiserman and Simpson, 2017; Littler, 2017; Piff et al, 2018; Piketty, 2019). The socioeconomic inequalities are made legitimate and necessary by the discourse of meritocracy and ultimately serve the rich and powerful. Those at the bottom are blamed for their alleged lack of talent or effort. Structural inequalities are disguised or discounted by the notion of equality of opportunity. The education system has a key role to play in this legitimation – the educational process is masked by notions of meritocracy and just reward (Bourdieu and Passeron, 1977). For Marshall et al (1997), social justice is not only about equal access to unequally rewarded positions, unequal outcomes that meritocracy brings still need to be justified. In other words, the inequality that the stratification principle of meritocracy causes is still open for moral assessment (Sayer, 2005).

In *The Tyranny of Merit*, political philosopher Michael Sandel (2020) explains that meritocracy legitimates inequality by assuming that it is the natural product of innate differences in talent and virtue: hardworkingness, intelligence, perseverance. People, therefore, feel that they deserve their income wealth, power and prestige. Yet the political aim to achieve meritocracy has not led to a fairer or better society but towards a society in which anger and frustration dominate. Winners believe they fully *earned* the rewards of their efforts, forgetting about the luck, circumstances (including family and the type of skills or talents the market happen to value) and public goods that allowed their success. Deservingness becomes entitlement. Meritocratic hubris has set in in which the elite look down on those who do not make it. The result has a corrosive effect on the way that success is interpreted, unable to recognise the common good and unable to give different types of work of recognition and esteem. Once people start to reflect on the contingency of talent and fortune, solidarity is much easier to achieve. Sandel explains that the meritocratic ethic happens within a context of growing credentialism and a strong belief that education will improve social mobility. Modern politics actively valorises credentialism through encouraging individuals to improve their lives by getting a university degree. This is combined with the 'rhetoric of rising', that if you try hard enough, you can achieve your goals, eroding the dignity, social recognition and esteem for non-graduate work and workers.

Similarly, David Goodhart (2020) argues that what he calls the cognitive society needs to provide status and dignity for non-graduate types of work.

Goodhart claims that the deservingness of the educated leads to the tyranny of the graduate class. He argues that with the rise of professionals associated with HE education (named 'Head' jobs), they have become a political tribe with their own interests and over time have used their position to devalue other types of work (see also Bovens and Wille, 2017).

The market is often seen as a legitimate meritocratic arbiter of value. Hecht's (2017) research on top income earners shows that the majority evaluate their own and others' incomes based on the idea that 'the market' is a neutral and fair instrument for the distribution of resources. They are generally not concerned about issues of distribution. Van Zanten (2015) observes that French upper- and middle-class families aim to preserve the image of an individual student's merit and autonomy. They conceal the control they exert over their children's educational and career trajectories. Brown et al (2016) show that graduates from elite universities in the UK and France acknowledged that they have been lucky to be in their position but maintain that hard work and determination led to their expected labour market success.

What is merit?

A third strand of criticism relates to what constitutes the concept of merit; what qualities, skills or dispositions can we include within the merit category (Sen et al, 2000)? This is historically and socially contingent but also open to being driven by power interests (Thornton, 2013; Sandel, 2020). Merit is socially constructed and different groups are in different positions to help define what counts as merit. Mijs (2016) reminds us that the definition of merit must favour some groups in society while putting others at a disadvantage. Social groups with wealth and status, in particular, can use the concept of merit to create social and economic advantages. Unequal outcomes are explained as differences in 'individual capacities' rather than systematic social factors. The role of luck may also be underplayed. Frank (2016) argues that luck intervenes by granting people merit, and by furnishing circumstances in which merit can translate into success. Despite their effort and intelligence, those who are merited owe a lot to luck.

Education itself can be used as meritocratic criteria to uphold the power of the advantaged classes. Brown (2013) argued that the drive for social mobility is actually set up more as a 'market' rather than a truly 'meritocratic' competition in the last decades. Instead of levelling the playing field, those from lower socioeconomic groups with disadvantaged backgrounds are given an opportunity to compete with those from more privileged backgrounds in a market competition. Meanwhile, government policies have been concentrated on enhancing the 'absolute' performance of children from disadvantaged backgrounds rather than improving the relative chances of them entering professional occupations compared to those from the middle classes.

Employability

A second key policy area that builds on some of the same assumptions on graduate work is the drive for greater employability of students. Graduate employability has been a core concept within Britain's HE policy context in the last few decades. It has been conceptualised and measured in many different ways (Moreau and Leathwood, 2006; Tomlinson and Holmes, 2017) and approached differently depending on the discipline (Römgens et al, 2020), but in general it represents the likelihood of (continued) employment of the individual (Yorke, 2006). It signifies how well skilled workers' human capital matches the demands of the economy, indicating the extent to which a graduate finds employment, remains in employment or obtains new employment (Hillage and Pollard, 1998; Thijssen et al, 2008). Employability depends on the extent to which the worker can invest time, effort and/or money in increasing or improving skills, knowledge or other characteristics. These skills could be discipline-specific knowledge and skills but also generic or transferable skills (such as communication, problem solving, personal qualities) (Bennett et al, 1999; Knight and Yorke, 2002). The two key pillars of employability are adaptability (the ability to shift to the demands of the labour market) and responsibilisation (workers becoming responsible for their labour market achievement).

The employability discourse not only highlights the individualised nature of skill formation, it also has distinct consequences in how we understand the role of HE. As described earlier, universities traditionally have had a role in vocational training, in particular for professional domains. This was accompanied by an understanding that a loose relationship between university education and the job content of graduate work exists, apart from fields such as law and medicine. In the 1990s, a new set of ideas on how HE can and should contribute to labour market outcomes gained more influence. It more clearly identified the role of HE in the production of an appropriately trained workforce that fits employers' needs. This required HE to identify what is it employers are looking for and shape HE curriculum accordingly. HE would need to instil marketable skills, including many non-technical skills such as communication and interpersonal skills that would improve their ability to maintain employment. So-called 'employability skills' would help graduates in the workplace. The UK Commission for Employment and Skills (UKCES) (2010) stated that there has been 'recognition that employers are looking for a broader set of generic employability skills' (p 6). These skills 'have been identified as a key element to ensuring that the employment and skills system is demand-led' (p 5). As a result, universities took on greater responsibility to show how their courses would contribute to earning power, demonstrating whether students are receiving value for money in the process. Universities continue to focus on employability as the foundation for graduate success (Kornelakis and Petrakaki, 2020). Their employability efforts are supported by a large body of literature on how universities should enhance their students' employability (for example Harvey, 2000; Hager and Holland, 2006; Yorke and Knight, 2006; Pegg et al, 2012).

The role of the government is vital in the graduate employability drive. Yorke argues (2006, p 3) that 'the employability of graduates has become an aim that governments around the world have, to varying extents, imposed on national HE systems'. The employability agenda, like the marketisation agenda, is predicated on the idea that universities should be accountable for their students' labour market opportunities. The pressure to ensure greater employability is very much in line with the need to make students (as consumers) responsible for their human capital investments. In policy documents, employability is directly linked with the value for money argument that has been a core feature of the marketisation drive:

> It is a top concern for business that students should leave university better equipped with a wider range of employability skills. All universities should be expected to demonstrate how their institution prepares its students for employment, including through training in modern workplace skills such as team working, business awareness, and communication skills. This information should help students choose courses that offer the greatest returns in terms of graduate opportunity. (DBIS, 2009, p 8)

It is accepted that graduate employability is, and should be, a key aim for HE providers, and therefore measured and benchmarked accordingly. Universities are expected to improve graduate employability by increasing the 'quality' of their courses and providing students with employability skills (understood as transferable skills needed by an individual to secure future employment opportunities) (HEFCE, 2010). Universities are incentivised through measurement and audit exercises, and learning outcome standards required by external accrediting bodies to address the government's employability agenda (DfE, 2016). Universities are expected to embed employability and/or enterprise and entrepreneurship education in subject curricula and actively think about the practical knowledge and skills deemed desirable by employers (Sewell and Dacre Pool, 2010; Blackmore et al, 2016; Durazzi, 2021). Work-based learning has also been introduced to provide students with work experiences, and extracurricular awards and recognition schemes aim to widen the student experience.

Universities must now closely monitor the labour market trajectories of their graduates and graduate employability is now measured internally as well as externally. They need to publish information on the employability of their graduates in the form of 'employability statements', explaining how they promote student job prospects. Key indicators such as labour market destinations and graduate starting salaries by institution (and subject) are published and regarded as evidence of how successful universities are in increasing student employability. Similar to the marketisation discourse, government policy here assumes a responsibility of HE institutions for labour market outcomes of graduates. It suggests that employability can be measured and captured through metrics and data, which should be available to students.

The dark side of employability

At first glance, the notion of graduate employability may seem benign and helpful for students to improve the labour market prospects of graduates. Yet as with the idea of meritocracy, a critical look reveals that it is a problematic concept. A whole range of criticism has been posed against the idea of graduate employability and its application (Tholen, 2015; Clarke, 2018; Tholen and Brown, 2017). Several objections are practical in nature. Some have pointed out that there is little consensus regarding the definition of the employability agenda or employability skills (Hallier, 2009). Many have questioned the extent to which current strategies are an effective means of developing transferable employability skills (Cranmer, 2006; Yorke, 2006; Holmes, 2013). Others question whether the skills developed in the classroom can be applied within the workforce (Boden and Nedeva, 2010; Tholen, 2019).

We can also take issue with the idea that HE needs to adjust to the demands of employers. Also, should we accept employer accounts of skill requirements? There exists significant variance in what employers expect from graduates. Accepting employer accounts of skill requirements at face value is also problematic. Employers may also not demand what universities teach. This is reflected in several empirical studies investigating employer skill requirements, demonstrating that hiring practices are not rewarding 'typical' graduate skills (Archer and Davidson, 2008; Wilton, 2011). They may recruit on personal qualities and characteristics that at best are tangibly related to university education or they may not necessarily be merit-based (Jackson, 2007). Some employers may need very specific skills. These job-specific skills can best be learned in the workplace or through specific on-the-job learning. There is only so much universities can do. As Mason et al (2009, p 26) state: 'There may be little to be gained from universities seeking to develop skills that are best acquired (or can only be acquired) after starting employment rather than beforehand.' The strong focus on the labour market in measuring employability leads to a universalist approach unable to meet the demands of employers and accurately define individual employability (Marginson, 2006; Jackson and Chapman, 2012).

Employability becomes the obligation of the individual to navigate a rapidly changing employment market, successfully maintain work and optimise earning power as well as transfer between jobs. The responsibilities of the worker largely absolve the government from addressing other inequalities. McCowan (2015, p 271) writes:

> The process of individualisation of responsibility for employment ... can be interpreted as an abrogation of responsibility on the part of the state. Instead of ensuring opportunities and welfare for all, the state is – in the name of fostering efficiency and economic competitiveness – allowing the wealthy to maintain their privileges and passing responsibility for disadvantage to the disadvantaged themselves. According to this view, employability is a sleight of hand, convincing people that their own employment success or failure does and should rest in their own hands, and thereby legitimising inequalities.

In line with the growing flexibilisation of the labour market, employability presents the shift towards a more transactional employment contract, replacing employment security with employability (Baruch, 2001).

Others have pointed out that social context is too often forgotten in defining graduate employability, leading to a myopic grasp of employment. Factors that impact on labour market conditions and individual opportunities include macroeconomic conditions, level of job vacancies, employer recruitment practices and government policy (McQuaid and Lindsay, 2005; Tholen, 2013). Brown and Hesketh (2004) maintain that graduate employability is not just about the individual skills and capabilities of graduates but there exists a relative dimension of employability. How well a graduate performs also depends on other graduates who enter the labour market. This relative dimension is crucial in understanding employability. Employability co-depends 'on how one stands relative to others within a hierarchy of job seekers' (Brown and Hesketh, 2004, p 25; see also the discussion of queuing theory in Chapter 7). This relative dimension is becoming increasingly important in the UK graduate labour market. There are signs that growth in the supply of graduates does not match the number of graduate-level jobs. Mass HE intensifies market competition and the struggle for positional advantage.

Too often employability is treated as a decontextualised signifier in so far as it overlooks how structural qualities of the economic, social and educational context interact with labour market opportunities (Morley, 2001; Thijssen et al, 2008). It ignores a wide range of factors that shape graduate employability such as social class, gender, disability, ethnicity, social networks and university status (Morley, 2001; Tomlinson, 2007; Mason et al, 2009; Holmes, 2013; Okay-Somerville and Scholarios, 2017; Burke et al, 2020; Merrill et al, 2020). The influence of social characteristics is far from a remnant from the past. They are very likely to stay with us. Because of large pools of qualified candidates, 'personal capital' – a wide range of various personal qualities – increasingly matters in recruitment (Brown et al, 2003).

The employability agenda is now baked into English HE provision as students' employability has been a key concern for the proponents of HE marketisation. The growing reliance on the 'consumer' to pay for their education can only be upheld if the return on education continues to be strong. Arguments made for the need for marketisation and choice in HE firmly insist that individual learners and institutions take responsibility for individual labour market success. The ongoing support for the idea that universities should teach 'relevant' skills became more solidified in the English context as tuition fees were allowed to rise. Greater transparency into what universities do to guarantee their students' future employability is thought to be needed to ensure that students can make more informed market decisions, ensuring graduates are in a position to be able to pay off their student loans.

Human Capital Theory

In Chapter 5, we saw how government policy on marketisation heavily relies on HCT. HCT is an economic theory that has dominated several policy areas, including economic and education policies. The theory became the cornerstone of policy thinking in promoting economic competitiveness, skill formation as well as wider social goals such as improving social mobility. HCT serves a wide economic purpose in directing how the economy should be managed and developed, shaping the blueprint for maintaining economic growth and economic competitiveness. In alignment with the idea of a knowledge economy and skill-biased technological change, HCT is the basis for an optimistic promise of skill and personal fulfilment for all able and willing to invest in education. The marketisation drive depends on the assumption of a narrow relationship between skills, productivity, jobs and earnings, which is what HCT offers. HCT also positions students, employers and universities as market actors which benefit from a well-regulated marketplace for skills. As a mainstream economic theoretical framework, there have been numerous critiques of HCT which have raised a wide range of objections. I will summarise a number of key ones here that demonstrate best that the ongoing reliance on HCT in understanding of graduate work is fraught with difficulties.

Earning without learning

In *The Death of Human Capital?* Brown et al (2020) argue against the dominance of HCT in thinking about economic and social progress. A key argument the authors make against its proponents is that more investment in education does not lead to higher earnings on a national and individual level. There remain large inequalities of earnings despite similar investments in education. Suppose one compares the average or median returns for graduate and non-graduate workers. In that case, there is a causal relationship between HE participation (learning) and wages (earning). Yet as we have seen in the previous chapter, when the data are disaggregated then stark differences in earnings become apparent in relation to different types of education and institutions, gender, class, race, ethnicity, industry and occupation as well as within-group inequalities. The authors point at the extreme outliers in growing earnings by the top decile earners often working in specific industries such as finance and/or being part of the wealthy elite unrelated to individual productivity. In short, wages do not reflect the investment in education in many cases. The authors also point out that global price competition is depressing wages for many graduates. An established body of literature outlined in the previous chapter highlights that many non-educational factors shape graduate earnings. Therefore, the importance of formal education in human capital has been overstated by HCT.

Productivity

The relationship between productivity and wages is likewise far from straightforward (Rosenfeld, 2021). A worker's productivity is shaped by numerous factors, many of them external, such as work organisation, management and use of technology. There are also wider economic systemic factors that compromise the relationship between wages and productivity. Rewards can be the result of rent-seeking rather than productivity. In other words, unproductive jobs can still be lucrative (Torvik, 2002) and distort the rates to return to education. It is not the individual human capital but rather the economic circumstances that make rents possible. Souto-Outero (2010) points out that rewards obtained in the labour market are to do with the labour market value of a profession rather than productivity. He explains that 'individual productivity occurs within a context that enables it' (p 402). To capture these influences, it requires a different type of analysis that needs to include salary surges in certain sectors and occupations (finance, law, business), the use of performance pay and other institutional differences such as tax laws and the role of unions. For instance, the exponential growth in the income of those at the top of the wage distribution has to be understood through a wider political-economic analysis (Piketty, 2020). The reasons for these extreme outliers in earnings cannot be fully understood by HCT (Brown et al, 2020).

Rationality

Another important criticism relates to the assumption that (young) people make rational, self-interested educational choices based on utility maximising and seeking a return on investment (Becker, 1994). In reality, they do not act as econometricians as Goldthorpe (2014, pp 270–271) has put it. Although human capital acknowledges that the utility for students does not necessarily have to be based on future income maximisation, this is what received all the attention. Yet students may act less as *homo economicus* than assumed (Budd, 2017; Muddiman, 2017). They do not 'self-select into colleges based on expected gain' (Borgen, 2015, p 34). They can choose to participate based on intrinsic motivation such as enjoyment and see their education at least partly as an end in itself. Also, students actively develop skills at university that may have little predictive value, and engage in various cultural, social or political activities that are not directly linked to any future careers. Students make key educational choices based on a wide range of rationales and motivations, including peer pressure, parents' expectations or the desire to leave home (Jenkins et al, 2001). Similarly, we know that social factors deeply influence educational outcomes in terms of how much education and what type of education is received. Social inequalities shape aspirations (for example Breen and Goldthorpe, 1997; Jackson et al, 2007; Abrahams, 2018; Grim et al, 2019), which hinders movement into higher levels of education and prestigious institutions (Boliver, 2011, 2013). HCT has little to say about this, although Becker's later work does engage with this issue (Becker and Murphy, 2000). Yet HCT remains limited in helping us understand educational choices by maintaining that they are the product of an individual rational decision-making process.

Why do employers value education?

The fourth strand of critique focuses on the assumption that employers seek higher qualifications because of the skills and knowledge that HE institutions impart. As we have seen in Chapter 5, the value of qualifications could lie elsewhere. The access to a higher level of education and the completion of it both may relate to personal characteristics such as perseverance or intelligence. Signalling theory does not assert that education itself makes one necessarily more productive. Employers may value educational qualifications and experience for various reasons.

Employers are projected to be interested first and foremost in the educational profile of candidates. In reality, the role of education in the hiring process is rather complex and far from uniform. A study on software engineers, financial analysts and press officers shows that between occupations the role and meaning differ considerably in relation to skill development, occupational identity, career development and access to the occupation (Tholen, 2019). Not all employers care much about formal education when they recruit nor does it take a central place in the workplace, even for skilled workers.

According to Marginson (2019), a key weakness of HCT is a lack of realism. In its view of HE as skill developer, HCT artificially integrates education and work. In reality, they represent two different domains that are only partially and ambiguously aligned. Marginson states:

> Higher education and work are different and separated social sites, though there are important overlaps in practice. This is not a relationship of identity, regularity or a linear continuum. Nor is it a dialectic, in which two contrasting parts form a unified system with a shared logic. Education and work are heterogeneous in relation to each other. ... Relations between higher education and work are also context-bound. They vary by country, field of study, type of institution, financing of education, occupation, industry, employment site and over time. (pp 297–298)

The UK educational context in particular demonstrates a loose relationship between education and work regarding skills development. In relation to other European countries, it has a high level of so-called vertical mismatches, the relatedness of subject and the degree and area of employment, especially in the graduate labour market. There is more vocational specificity in education, and predictable education-to-work pathways, in countries such as Germany and Austria compared to the UK, Ireland and the US where we find very loose linkages between occupational groups, education and certification (albeit with considerable variance between occupations, as found by Bol et al 2019). Graduates from any field can fill many graduate-level jobs. Graduates depart from their field of study and may never return. As a result, level of education and institution attended are more significant than field of study for employers in these countries. It has been suggested that signalling theory is more valid than HCT for these types of graduate labour markets (Tholen, 2013; Di Stasio and van de Werfhorst, 2016).

Humankind

A final strain of critique highlights human capital's damaging impact on how people perceive themselves and others. For HCT theorists and in particular Gary Becker (1993, 1994), any kind of human behaviour could be analysed within the framework of the utility maximisation calculus (including training and education). HCT reduces the individual to atomic stimulus–response subjects primarily engaged in life to optimise their human capital investments. As such, it does not promote a wide enough view of human development. HCT can be considered as a fundamentally neoliberal economic framework (Foucault, 2008). In particular, Gary Becker's foundational work draws on the notion that market competition would lead to optimum investment in human capital. In HCT the individual is positioned as a market actor investor in education and training, responsible for their own labour market position and success. The notion of employability becomes the measure of how well the individual has succeeded to match their human capital profile to labour market demands (Thijssen et al, 2008). Foucault (2008), in his discussion of neoliberalism in his lecture at the Collège de France on the 'Birth of Biopolitics', recognised the radicality of HCT's view of humans early on. He remarks that economics traditionally has seen workers predominantly as persons of exchange. They sell their labour power based on labour market supply and demand. In HCT, workers are active economic subjects and are presented as enterprises responsible for allocating their time and labour and skill development according to the maximisation of utility. Human beings become defined by a calculative mentality and act in predictable ways. Foucault (2008) notes that the worker in HCT is 'an entrepreneur of himself, being for himself his own capital, being for himself his own producer, being for himself the source of earnings' (p 226). This logic spills to all areas of life, in every action including crime, marriage, education or love. All can be framed as an investment and calculated in terms of cost and benefits. The logic of interest and competition will become all-dominating. We should note again that Becker himself, unlike his followers, has put forward nuance in his view of the individual, acknowledging the complexity and the reductionist purpose of theories (Becker et al, 2012).

Building on the work of Foucault, political theorist Wendy Brown (2015, pp 37–38) warns that HCT represents a neoliberal view that makes individuals responsible for their labour market success without offering a guarantee of security, protection or even survival. It focuses on market winners and losers, not equal treatment or protection. These sentiments are echoed by Fleming (2017) who, as we have seen earlier, observes that an extreme version of self-interested individualism in HCT enabled the individualising of employment which has aided economic insecurity, low productivity, diminished autonomy and personal debt.

HCT's greatest success is becoming so mainstream in our thinking that we no longer recognise it as a theory. Yet since its conception, it has been under severe criticism for the various assumptions on earnings, productivity, skills and human agency. These maintain that HCT:

- misunderstands the relationship between education and work;
- essentialises the role of education in skill development and graduate premium;
- places unrealistic assumptions on the self-interest and rationality of workers and employers;
- misreads the relationship between education and productivity;
- misinterprets why employers demand education;
- offers a reductionist view of human beings.

The many fundamental issues raised against HCT have deep implications on the validity of the marketisation discourse. Why should we accept argumentation build on a theoretical framework that shows severe flaws in areas that are crucial for the policy discourse on marketisation?

Conclusion

This chapter has shown that the political notion of meritocracy, the trust in employability as the individual solution to labour market issues and the belief in HCT as the cornerstone of economic and educational development share many of the same assumptions with the marketisation discourse. And without ascribing any agency to these ideas, all three validate the understanding of work that grounds the promotion of the marketisation of HE.

We have also seen that all three are problematic in their own right. Notions of merits are used to maintain inequalities within capitalism and help create educational systems focused on the life opportunities of the few rather than the many. Likewise, the political aim to increase students' employability as a goal in itself is beset with issues. The individualistic interpretation of the concept combined with pressure on HE to improve graduates' employability makes the promise of graduate employability a myth (Tholen and Brown, 2017). Finally, HCT positions students as market actors making economic decisions in their human capital investment. It misunderstands the relationship between education and labour market outcomes. It maintains that as long as there is a healthy graduate premium, HE will become the key to individual prosperity while answering the modern economy's technological demands. This supply-side solution has run into trouble. As Brown et al (2020, p 133) explain, the 'fundamental problem is not that there is a shortage of the relevant skills that employers demand but that there is a lack of good, quality jobs' (p 133).

10

Conclusion

Introduction

This book argues that the drive for marketisation is motivated by a false understanding of graduate work. The research evidence shows that many of the economic assumptions that underpin government higher education (HE) policy need to be challenged. We need an honest discussion about how well labour needs justify the marketisation of HE. The relatively high level of marketisation has fundamentally changed the HE sector in all the nations of the UK, especially in England. In the last 20 years, the increase in a state-regulated market to coordinate HE has been a leitmotif within the HE sector. It has altered income streams, incentive structure, work practices, curricula, the role of the student and much more. How one evaluates marketisation and its effects will depend on other moral and political views such as the role of education in society and the relationship between state and market. The pursuit of the market and competition between universities and courses may have made education provision more responsive to the demands of the consumer of HE. Yet, the policy pressure for greater student choice, institutional accountability and recognition of customer–provider relationships may have led to forms of consumerism. The pressure for universities to deliver employability and drive economic prosperity through human capital development has made universities devalue their other aims. Marketisation has added financial instability throughout the sector. Transferring the cost of HE to students has improved university funding. However, it leaves major questions about the affordability of HE for students and the taxpayer. Private sector managerialism and rationalism found in the governance of universities has changed the role of the academic, including their autonomy. Even from an economic perspective, there are clear limits to marketisation in HE (see G. Williams, 2013).

Efforts to increase competition and choice in the system may result from haphazard policymaking, but we can see that marketisation is politically motivated. The ideological rationales for it can be found throughout policy documents and in political speeches and interviews with politicians.

Over time, the spirit of marketisation has coloured our perception of what HE is for, how HE should be run, and who should pay for it. Increasingly HE is spoken of in economic instrumentalist terms that fit right in with what the marketised system aims to do; establish the value of HE in market terms. Recently Sir Peter Lampl, the chairman of the Sutton Trust, established to improve social mobility in the UK, worried that taxpayers' money is being wasted. Employers are not getting the skills they need because too many young people are going to university (Mathers, 2021). Students have been in a competitive selective HE system for the longest time. However, gradually discussions about merit and opportunity have been informed by issues of choice and competition. For instance, the 'pressure-selling' of place offers to school-leavers has become common practice, signalling a marketplace based on consumerist values (Adams, 2019b). Academics also have adapted to the marketised system and are acutely aware of it but often feel powerless. In a mental health survey with UK academics, it was shown that the culture of performativity has resulted in target-driven management approaches, causing anxiety and pressure (O'Brien and Guiney, 2018). As one participant wrote: 'You have to do all you can to keep student numbers high. Otherwise, next year one of your colleagues might lose their job' (p 12). Marketisation has also shifted the value system under which academics are working. As one academic reflects on the overt control which he experiences working in UK academia: 'The marketisation of higher education makes working in a UK university feel like working in a business' (Anonymous, 2018).

Despite the resistance against marketisation, it has continued to grow and become an integral dimension of the HE sector. This book has started asking the question how with each passing government, more and more forms of marketisation are implemented? Here the book does not claim to offer a full overview of all the forces that made marketisation possible and desirable (see, for a more comprehensive answer, McCaig, 2018). Instead, it has aimed to elucidate one key rationale that has underpinned the policy thinking on HE. Marketisation would turn HE into a more flexible and efficient institution in delivering its economic aims. It would be better able to ensure value for money and improve the sector's responsiveness to the economy's needs. The interests of employers, students, the taxpayer and the state are deemed to align. Marketisation improves the human capital investments made by students and demanded by employers within the modern graduate labour market. A well-functioning market in HE is needed to allow students to choose the right course and universities to be more adaptable to and focused on the needs of businesses. The improved skill profile of the workforce plus that lower public cost would benefit the taxpayers and the state. Ideas about the labour market and economy have helped shape HE reform, building on conceptions on the nature of Western economic development, globalisation and the nature of modern high-skilled work. The HE sector had been theoretically framed as the key facilitator of economic success and individual labour market opportunity. The need for increasing competition, choice and personal responsibility thus made sense.

In Chapters 3, 4, and 5, the book challenges the assumptions found in policy documents by examining the work graduates perform and the rewards they receive as well as the economic and societal relations they find themselves in. The education policy overestimates how important HE is in directing modern work and the graduate labour market. The idea that investment in education will give graduates privileged opportunities to become high-waged, high-skilled knowledge workers is not quite supported by research on occupational change, earnings, skill use and work conditions.

What can the case of England tell us about marketisation in HE?

The book's analysis of the English HE system can provide comparative insights into national contexts, especially in relation to countries in which marketisation is in a less advanced stage. HE sectors within continental Europe are moving in England's direction, as distinct features of markets are apparent within its management in particular (Slaughter and Cantwell, 2012). According to Marginson (2007, p 42), '[p]artial marketisation is a feature of many if not most national systems'. Every national context may have unique aspects that shape how and where marketisation occurs. Yet, the case of England may serve as a case study on how economic discourses support changes in policy on HE marketisation. Given the global appeal of the ideal of the knowledge society as well as Human Capital Theory (HCT), there may be parallels and connections with other national policy contexts.

Marketisation as a process is historically contingent. For instance, the financial crisis of 2008 put pressure on all forms of public spending, leading to the Browne Review. The dominance of the Conservative government may also have made market-led development more likely. The HE sector itself has also played a key role. In its response to market initiatives, university hierarchies seemed ready to embrace the language and ethos of marketisation. It is essential to understand marketisation as much as a political/ideological process as an economic phenomenon (Furedi, 2011, p 2). For those who regard marketisation in HE as part of a larger neoliberal movement affecting the public sector, policy initiatives that demand more marketisation seemed predictable within the English context (Canaan and Shumar, 2008). Yet, we need to be careful not to be deterministic. Marketisation in HE was achieved slowly, and its development was far from certain. It needed to be defended and sold as the rational or sensible thing to do and accepted within both political and stakeholder circles. Although we may associate marketisation with conservative or free-market politics, it has also found support among the centre-left. This book has not examined the specific political contexts and detailed histories in which these policies came about, yet it does demonstrate that policymakers heavily rely on distinct policy discourses that offer specific views on the modern world, including the economy and labour market.

What is higher education for?

Marketisation in HE has been resisted by many inside and outside academia (McGettigan, 2013; Docherty, 2014; Giroux, 2014). The analysis offered in this book may help with opposing it by challenging some the argumentation for marketisation. Once we accept a more realistic understanding of the role of HE in the economy and labour market, we have a better view of what HE can and should deliver and how this serves its stakeholders. Policymakers can, of course, advance the state-regulated market in HE for various reasons. Yet if the reasons are driven by the policy discourse examined in this book, it should be questioned and resisted. Given that the consequences of marketisation are immense, its rationales need much more scrutiny. This could help strengthen a rejection of the dominance of economics' instrumental purpose of universities. Currently, the perceived purpose of the university is overly reliant on the idea that within the knowledge-based society, universities are in the service of economic development. Over time, unmet employer skills demand and employability needs of students were regarded as *the* key problems of the English HE system. Also, affordability issues were directly measured in relation to the economic benefits, justifying a higher contribution of students. Economic gains of HE were problematised and prioritised, and other issues muted. HE's effectiveness and quality were measured, audited and assessed through consumer market mechanisms.

Within policy debates, university education is seen predominantly in relation to the economy and towards improving productivity, productive knowledge and human capital development. The obsession with viewing education in solely economistic terms has become hardwired in policy circles in many Western countries (Spring, 2015). Greater scrutiny of what HE is for and how it contributes to a wider set of objectives is needed. This is not to say that it should ignore the state finances or the needs of employers as stakeholders. A renewed understanding of the role of universities in the economy and labour market may serve debates about the purposes of HE or universities specifically (Willetts, 2017; Collini, 2018). It also allows alternative understandings of what universities are and how they (should) relate to their students, society, economy and other stakeholders.

In recent decades, many have had concern for the disappearance of the wider non-economic public role that universities should, in their eyes, take (Teixeira, 2011; J. Williams, 2013; Ashwin, 2020). The university is imagined as having lost its initial characteristics to service a market-driven utilitarian project, including its traditional values and ideals (Marginson, 1997; Potts, 2005; Boden and Epstein, 2006; Naidoo and Williams, 2015). Recent policies represent a capitalist takeover of HE in which the outputs or results have become products to be sold, bought and traded, including research and teaching. In this commodification or economisation of HE, economic value is attributed to all its activities (Berman, 2015).

The instrumental economic approach to the role of universities within society ignores their social role. Other purposes for universities such as to foster human understanding through open-ended enquiry have been overshadowed. The tradition of regarding universities foremost as sites of intellectual development, social progress and personal growth seems to fade away. There is no longer room to pursue many of their roles in a marketised system as institutions are incentivised to focus on a limited number of commercially viable activities. Gibbs (2001) writes:

> Under pressure from a short-termist market and in order to compete for students, the temptation for universities is to neglect the well-being of their students and concentrate on measuring the financial aspect of their success. In doing this, universities may be compromising the trusting relationship within which personal well-being can flourish. They risk the loss of community, for they ask scholars to participate on terms that they could reasonably reject, for their ends become private rather than public. (p 91)

One specific example of the demise of HE's social role is the perceived loss of the public mission. HE is constructed as having public aims, including creating a democratic debate, supporting society in creating solutions to its problems and offering an education that equips students for the public service professions (Calhoun, 2006). Shapiro (2005) emphasises the need for the HE institutions to move beyond narrow self-serving concerns and enforce social change to reflect the nature of a society that its members desire. HE's public role is in decline due to increasing marketisation (De La Fuente, 2002; Heller, 2016; Wright and Shore, 2017). With a loss of public funding comes the loss of a political consensus about universities' wider benefits, which previously justified public spending on HE (Simons and Masschelein, 2009). Marketisation threatens the social contract between HE and society whereby universities receive privileges (autonomy and financial support) in exchange for serving the public good (Brown, 2011b; see also Holmwood and Bhambra, 2012; Holmwood, 2014). Lynch (2006) warns us 'that the danger with this advancing marketised individualism is that it will further weaken public interest values among those who are university educated' (p 2).

The future

The COVID-19 pandemic has shown the impact of the ongoing marketisation of HE (Moore, 2021). In the summer of 2021, there were discussions of A-level grade inflation due to the teacher-assessment method. The latter resulted in higher grades compared to previous years with as many as 45 per cent of students getting top A★ grades at A-level (Adams et al, 2021), giving more students access to HE courses. This led to an oversubscription of courses based on offers awarded. The most selective institutions had taken the largest share of increased recruitment as they had made offers before the new grading method was announced (McKie, 2021). This, in turn, made mid- and lower-ranking universities extremely nervous (Staton, 2021c). The market competition and the pressure for recruitment targets intensify when there is a sudden change in demand. The volatility within the system and the stakes involved for universities and school-leavers will further solidify efforts to attract students and allocate effort and resources to do so. And thus universities cannot easily change direction.

The COVID-19 crisis also exposed the control the state continues to exercise to deliver HE in the market mould. In July 2020, Education Secretary Gavin Williamson made it a condition that universities facing bankruptcy must close 'low value' courses (as well as demonstrate commitment to free speech) in order to receive government loans. Low value courses were defined as those associated with low graduate pay, high drop-out rates or whose graduates did not often end up in skilled employment. In August 2021, there were severe uncertainties about the spread of COVID-19 in the autumn and safety concerns within the HE sector about returning to face-to-face teaching. Williamson expected universities to be offering face-to-face teaching, 'unless there's unprecedented reasons' (Cowburn, 2021). He stated that universities that did not return to face-to-face teaching that academic year should not be charging full fees. Again, the market regulator (OfS) was used to set the expectations around education provision. Williamson warned that it would be given 'all the power and all the backing in order to pursue those universities that aren't delivering enough for students that are paying their fees' (Cowburn, 2021). We may be moving from a state-regulated market to a state-directed market in HE.

The COVID-19 pandemic also led to dissatisfied students who became aware that they were paying for mostly online courses which they felt as consumers signalled low value for money (Bundock, 2021). Debates emerged on whether the affected students should be offered fee refunds paid for by universities or whether the government should offer rebates by cutting the amount students have to repay for the tuition fee and living-cost loans (Fazackerley, 2021). This shows that the HE market is an unusual market with uncertainty about who is responsible for what. Yet it also fundamentally demonstrates that issues in HE quality are now directly linked to how well the market functions, utilising the language of the market.

The future is open but as it stands there is little room for optimism for those who would like to see marketisation rolled back. There has been considerable attention to improving other types of post-compulsory forms of education such as (degree) apprenticeship. Yet this drive does not reduce the marketisation of HE in itself. And as argued in the previous chapter, there are vested interests in maintaining the policy discourse on graduate work and the labour market. The marketisation of HE relies on powerful adjacent political 'allies' which may make it more difficult for some to accept arguments against it.

And yet the resistance against marketisation will also remain. For instance, there continue to be voices that would like to reduce or scrap tuition fees, most notably some within the Labour Party. Yet, it is far from unlikely that students will bear even more of the financial burden, especially in post-COVID-19 times in which UK politicians will need to address the large government debt due to increased borrowing. A Higher Education Policy Institute report proposes that students pay back more of their loan (Hillman, 2021). This could involve lowering the salary at which students repay the loan and extending the loan period from 30 to 35 years. The report has received positive feedback from politicians, including former universities minister Jo Johnson (Staton, 2021d).

Concerns about the costs of the current fees system for the taxpayer may also shape HE policy in the future. It could lead to lowering the cap for tuition fees for specific courses or changes to student loan repayment thresholds, although it could also look more radical. In 2014, former universities minister David Willetts proposed on *Newsnight* that HE institutions in the future could be buying the student debts of their own graduates (Cook, 2014). It would come with variable tuition fees and shift the financial risk of low-earning graduates to HE institutions. They would also profit if their graduates repaid more of their debt. It would incentivise institutions to offer courses that the labour market demands and rewards accordingly. Since then, the idea of financialising student debt to lower the risk has been proposed various times (Dickinson, 2021). These ideas are underpinned by the same assumptions about the graduate labour market and the relationship between HE and labour market demand. Yet now universities become further responsible for the labour market outcomes of their students.

The future of HE systems in the UK and beyond may continue to hold support for the idea that the best or appropriate way to manage, coordinate and fund HE and its activities is by relying on the markets and competition. Policymakers may uphold and feel strengthened by the policy narrative outlined in this book. Alternatively, we could move on from this policy discourse, realising that it forms an impediment to creating an HE system that is of value in itself rather than a function of the market benefits it offers. Here it may open up opportunities to actively reduce inequalities in society. Too often, the current system redresses existing disparities in society and the economy by offering overly optimistic meritocratic human capital solutions to social justice issues. A renewed policy narrative could be based on wider measures of quality of teaching than those based on satisfaction surveys and labour market outcomes. It could also actively try to reduce consumerism. Discussions about the ideal distribution between taxpayers and users in covering the costs of HE will not go away. Likewise, employers remain natural stakeholders in HE and universities may want a closer relationship to deliver more vocational degrees such as degree apprenticeships. These conversations will all benefit from a more realistic understanding of the relationship between education, skill, jobs and earnings. This book hopefully contributes towards this aspiration.

References

Abel, W., Burnham, R. and Corder, M. (2016) 'Wages, productivity and the changing composition of the UK workforce', *Bank of England Quarterly Bulletin*, 56(1), pp 12–22. Available at: https://ideas.repec.org/a/boe/qbullt/0193.html (Accessed: 26 August 2021).

Abrahams, J. (2018) 'Option blocks that block options: Exploring inequalities in GCSE and A Level options in England', *British Journal of Sociology of Education*, 39(8), pp 1143–1159.

Acemoglu, D. (1998) 'Why do new technologies complement skills? Directed technical change and wage inequality', *The Quarterly Journal of Economics*, 113(4), pp 1055–1089.

Acemoglu, D. (2002) 'Technical change, inequality, and the labor market', *Journal of Economic Literature*, 40(1), pp 7–72.

Acemoglu, D. and Autor, D. (2011) 'Lectures in labor economics: Lecture notes, MIT'. Available at: https://economics.mit.edu/files/4689 (Accessed: 5 April 2022).

Acemoglu, D. and Autor, D. (2012) 'What does human capital do? A review of Goldin and Katz's *The Race between Education and Technology*', *Journal of Economic Literature*, 50(2), pp 426–463.

Acemoglu, D. and Restrepo, P. (2018) 'The race between man and machine: Implications of technology for growth, factor shares, and employment', *American Economic Review*, 108(6), pp 1488–1542.

Acker, J. (2006) 'Inequality regimes: Gender, class, and race in organizations', *Gender & Society*, 20(4), pp 441–464.

Adamecz-Völgyi, A., Henderson, M. and Shure, N. (2020) 'Is "first in family" a good indicator for widening university participation?', *Economics of Education Review*, 78, p 102038.

Adams, A. (2018) 'Technology and the labour market: The assessment', *Oxford Review of Economic Policy*, 34(3), pp 349–361.

Adams, R. (2019a) 'Graduate gender pay gap is widening, official figures reveal', *The Guardian*, 29 March. Available at: http://www.theguardian.com/education/2019/mar/29/graduate-gender-pay-gap-is-widening-official-figures-reveal (Accessed: 26 August 2021).

Adams, R. (2019b) 'Universities "pressure-selling" place offers to school-leavers', *The Guardian*, 25 January. Available at: http://www.theguardian.com/education/2019/jan/25/universities-pressure-selling-place-offers-to-school-leavers (Accessed: 27 August 2021).

Adams, R. (2022) 'OfS publishes plans to punish English universities for poor value for money', *The Guardian*. Available at: https://www.theguardian.com/education/2022/jan/20/ofs-publishes-plans-to-punish-english-universities-for-poor-value-for-money (Accessed: 20 January 2022).

Adams, R., McIntyre, N. and Kirk, A. (2021) 'Nearly 45% of A-level entries across UK awarded top grades', *The Guardian*, 10 August. Available at: http://www.theguardian.com/education/2021/aug/10/a-level-entries-across-uk-awarded-top-grades (Accessed: 27 August 2021).

Aldred, J. (2019) *Licence to be Bad: How Economics Corrupted Us.* London: Allen Lane.

Alesina, A. and Angeletos, G.-M. (2005) 'Fairness and redistribution', *American Economic Review*, 95(4), pp 960–980.

Alvesson, M. (2001) 'Knowledge work: Ambiguity, image and identity', *Human Relations*, 54(7), pp 863–886.

Alvesson, M. (2004) *Knowledge Work and Knowledge-Intensive Firms.* Oxford and New York: Oxford University Press.

Anderson, K.T. and Holloway, J. (2020) 'Discourse analysis as theory, method, and epistemology in studies of education policy', *Journal of Education Policy*, 35(2), pp 188–221.

Anderson, V. and Tomlinson, M. (2021) 'Signaling standout graduate employability: The employer perspective', *Human Resource Management Journal*, 31(3), pp 675–693.

Anonymous (2018) 'Working in a UK university is starting to feel like working for a business', *The Guardian*, 23 February. Available at: http://www.theguardian.com/higher-education-network/2018/feb/23/lecturing-in-a-uk-university-is-starting-to-feel-like-working-in-a-business (Accessed: 27 August 2021).

Appiah, K.A. (2018) 'The myth of meritocracy: Who really gets what they deserve?', *The Guardian*, 19 October. Available at: http://www.theguardian.com/news/2018/oct/19/the-myth-of-meritocracy-who-really-gets-what-they-deserve (Accessed: 26 August 2021).

Araki, S. (2020) 'Educational expansion, skills diffusion, and the economic value of credentials and skills', *American Sociological Review*, 85(1), pp 128–175.

Archer, W. and Davidson, J. (2008) *Graduate Employability: What Do Employers Think and Want?* London: The Council for Industry and Higher Education.

Arntz, M., Gregoryi, T. and Zierahni, U. (2021) 'The impact of artificial intelligence on the labour market: What do we know so far?', OECD Social, Employment and Migration Working Papers 256.

Arum, R. and Roksa, J. (2010) *Academically Adrift: Limited Learning on College Campuses.* Chicago: University of Chicago Press.

Ashley, L. and Empson, L. (2013) 'Differentiation and discrimination: Understanding social class and social exclusion in leading law firms', *Human Relations*, 66(2), pp 219–244.

Ashwin, P. (2020) *Transforming University Education: A Manifesto.* London: Bloomsbury.

Askehave, I. (2007) 'The impact of marketization on higher education genres: The international student prospectus as a case in point', *Discourse Studies*, 9(6), pp 723–742.

Atkinson, R.D. and Wu, J. (2017) *False Alarmism: Technological Disruption and the U.S. Labor Market, 1850–2015*. Information Technology and Innovation Foundation. Available at: http://www2.itif.org/2017-false-alarmism-technological-disruption.pdf?_ga=2.122339278.493393312.162 9819756-1030088995.1629819756 (Accessed: 24 August 2021).

Augar, P. (2019) *Independent Panel Report to the Review of Post-18 Education and Funding*. London: Department for Education.

Autor, D.H. (2015) 'Why are there still so many jobs? The history and future of workplace automation', *Journal of Economic Perspectives*, 29(3), pp 3–30.

Autor, D.H. and Dorn, D. (2013) 'The growth of low-skill service jobs and the polarization of the US labor market', *The American Economic Review*, 103(5), pp 1553–1597.

Autor, D.H., Katz, L.F. and Krueger, A.B. (1998) 'Computing inequality: Have computers changed the labor market?', *The Quarterly Journal of Economics*, 113(4), pp 1169–1213.

Avent-Holt, D., Henriksen, L.F., Hägglund, A.E., Jung, J., Kodama, N., Melzer, S.M., Mun, E., Rainey, A. and Tomaskovic-Devey, D. (2020) 'Occupations, workplaces or jobs?: An exploration of stratification contexts using administrative data', *Research in Social Stratification and Mobility*, 70, p 100456 https://doi.org/10.1016/j.rssm.2019.100456

Bailey, O. and Harrop, A. (2018) 'UK: Preparing for a digital revolution', in Neufiend, J., O'Reilly, J. and Ranft, F. (eds) *Work in the Digital Age*. London: Policy Network, pp 333–343.

Baker, S. (2021) 'Average classroom master's fee jumps £1,200 for UK students', *Times Higher Education (THE)*, 10 August. Available at: https://www.timeshighereducation.com/news/average-classroom-masters-fee-jumps-1200-pounds-for-uk-students (Accessed: 22 August 2021).

Baethge, M. and Wolter, A (2015) 'The German skill formation model in transition: From dual system of VET to higher education?', *Journal for Labour Market Research*, 48(2): 97–112.

Balaram, B., Warden, J. and Wallace-Stephens, F. (2017) *Good Gigs: A Fairer Future for the UK's Gig Economy*. London: RSA.

Baldwin, G. and James, R. (2000) 'The market in Australian higher education and the concept of student as informed consumer', *Journal of Higher Education Policy and Management*, 22(2), pp 139–148.

Baldwin, R.E. (2019) *The Globotics Upheaval: Globalization, Robotics, and the Future of Work*. Oxford: Oxford University Press.

Ball, S.J. (1993) 'What is policy? Texts, trajectories and toolboxes', *Discourse: Studies in the Cultural Politics of Education*, 13(2), pp 10–17.

Ball, S.J. (2003) 'The teacher's soul and the terrors of performativity', *Journal of Education Policy*, 18(2), pp 215–228.

Ball, S.J. (2012a) 'Performativity, commodification and commitment: An I-spy guide to the neoliberal university', *British Journal of Educational Studies*, 60(1), pp 17–28.

Ball, S.J. (2012b) 'The making of a neoliberal academic', *Research in Teacher Education*, 2(1), pp 29–31.

Ball, S.J. (2015) 'What is policy? 21 years later: Reflections on the possibilities of policy research', *Discourse: Studies in the Cultural Politics of Education*, 36(3), pp 306–313.

Ball, S.J. (2017) *The Education Debate*, third edition. Bristol: Policy Press.

Barber, M., Donnelly, K. and Rizvi, S. (2013) *An Avalanche is Coming: Higher Education and the Revolution Ahead*. London: IPPR. Available at: http://vo.hse.ru/en/2013--3/100508881.html (Accessed: 22 August 2021).

Barone, C. and Ortiz, L. (2011) 'Overeducation among European university graduates: A comparative analysis of its incidence and the importance of higher education differentiation', *Higher Education*, 61(3), pp 325–337.

Barnett, R. (2003) *Beyond All Reason: Living With Ideology in the University*. Buckingham: SRHE and Open University Press.

Baruch, Y. (2001) 'Employability: A substitute for loyalty?', *Human Resource Development International*, 4(4), pp 543–566.

Battu, H., Belfield, C.R. and Sloane, P.J. (2000) 'How well can we measure graduate over-education and its effects?', *National Institute Economic Review*, 171(1), pp 82–93.

Batty, D. (2020) Hundreds of university staff to be made redundant due to coronavirus. *The Guardian*. 2 April. Available at: https://www.theguardian.com/education/2020/apr/02/hundreds-of-university-staff-made-redundant-due-to-coronavirus (Accessed: 6 April 2022).

BBC (2016) 'Student grants replaced by loans', *BBC News*, 1 August. Available at: https://www.bbc.com/news/education-36940172 (Accessed: 21 August 2021).

Beaudry, P., Green, D.A. and Sand, B.M. (2016) 'The great reversal in the demand for skill and cognitive tasks', *Journal of Labor Economics*, 34(S1), pp S199–S247.

Becker, G.S. (1964) *Human Capital: A Theoretical and Empirical Analysis, with Special Reference to Education*. Chigago: University of Chicago Press.

Becker, G.S. (1993) 'Nobel lecture: The economic way of looking at behavior', *Journal of Political Economy*, 101(3), pp 385–409.

Becker, G.S. (1994) *Human Capital: A Theoretical and Empirical Analysis with Special Reference to Education*, third edition. Chicago: University of Chicago Press.

Becker, G.S. (1996) *Accounting for Tastes*. Cambridge: Harvard University Press.

Becker, G.S. and Murphy, K.M. (2000) *Social Economics: Market Behavior in a Social Environment.* Cambridge, MA: Belknap Press.

Becker, G.S., Ewald, F. and Harcourt, B.E. (2012) *'Becker on Ewald on Foucault on Becker': American Neoliberalism and Michel Foucault's 1979 'Birth of Biopolitics' Lectures.* Working Paper No. 654, Coase-Sandor Institute for Law & Economics.

Belfield, C., Britton, J., Buscha, F., Dearden, L., Dickson, M., van der Erve, L., Sibieta, L., Vignoles, A., Walker, I. and Zhu, Y. (2018) *The Impact of Undergraduate Degrees on Early-career Earnings.* London: Department for Education.

Bell, D. (1972) 'On equality: I. Meritocracy and equality', *Public Interest,* 29, pp 29–68.

Bell, D. (1973) *The Coming of the Post-Industrial Society: A Venture in Social Forecasting,* first edition. New York: Basic Books.

Benko, C., Anderson, A. and Vickberg, S. (2011) 'The corporate lattice', *Deloitte Insights.* Available at: https://www2.deloitte.com/us/en/insights/deloitte-review/issue-8/the-corporate-lattice-rethinking-careers-in-the-changing-world-of-work.html (Accessed: 25 August 2021).

Bennett, N., Dunne, E. and Carré, C. (1999) 'Patterns of core and generic skill provision in higher education', *Higher Education,* 37(1), pp 71–93.

Berman, E., Bound, J. and Machin, S. (1998) 'Implications of skill-biased technological change: International evidence', *The Quarterly Journal of Economics,* 113(4), pp 1245–1279.

Berman, E.P. (2015) *Creating the Market University: How Academic Science Became an Economic Engine.* Princeton: Princeton University Press.

Besbris, M. and Petre, C. (2020) 'Professionalizing contingency: How journalism schools adapt to deprofessionalization', *Social Forces,* 98(4), pp 1524–1547.

Bessen, J. (2016) 'How computer automation affects occupations: Technology, jobs, and skills', *Boston University School of Law, Law and Economics Research Paper,* No. 15–49. Available at: https://scholarship.law.bu.edu/faculty_scholarship/813 (Accessed: 5 April 2022).

Birch, K. (2020) 'Technoscience rent: Toward a theory of *rentiership* for technoscientific capitalism', *Science, Technology, & Human Values,* 45(1), pp 3–33.

Black, S.E., Devereux, P.J., Lundborg, P. and Majlesi, K. (2020) 'Poor little rich kids? The role of nature versus nurture in wealth and other economic outcomes and behaviours', *The Review of Economic Studies,* 87(4), pp 1683–1725.

Blackmore, P., Bulaitis, Z., Jackman, A. and Tan, E. (2016) *Employability in Higher Education: A Review of Practice and Strategies around the World.* London: Pearson.

Blair, P.Q. and Deming, D.J. (2020) 'Structural increases in demand for skill after the great recession', *AEA Papers and Proceedings*, 110, pp 362–365.

Blair, T. and Schröder, G. (1999) *Europe: The Third Way/die neue Mitte.* London: Labour Party and SPD.

Blau, P.M. and Duncan, O.D. (1967) *The American Occupational Structure.* Hoboken: John Wiley & Sons Inc.

Bloodworth, J. (2016) *The Myth of Meritocracy: Why Working-Class Kids Still Get Working-Class Jobs.* London: Biteback Publishing.

Bloome, D., Dyer, S. and Zhou, X. (2018) 'Educational inequality, educational expansion, and intergenerational income persistence in the United States', *American Sociological Review*, 83(6), pp 1215–1253.

Boden, R. and Epstein, D. (2006) 'Managing the research imagination? Globalisation and research in higher education', *Globalisation, Societies and Education*, 4(2), pp 223–236.

Boden, R. and Nedeva, M. (2010) 'Employing discourse: Universities and graduate "employability"', *Journal of Education Policy*, 25(1), pp 37–54.

Bok, D.C. (2005) *Universities in the Marketplace: The Commercialization of Higher Education.* Princeton: Princeton University Press.

Bol, T. (2015) 'Has education become more positional? Educational expansion and labour market outcomes, 1985–2007', *Acta Sociologica*, 58(2), pp 105–120.

Bol, T. and Weeden, K.A. (2015) 'Occupational closure and wage inequality in Germany and the United Kingdom', *European Sociological Review*, 31(3), pp 354–369.

Bol, T., Ciocca Eller, C., van de Werfhorst, H.G. and DiPrete, T.A. (2019) 'School-to-work linkages, educational mismatches, and labor market outcomes', *American Sociological Review*, 84(2), pp 275–307.

Boliver, V. (2011) 'Expansion, differentiation, and the persistence of social class inequalities in British higher education', *Higher Education*, 61(3), pp 229–242.

Boliver, V. (2013) 'How fair is access to more prestigious UK universities?: How fair is access to more prestigious UK universities?', *The British Journal of Sociology*, 64(2), pp 344–364.

Bolton, P. (2021) 'Higher education funding in England'. Available at: https://commonslibrary.parliament.uk/research-briefings/cbp-7973/ (Accessed: 22 August 2021).

Borgen, N.T. (2015) 'College quality and the positive selection hypothesis: The "second filter" on family background in high-paid jobs', *Research in Social Stratification and Mobility*, 39, pp 32–47.

Borgen, N.T. and Mastekaasa, A. (2018) 'Horizontal stratification of higher education: The relative importance of field of study, institution, and department for candidates' wages', *Social Forces*, 97(2), pp 531–558.

Bound, J. and Johnson, G. (1992) 'Changes in the structure of wages in the 1980's: An evaluation of alternative explanations', *American Economic Review*, 82(3), pp 371–392.

Bourdieu, P. (1986) 'The forms of capital', in Richardson, J. (ed) *Handbook of Theory and Research for the Sociology of Education*. New York: Greenwood, pp 241–258.

Bourdieu, P. and Passeron, J.C. (1977) *Reproduction in Education, Society, and Culture*. Beverly Hills: SAGE.

Bovens, M.A.P. and Wille, A. (2017) *Diploma Democracy: The Rise of Political Meritocracy*, first edition. New York: Oxford University Press.

Bragg, S. (2007) ' "Student voice" and governmentality: The production of enterprising subjects?', *Discourse: Studies in the Cultural Politics of Education*, 28(3), pp 343–358.

Breen, R. and Goldthorpe, J.H. (1997) 'Explaining educational differentials: Towards a formal rational action theory', *Rationality and Society*, 9(3), pp 275–305.

Breen, R., Luijkx, R., Müller, W. and Pollak, R. (2009) 'Nonpersistent inequality in educational attainment: Evidence from eight European countries', *American Journal of Sociology*, 114(5), pp 1475–1521.

Breen, R., Luijkx, R., Muller, W. and Pollak, R. (2010) 'Long-term trends in educational inequality in Europe: Class inequalities and gender differences', *European Sociological Review*, 26(1), pp 31–48.

Brinkley, I., Fauth, R., Mahdon, M. and Theodoropoulou, S. (2009) *Knowledge Workers and Knowledge Work*. London: The Work Foundation.

Britton, J., Dearden, L., Shephard, N. and Vignoles, A. (2016) *How English Domiciled Graduate Earnings Vary with Gender, Institution Attended, Subject and Socio-economic Background*. London: IFS. Available at: https://ifs.org.uk/uploads/publications/wps/wp201606.pdf (Accessed: 5 April 2022).

Britton, J., Dearden, L., van der Erve, L. and Waltmann, B. (2020) *The Impact of Undergraduate Degrees on Lifetime Earnings*. London: IFS. Available at: https://ifs.org.uk/uploads/R167-The-impact-of-undergraduate-degrees-on-lifetime-earnings.pdf (Accessed: 5 April 2022).

Britton, J., Dearden, L. and Waltmann, B. (2021) *The Returns to Undergraduate Degrees by Socio-economic Group and Ethnicity*. London: IFS. Available at: https://ifs.org.uk/uploads/R186-The-returns-to-undergraduate-degrees.pdf (Accessed: 26 August 2021).

Brooks, R. (2018) 'The construction of higher education students in English policy documents', *British Journal of Sociology of Education*, 39(6), pp 745–761.

Brown, D. (2001) 'The social sources of educational credentialism: Status cultures, labor markets, and organizations', *Sociology of Education*, 74, pp 19–34.

Brown, P. (2013) 'Education, opportunity and the prospects for social mobility', *British Journal of Sociology of Education*, 34(5–6), pp 678–700.

Brown, P. and Hesketh, A. (2004) *The Mismanagement of Talent: Employability and Jobs in the Knowledge Economy*. Oxford and New York: Oxford University Press.

Brown, P. and Lauder, H. (2006) 'Globalisation, knowledge and the myth of the magnet economy', *Globalisation, Societies and Education*, 4(1), pp 25–57.

Brown, P., Hesketh, A. and Wiliams, S. (2003) 'Employability in a knowledge-driven economy', *Journal of Education and Work*, 16(2), pp 107–126.

Brown, P., Lauder, H. and Ashton, D. (2012) *The Global Auction: The Broken Promises of Education, Jobs, and Incomes*. New York: Oxford University Press.

Brown, P., Power, S., Tholen, G. and Allouch, A. (2016) 'Credentials, talent and cultural capital: A comparative study of educational elites in England and France', *British Journal of Sociology of Education*, 37(2), pp 191–211.

Brown, P., Lauder, H. and Cheung, S.Y. (2020) *The Death of Human Capital? Its Failed Promise and How to Renew It*. New York: Oxford University Press.

Brown, R. (2011a) 'Introduction', in Brown, R. (ed) *Higher Education and the Market*. London and New York: Routledge, pp 1–6.

Brown, R. (2011b) 'Taming the beast', in Brown, R. (ed) *Higher Education and the Market*. London and New York: Routledge, pp 158–200.

Brown, R. (2013) *Everything for Sale? The Marketization of UK Higher Education*. London: Routledge.

Brown, W. (2015) *Undoing the Demos: Neoliberalism's Stealth Revolution*. New York: Zone Books.

Browne, J. (2010) *Securing a Sustainable Future in Higher Education*. London: Department of Business Innovation and Skills.

Brynin, M. (2013) 'Individual choice and risk: The case of higher education', *Sociology*, 47(2), pp 284–300.

Brynjolfsson, E. and Mitchell, T. (2017) 'What can machine learning do? Workforce implications', *Science*, 358(6370), pp 1530–1534.

Budd, R. (2017) 'Undergraduate orientations towards higher education in Germany and England: Problematizing the notion of "student as customer"', *Higher Education*, 73(1), pp 23–37.

Bukodi, E. and Goldthorpe, J.H. (2011) 'Class origins, education and occupational attainment in Britain: Secular trends or cohort-specific effects?', *European Societies*, 13(3), pp 347–375.

Bukodi, E. and Goldthorpe, J.H. (2013) 'Decomposing "social origins": The effects of parents' class, status, and education on the educational attainment of their children', *European Sociological Review*, 29(5), pp 1024–1039.

Bukodi, E. and Goldthorpe, J.H. (2016) 'Educational attainment – relative or absolute – as a mediator of intergenerational class mobility in Britain', *Research in Social Stratification and Mobility*, 43, pp 5–15.

Bukodi, E. and Goldthorpe, J.H. (2018) *Social Mobility and Education in Britain: Research, Politics and Policy*. Cambridge: Cambridge University Press.

Bukodi, E., Goldthorpe, J.H., Halpin, B. and Waller, L. (2016) 'Is education now class destiny? Class histories across three British birth cohorts', *European Sociological Review*, 32(6), pp 835–849.

Bukodi, E., Goldthorpe, J.H. and Zhao, Y. (2021) 'Primary and secondary effects of social origins on educational attainment: New findings for England', *The British Journal of Sociology*, 72(3), pp 627–650.

Bundock, L. (2021) 'COVID-19: University students on brink of strike action over online tuition', *Sky News*. Available at: https://news.sky.com/story/covid-19-university-students-on-brink-of-strike-action-over-onl ine-tuition-12186979 (Accessed: 27 August 2021).

Burke, C., Scurry, T. and Blenkinsopp, J. (2020) 'Navigating the graduate labour market: The impact of social class on student understandings of graduate careers and the graduate labour market', *Studies in Higher Education*, 45(8), pp 1711–1722.

Burrell, J. and Fourcade, M. (2021) 'The society of algorithms', *Annual Review of Sociology*, 47(1), pp 213–237.

Burris, B.H. (1993) *Technocracy at Work*. New York: SUNY Press.

Busch, F. (2018) 'Occupational devaluation due to feminization? Causal mechanics, effect heterogeneity, and evidence from the United States, 1960 to 2010', *Social Forces*, 96(3), pp 1351–1376.

By, R.T., Diefenbach, T. and Klarner, P. (2008) 'Getting organizational change right in public services: The case of European higher education', *Journal of Change Management*, 8(1), pp 21–35.

Cabinet Office (2009) *Unleashing Aspiration: The Final Report of the Panel on Fair Access to the Professions*. London: TSO.

Cabinet Office (2011) *Opening Doors, Breaking Barriers: A Strategy for Social Mobility*. London: HM Government.

Calhoun, C. (2006) 'The university and the public good', *Thesis Eleven*, 84(1), pp 7–43.

Cameron, D. (2010) *PM's Speech on Education*. Available at: https://www.gov.uk/government/speeches/pms-speech-on-education (Accessed: 23 August 2021).

Cameron, D. (2011) 'David Cameron's education speech in full', *Politics.co.uk*. Available at: https://www.politics.co.uk/comment-analysis/2011/09/09/david-camerons-education-speech-in-full/ (Accessed: 23 August 2021).

Canaan, J.E. and Shumar, W. (eds) (2008) *Structure and Agency in the Neoliberal University*. New York: Routledge.

Cantwell, B., Marginson, S. and Smolentseva, A. (eds) (2018) *High Participation Systems of Higher Education*. Oxford and New York: Oxford University Press.

Caplan, B.D. (2018) *The Case against Education: Why the Education System is a Waste of Time and Money.* Princeton: Princeton University Press.

Cappelli, P. (2020) 'The return on a college degree: The US experience', *Oxford Review of Education*, 46(1), pp 30–43.

Chang, H. (2011) *23 Things They Don't Tell You about Capitalism.* London: Penguin.

Chapleo, C. (2010) 'What defines "successful" university brands?', *International Journal of Public Sector Management*, 23(2), pp 169–183.

Chevalier, A. (2003) 'Measuring over-education', *Economica*, 70(279), pp 509–531.

Christophers, B. (2020) *Rentier Capitalism: Who Owns the Economy, and Who Pays for It?* London and New York: Verso.

Clarke, M. (2018) 'Rethinking graduate employability: The role of capital, individual attributes and context', *Studies in Higher Education*, 43(11), pp 1923–1937.

Coates, K. (2016) 'Playing to the numbers', *Prometheus*, 34(1), pp 73–77.

Cockayne, D. (2016) 'Sharing and neoliberal discourse: The economic function of sharing in the digital on-demand economy', *Geoforum*, 77(6), pp 73–82.

Codagnone, C., Abadie, F. and Biagi, F. (2016) *The Future of Work in the 'Sharing Economy'.* Luxembourg: Publications Office. Available at: https://data.europa.eu/doi/10.2791/431485 (Accessed: 24 August 2021).

Coleman, J.S. (1988) 'Social capital in the creation of human capital', *American Journal of Sociology*, 94, pp S95–S120.

Collini, S. (2018) *Speaking of Universities.* London: Verso.

Collins, R. (1979) *The Credential Society: An Historical Sociology of Education and Stratification.* New York: Academic Press.

Commons Education Committee (2017) *Value for Money in Higher Education.* Available at: https://publications.parliament.uk/pa/cm201719/cmselect/cmeduc/343/34302.htm (Accessed: 22 August 2021).

Conboye, J. and Warwick-Ching, L. (2021) ' "I feel left behind": Graduates struggle to secure good jobs', *Financial Times*, 28 June. Available at: https://www.ft.com/content/2fc4e1f4-a5e8-4cbd-9bd8-f51a43b01417 (Accessed: 25 August 2021).

Confederation of British Industry (CBI) and National Union of Students (NUS) (2011) *Working Towards Your Future: Making the Most of Your Time in Higher Education.* London: CBI. Available at: www.cbi.org.uk/pdf/cbi-nus-employability-report.pdf (Accessed: 4 October 2011).

Connell, I. and Galasiński, D. (1998) 'Academic mission statements: An exercise in negotiation', *Discourse & Society*, 9(4), pp 457–479.

Conte, A. and Vivarelli, M. (2007) 'Imported skill biased technological change in developing countries', *The Developing Economies*, 49(1), pp 36–65.

Cook, C. (2014) 'Student loans overhaul discussed by ministers', *BBC News*, 29 July. Available at: https://www.bbc.co.uk/news/education-28528824 (Accessed: 21 December 2021).

Cornell, B., Hewitt, R. and Bekhradnia, B. (2020) *Mind the (Graduate Gender Pay) Gap*. London: Higher Education Policy Institute.

Cortes, G.M. and Salvatori, A. (2019) 'Delving into the demand side: Changes in workplace specialization and job polarization', *Labour Economics*, 57, pp 164–176.

Coughlan, S. (2020) '"Grade inflation" in top degree grades stopping', *BBC News*, 17 January. Available at: https://www.bbc.com/news/education-51136349 (Accessed: 22 August 2021).

Cowburn, A. (2021) 'Williamson says universities shouldn't charge full tuition fees if they fail to deliver what students "expect"', *The Independent*, 10 August. Available at: https://www.independent.co.uk/news/uk/politics/gavin-williamson-students-universities-tuition-b1899879.html (Accessed: 27 August 2021).

Cranmer, S. (2006) 'Enhancing graduate employability: Best intentions and mixed outcomes', *Studies in Higher Education*, 31(2), pp 169–184.

Crawford, C. and van der Erve, L. (2015) 'Does higher education level the playing field? Socio-economic differences in graduate earnings', *Education Sciences*, 5(4), pp 380–412.

Crawford, C., Gregg, P., Macmillan, L., Vignoles, A. and Wyness, G. (2016) 'Higher education, career opportunities, and intergenerational inequality', *Oxford Review of Economic Policy*, 32(4), pp 553–575.

Cunningham, W.V. and Villaseñor, P. (2016) 'Employer voices, employer demands, and implications for public skills development policy connecting the labor and education sectors', *The World Bank Research Observer*, 31(1), pp 102–134.

David, M. (2016) 'Fabricated world class: Global university league tables, status differentiation and myths of global competition', *British Journal of Sociology of Education*, 37(1), pp 169–189.

De La Fuente, J.R. (2002) 'Academic freedom and social responsibility', *Higher Education Policy*, 15(4), pp 337–339.

Deem, R. (2001) 'Globalisation, new managerialism, academic capitalism and entrepreneurialism in universities: Is the local dimension still important?', *Comparative Education*, 37(1), pp 7–20.

Deem, R. and Brehony, K.J. (2005) 'Management as ideology: The case of "new managerialism" in higher education', *Oxford Review of Education*, 31(2), pp 217–235.

Deem, R., Hillyard, S. and Reed, M.I. (2007) *Knowledge, Higher Education, and the New Managerialism: The Changing Management of UK Universities*. Oxford and New York: Oxford University Press.

Delaney, J., McGuinness, S., Pouliakas, K. and Redmond, P. (2020) 'Educational expansion and overeducation of young graduates: A comparative analysis of 30 European countries', *Oxford Review of Education*, 46(1), pp 10–29.

Delanty, G. (2003) 'Ideologies of the knowledge society and the cultural contradictions of higher education', *Policy Futures in Education*, 1(1), pp 71–82.

Dellot, B. (2017) '8 key takeaways from our new report on AI, robotics and automation', *The RSA*. Available at: https://www.thersa.org/blog/2017/09/8-key-takeaways-from-our-new-report-on-ai-robotics-and-automation (Accessed: 24 August 2021).

Dellot, B. and Wallace-Stephens, F. (2017) *The Age of Automation Artificial Intelligence, Robotics and the Future of Low-skilled Work*. London: RSA.

Deming, D.J. (2017) 'The growing importance of social skills in the labor market', *The Quarterly Journal of Economics*, 132(4), pp 1593–1640.

Department for Business, Innovation and Skills (DBIS) (2009) *Higher Ambitions: The Future of Universities in a Knowledge Economy*. London: DBIS.

Department for Business, Innovation and Skills (DBIS) (2011) *Students at the Heart of the System*. London: DBIS.

Department for Business, Innovation and Skills (DBIS) (2015) *Fulfilling Our Potential: Teaching Excellence, Social Mobility and Student Choice*. London: HM Government.

Department for Business, Innovation and Skills (DBIS) (2016) *Success as a Knowledge Economy: Teaching Excellence, Social Mobility and Student Choice*. London: HM Government.

Department for Education (DfE) (2016) *Teaching Excellence Framework: Year Two Specification*. London: DfE.

Department for Education (DfE) (2018) *Value for Money in Higher Education, Seventh Report of Session 2017–19*. London: DfE.

Department for Education (DfE) (2019) *Graduate Outcomes (LEO): Outcomes in 2016 to 2017, GOV.UK*. Available at: https://www.gov.uk/government/statistics/graduate-outcomes-leo-outcomes-in-2016-to-2017 (Accessed: 26 August 2021).

Department of Education and Science (DES) (1987) *Higher Education: Meeting the Challenge*. London: HMSO.

Department for Education and Skills (DfES) (2003) *The Future of Higher Education*. London: HMSO.

Department of Innovation, Universities and Skills (DIUS) (2008) *Higher Education at Work: High Skills, High Value*. London: DIUS.

Desjardins, R. and Rubenson, K. (2011) 'An analysis of skill mismatch using direct measures of skills', *OECD Education Working Papers*, 63.

Di Stasio, V. (2017) 'Who is ahead in the labor queue? Institutions' and employers' perspective on overeducation, undereducation, and horizontal mismatches', *Sociology of Education*, 90(2), pp 109–126.

Di Stasio, V. and van de Werfhorst, H.G. (2016) 'Why does education matter to employers in different institutional contexts? A vignette study in England and the Netherlands', *Social Forces*, 95(1), pp 77–106.

Di Stasio, V., Bol, T. and van de Werfhorst, H.G. (2016) 'What makes education positional? Institutions, overeducation and the competition for jobs', *Research in Social Stratification and Mobility*, 43, pp 53–63.

Dickinson, J. (2021) 'We need an alternative to human capital theory as a basis for university funding', *Wonkhe*. Available at: https://wonkhe.com/blogs/we-need-an-alternative-to-human-capital-theory-as-a-basis-for-university-funding/ (Accessed: 22 December 2021).

Dill, D.D. (1997) 'Higher education markets and public policy', *Higher Education Policy*, 10(3), pp 167–185.

Dill, D.D. (2003) 'Allowing the market to rule: The case of the United States', *Higher Education Quarterly*, 57(2), pp 136–157.

Dizik, A. (2017) 'The downside of limitless career options', *BBC*, 26 June. Available at: https://www.bbc.com/worklife/article/20170626-the-downside-of-limitless-career-options (Accessed: 25 August 2021).

Docherty, T. (2014) *Universities at War*. Los Angeles: SAGE.

Donelan, M. (2020) 'Universities minister calls for true social mobility', *GOV.UK*. Available at: https://www.gov.uk/government/speeches/universities-minister-calls-for-true-social-mobility (Accessed: 26 August 2021).

Donnelly, M. and Gamsu, S. (2019) 'The field of graduate recruitment: Leading financial and consultancy firms and elite class formation', *The British Journal of Sociology*, 70(4), pp 1374–1401.

Donnelly, R. (2006) 'How "free" is the free worker?: An investigation into the working arrangements available to knowledge workers', *Personnel Review*, 35(1), pp 78–97.

Donovan, S.A. and Bradley, D.H. (2018) *Real Wage Trends, 1979 to 2019*. Washington, DC: Congressional Research Service. Available at: https://purl.fdlp.gov/GPO/gpo114551 (Accessed: 26 August 2021).

Dore, R. (1976) *The Diploma Disease: Education, Qualification and Development*. Berkeley: University of California Press.

Dörfler, L. and van de Werfhorst, H.G. (2009) 'Employers' demand for qualifications and skills: Increased merit selection in Austria, 1985–2005', *European Societies*, 11(5), pp 697–721.

Dorling, D. (2019) *Inequality and the 1%*. London: Verso Books.

Dromey, J. (2018) *Power to the People: How Stronger Unions can Deliver Economic Justice*. London: Resolution Foundation. Available at: http://www.ippr.org/research/publications/power-to-the-people (Accessed: 26 August 2021).

Du Gay, P. (1995) *Consumption and Identity at Work*, first edition. London and Thousand Oaks: SAGE.

Durazzi, N. (2021) 'Opening universities' doors for business? Marketization, the search for differentiation and employability in England', *Journal of Social Policy*, 50(2), pp 386–405.

Duta, A., Wielgoszewska, B. and Iannelli, C. (2021) 'Different degrees of career success: Social origin and graduates' education and labour market trajectories', *Advances in Life Course Research*, 47(1), p 100376. doi: 10.1016/j.alcr.2020.100376.

Eckhardt, G.M. and Bardhi, F. (2015) 'The sharing economy isn't about sharing at all', *Harvard Business Review*, 28 January. Available at: https://hbr.org/2015/01/the-sharing-economy-isnt-about-sharing-at-all (Accessed: 24 August 2021).

The Economist (2018) 'English universities compete harder for applicants', *The Economist*, 23 August. Available at: https://www.economist.com/britain/2018/08/23/english-universities-compete-harder-for-applicants (Accessed: 22 August 2021).

Eeckhout, J. (2021) *The Profit Paradox: How Thriving Firms Threaten the Future of Work*. Princeton: Princeton University Press.

Elliott, L. (2018) 'Some praise our gig economy flexibility. I call it exploitation', *The Guardian*, 26 April. Available at: http://www.theguardian.com/commentisfree/2018/apr/26/gig-economy-flexibility-exploitation-record-employment-low-wages-zero-hours (Accessed: 24 August 2021).

Enders, J., de Boer, H. and Weyer, E. (2013) 'Regulatory autonomy and performance: The reform of higher education re-visited', *Higher Education*, 65(1), pp 5–23.

Ertl, H. and Sloane, P. (2004) 'A comparison of VET structures in Germany and England: contexts of complex teaching-learning environments', in Mulder, R. and Sloane, P. (eds), *New Approaches to Vocational Education in Europe*. Oxford: Symposium Books, 27–43.

Evetts, J. (2009) 'New professionalism and new public management: Changes, continuities and consequences', *Comparative Sociology*, 8(2), pp 247–266.

Fairclough, N. (1993) 'Critical discourse analysis and the marketization of public discourse: The universities', *Discourse & Society*, 4(2), pp 133–168.

Falcon, J. and Bataille, P. (2018) 'Equalization or reproduction? Long-term trends in the intergenerational transmission of advantages in higher education in France', *European Sociological Review*, 34(4), pp 335–347.

Fazackerley, A. (2018) 'Cut-throat A-level season "pushing some universities towards insolvency"', *The Guardian*, 28 August. Available at: http://www.theguardian.com/education/2018/aug/28/alevel-season-pushing-universities-towards-insolvency (Accessed: 22 August 2021).

Fazackerley, A. (2020) 'Alarm at Ofsted-style plan to rank universities by graduate earnings', *The Guardian*, 11 February. Available at: http://www. theguardian.com/education/2020/feb/11/alarm-at-ofsted-style-plan-to-rank-universities-by-graduate-earnings (Accessed: 21 August 2021).

Fazackerley, A. (2021) 'Foot the bill for refunding student fees, Downing Street told', *The Guardian*, 8 January. Available at: http://www.theguard ian.com/education/2021/jan/08/foot-the-bill-for-refunding-student-fees-downing-street-told (Accessed: 27 August 2021).

Felstead, A., Gallie, D., Green, F. and Henseke, G. (2020) 'Getting the measure of employee-driven innovation and its workplace correlates', *British Journal of Industrial Relations*, 58(4), pp 904–935.

Ferlie, E., Musselin, C. and Andresani, G. (2008) 'The steering of higher education systems: A public management perspective', *Higher Education*, 56(3), pp 325–348.

Fernández-Macías, E. and Hurley, J. (2017) 'Routine-biased technical change and job polarization in Europe', *Socio-Economic Review*, 15(3), pp 563–585.

Fiel, J.E. (2020) 'Great equalizer or great selector? Reconsidering education as a moderator of intergenerational transmissions', *Sociology of Education*, 93(4), pp 353–371.

Figueiredo, H., Teixeira, P. and Rubery, J. (2013) 'Unequal futures? Mass higher education and graduates' relative earnings in Portugal, 1995–2009', *Applied Economics Letters*, 20(10), pp 991–997.

Figueiredo, H., Biscaia, R., Rocha, V. and Teixeira, P. (2015) 'Should we start worrying? Mass higher education, skill demand and the increasingly complex landscape of young graduates' employment', *Studies in Higher Education*, 42(8), pp 1401–1420.

Finegold, D. and Soskice, D. (1988) 'The failure of training in Britain: Analysis and prescription', *Oxford Review of Economic Policy*, 4(3), pp 21–53.

Fleming, P. (2017) 'The human capital hoax: Work, debt and insecurity in the era of Uberization', *Organization Studies*, 38(5), pp 691–709.

Flisi, S., Goglio, V., Meroni, E.C., Rodrigues, M. and Vera-Toscano, E. (2017) 'Measuring occupational mismatch: Overeducation and overskill in Europe—evidence from PIAAC', *Social Indicators Research*, 131(3), pp 1211–1249.

Foroohar, R. (2021) 'Five lessons from 25 years of corporate wealth creation', *Financial Times*, 30 May. Available at: https://www.ft.com/content/5f4c5 8ca-4320-424c-9afc-7c0bf5667169 (Accessed: 26 August 2021).

Foskett, N. (ed) (1996) *Markets in Education: Policy, Process and Practice. Volume 2, Markets in Post-compulsory Education*. Southampton: Centre for Research in Education Marketing, School of Education, University of Southampton.

Foskett, N. (2011) 'Markets, government, funding and the marketisation of higher education', in Molesworth, M., Scullion, R. & Nixon, E. (eds), *The Marketisation of Higher Education and the Student as Consumer*. London: Routledge, pp 25–38.

Foucault, M. (2008) *The Birth of Biopolitics: Lectures at the Collège de France, 1978–79*. Translated by G. Burchell. New York: Palgrave Macmillan.

Frank, D.J. and Meyer, J.W. (2020) *The University and the Global Knowledge Society*. Princeton: Princeton University Press.

Frank, R.H. (2016) *Success and Luck: Good Fortune and the Myth of Meritocracy*, illustrated edition. Princeton: Princeton University Press.

Frase, P. (2016) *Four Futures: Life After Capitalism*. Brooklyn: Verso Books.

Freeman, R. (1976) *The Overeducated American*. New York: Academic Press.

Frenkel, S., Korczynski, M., Donoghue, L. and Shire, K. (1995) 'Reconstituting work: Trends towards knowledge work and info-normative control', *Work, Employment & Society*, 9(4), pp 773–796.

Frey, C. and Osborne, M.A. (2013) 'The future of employment: How susceptible are jobs to computerisation?', Oxford Martin School, University of Oxford Working Paper. Available at: https://www. oxfordmartin. ox.ac.uk/downloads/academic/future-of-employment.pdf (Accessed: 6 April 2022).

Furedi, F. (2011) 'Introduction to the marketisation of higher education and the student as consumer', in Molesworth, M., Scullion, R. and Nixon, E. (eds), *The Marketisation of Higher Education and the Student as Consumer*. London: Routledge, pp 1–8.

Gallie, D., Felstead, A., Green, F. and Henseke, G. (2018) *Participation at Work in Britain: First Findings from the Skills and Employment Survey 2017*. London: Centre for Learning and Life Chances in Knowledge Economies and Societies, UCL Institute of Education.

Gardiner, L. and Corlett, A. (2015) *Looking Through the Hourglass: Hollowing Out of the UK Jobs Market Pre- and Post-crisis*. London: Resolution Foundation. Available at: https://www.resolutionfoundation.org/app/uplo ads/2015/03/Polarisation-full-slide-pack.pdf (Accessed: 6 April 2022).

Garibaldi, P. (2006) *Personnel Economics in Imperfect Labour Markets*, illustrated edition. Oxford and New York: Oxford University Press.

Gibbs, P. (2001) 'Higher education as a market: A problem or solution?', *Studies in Higher Education*, 26(1), pp 85–94.

Giddens, A. (2000) *The Third Way and Its Critics*. Cambridge and Malden: Polity Press and Blackwell Publishers.

Giroux, H.A. (2014) *Neoliberalism's War on Higher Education*. Chicago: Haymarket Books.

Gleadle, P., Hodgson, D. and Storey, J. (2012) ' "The ground beneath my feet": Projects, project management and the intensified control of R&D engineers', *New Technology Work and Employment*, 27(3), pp 163–177.

Godin, B. (2006) 'The knowledge-based economy: Conceptual framework or buzzword?', *The Journal of Technology Transfer*, 31(1), pp 17–30.

Goldin, C. and Katz, L.F. (2009) *Race between Education and Technology*. Cambridge, MA: Harvard University Press.

Goldthorpe, J.H. (1996) 'Problems of "meritocracy"', in Erikson, R. and Jonsson, J.O. (eds) *Can Education be Equalized?* Colorado: Westview Press, pp 255–287.

Goldthorpe, J.H. (2014) 'The role of education in intergenerational social mobility: Problems from empirical research in sociology and some theoretical pointers from economics', *Rationality and Society*, 26(3), pp 265–289.

Goldthorpe, J.H. and Jackson, M. (2006) 'Education-based meritocracy: Barriers to its realisation', in Lareau, A. and Conley, D. (eds) *Social Class: How Does It Work?* New York: Russell Sage Foundation, pp 93–117.

Goodhart, D. (2020) *Head Hand Heart: The Struggle for Dignity and Status in the 21st Century*. London: Allen Lane.

Goos, M., Manning, A. and Salomons, A. (2014) 'Explaining job polarization: Routine-biased technological change and offshoring', *American Economic Review*, 104(8), pp 2509–2526.

Gore, G. (2018) 'UK universities turn to private market as debts rack up', *IFR*. Available at: https://www.ifre.com/story/1516984/uk-universit ies-turn-to-private-market-as-debts-rack-up-dhp0nmdjz5 (Accessed: 22 August 2021).

gov.uk (2021) 'Graduate outcomes, by degree subject and university', *gov. uk*. Available at: https://assets.publishing.service.gov.uk/government/uplo ads/system/uploads/attachment_data/file/573831/SFR60_2016_LEO_m ain_text_v1.1.pdf (Accessed: 26 August 2021).

Green, F. and Zhu, Y. (2010) 'Overqualification, job dissatisfaction, and increasing dispersion in the returns to graduate education', *Oxford Economic Papers*, 62(4), pp 740–763.

Green, F. and Henseke, G. (2016) 'The changing graduate labour market: Analysis using a new indicator of graduate jobs', *IZA Journal of Labor Policy*, 5(1), p 14. Available at: https://doi.org/10.1186/s40173-016-0070-0 (Accessed: 6 April 2022).

Green, F. and Kynaston, D. (2019) *Engines of Privilege: Britain's Private School Problem*. London: Bloomsbury.

Green, F., Henseke, G. and Vignoles, A. (2017) 'Private schooling and labour market outcomes', *British Educational Research Journal*, 43(1), pp 7–28.

Gregg, P., Jonsson, J.O., Macmillan, L. and Mood, C. (2017) 'The role of education for intergenerational income mobility: A comparison of the United States, Great Britain, and Sweden', *Social Forces*, 96(1), pp 121–152.

Grim, J., Moore-Vissing, Q. and Mountford-Zimdars, A. (2019) 'A comparative study of the factors shaping postsecondary aspirations for low-income students in greater Boston and greater London', *British Journal of Sociology of Education*, 40(6), pp 826–843.

Gruber, T. (2014) 'Academic sell-out: How an obsession with metrics and rankings is damaging academia', *Journal of Marketing for Higher Education*, 24(2), pp 165–177.

Gruening, G. (2001) 'Origin and theoretical basis of new public management', *International Public Management Journal*, 4(1), pp 1–25.

Gugushvili, A., Bukodi, E. and Goldthorpe, J.H. (2017) 'The direct effect of social origins on social mobility chances: "Glass floors" and "glass ceilings" in Britain', *European Sociological Review*, 33(2), pp 305–316.

Gyimah, S. (2018) 'Speech at UUK annual conference', *GOV.UK*. Available at: https://www.gov.uk/government/speeches/universities-minister-spe aks-at-uuk-annual-conference (Accessed: 23 August 2021).

Hager, P.J. and Holland, S. (eds) (2006) *Graduate Attributes, Learning and Employability*. Dordrecht: Springer.

Hale, T. (2018) 'The financial plumbing of university education', *Financial Times*, 11 December. Available at: https://www.ft.com/content/d8652 eba-8111-3379-8eef-86166a1eba01 (Accessed: 22 August 2021).

Halford, S. and Leonard, P. (1998) 'New identities? Professionalism, managerialism and the construction of self', in Exworthy, M. and Halford, S. (eds), *Professionals and the New Managerialism in the Public Sector*. Buckingham: Open University, pp 102–121. Available at: https://eprints. soton.ac.uk/33846/ (Accessed: 25 August 2021).

Hall, P.A. and Soskice, D. (2001) *Varieties of Capitalism: The Institutional Foundations of Comparative Advantage*. Oxford: Oxford University Press.

Hall, R. (2020) 'Universities brace for the biggest ever clearing day', *The Guardian*, 13 August. Available at: http://www.theguardian.com/educat ion/2020/aug/12/its-a-buyers-market-universities-brace-for-the-bigg est-clearing-day-yet (Accessed: 22 August 2021).

Hall, R. (2021) 'Disadvantaged graduates earn half as much as privileged peers in first job', *The Guardian*, 12 November. Available at: https://www. theguardian.com/money/2021/nov/12/disadvantaged-graduates-earn-half-as-much-as-privileged-peers-in-first-job (Accessed: 22 August 2021).

Hall, S. and Weale, S. (2019) 'Universities spending millions on marketing to attract students', *The Guardian*, 2 April. Available at: http://www.theg uardian.com/education/2019/apr/02/universities-spending-millions-on-marketing-to-attract-students (Accessed: 22 August 2021).

Hallier, J. (2009) 'Rhetoric but whose reality? The influence of employability messages on employee mobility tactics and work group identification', *The International Journal of Human Resource Management*, 20(4), pp 846–868.

Hanushek, E.A. and Woessmann, L. (2015) *The Knowledge Capital of Nations: Education and the Economics of Growth*. Cambridge, MA: MIT Press.

Harvey, L. (2000) 'New realities: The relationship between higher education and employment', *Tertiary Education and Management*, 6(1), pp 3–17.

Hayes, C. (2013) *Twilight of the Elites: America After Meritocracy*. New York: Broadway Books.

Hazelkorn, E. (2015) *Rankings and the Reshaping of Higher Education: The Battle for World-Class Excellence*, second edition. Houndmills and New York: Palgrave Macmillan.

Head, S. (2014) 'Toward a new industrial state', *Policy Options*. Available at: https://policyoptions.irpp.org/magazines/old-politics-new-politics/head/ (Accessed: 24 August 2021).

Hecht, K. (2017) 'A relational analysis of top incomes and wealth: Economic evaluation, relative (dis)advantage and the service to capital', Department of Sociology Working paper 11, London School of Economics. Available at: http://www.lse.ac.uk/International-Inequalities/Assets/Documents/Working-Papers/Katharina-Hecht-A-Relational-Analysis-of-Top-Incomes-and-Wealth.pdf (Accessed: 26 August 2021).

Heiserman, N. and Simpson, B. (2017) 'Higher inequality increases the gap in the perceived merit of the rich and poor', *Social Psychology Quarterly*, 80(3), pp 243–253.

Heller, H. (2016) *The Capitalist University: The Transformations of Higher Education in the United States, 1945–2016*. London: Pluto Press.

Henehan, K. and Rose, H. (2018) *Opportunities Knocked? Exploring Pay Penalties among the UK's Ethnic Minorities*. London: Resolution Foundation. Available at: https://www.resolutionfoundation.org/app/uploads/2018/07/Opportunities-Knocked.pdf (Accessed: 26 August 2021).

Henkel, M. (1997) 'Academic values and the university as corporate enterprise', *Higher Education Quarterly*, 51(2), pp 134–143.

Henseke, G., Felstead, A., Gallie, D. and Green, F. (2018) *Skills Trends at Work in Britain: First Findings from the Skills and Employment Survey 2017*. London: Centre for Learning and Life Chances in Knowledge Economies and Societies, UCL Institute of Education. Available at: https://orca.cardiff.ac.uk/113355/1/2_Skills_at_Work_Minireport_Final_edit.pdf (Accessed: 25 August 2021).

Higher Education Funding Council for England (HEFCE) (2010) *Employability Statements Circular Letter Number 12/2010*. Available at: https://webarchive.nationalarchives.gov.uk/ukgwa/*/http:/www.hefce.ac.uk/ (Accessed: 6 April 2022).

Higher Education Policy Institute (HEPI) (2018) *Turning the Corner on Value for Money*. Available at: https://www.hepi.ac.uk/2018/06/07/turning-cor ner-value-money-2018-hepi-advance-student-academic-experience-sur vey-highlights-students-belief-value-money-higher-education-improving/ (Accessed: 22 August 2021).

Hill, S. (2017) *Raw Deal: How the 'Uber Economy' and Runaway Capitalism are Screwing American Workers*. New York: St. Martin's Press.

Hillage, J. and Pollard, E. (1998) *Employability: Developing a Framework for Policy Analysis*. London: Department for Education and Employment.

Hillman, N. (2021) *No Easy Answers: English Student Finance and the Spending Review*. London: Higher Education Policy Institute. Available at: https://www.hepi.ac.uk/wp-content/uploads/2021/06/No-easy-answ ers-English-student-finance-in-the-spending-review.pdf (Accessed: 22 August 2021).

Hillman, N., Dickinson, J., Rubbra, A. and Klamann, Z. (2018) *Where Do Student Fees Really Go?: Following the Pound*. Higher Education Policy Institute. Available at: https://www.hepi.ac.uk/wp-content/uploads/2018/ 11/Following-the-pound-1.pdf (Accessed: 22 August 2021).

Hirsch, F. (1976) *Social Limits to Growth*. Cambridge, MA: Harvard University Press.

Holland, D., Liadze, I., Rienzo, C. and Wilkinson, D. (2013) 'The relationship between graduates and growth across countries', BIS Research Paper 146. London: BIS.

Holman, D. and Rafferty, A. (2018) 'The convergence and divergence of job discretion between occupations and institutional regimes in Europe from 1995 to 2010', *Journal of Management Studies*, 55(4), pp 619–647.

Holmes, C. (2013) 'Has the expansion of higher education led to greater economic growth?', *National Institute Economic Review*, 224(1), pp R29–R47.

Holmes, C. and Mayhew, K. (2012) *The Changing Shape of the UK Job Market and its Implications*. London: Resolution Foundation.

Holmes, L. (2013) 'Competing perspectives on graduate employability: Possession, position or process?', *Studies in Higher Education*, 38(4), pp 538–554.

Holmwood, J. (2014) 'From social rights to the market: Neoliberalism and the knowledge economy', *International Journal of Lifelong Education*, 33(1), pp 62–76.

Holmwood, J. (2016) '"The turn of the screw"; Marketization and higher education in England', *Prometheus*, 34(1), pp 63–72.

Holmwood, J. and Bhambra, G.K. (2012) 'The attack on education as a social right', *South Atlantic Quarterly*, 111(2), pp 392–401.

Horowitz, J. (2018) 'Relative education and the advantage of a college degree', *American Sociological Review*, 83(4), pp 771–801.

House of Commons Education Committee (2018a) 'Universities must focus on value for money'. Available at: https://committees.parliament.uk/committee/203/education-committee/news/102476/universities-must-focus-on-value-for-money/ (Accessed: 23 August 2021).

House of Commons Education Committee (2018b) 'Value for money in higher education', Seventh Report of Session 2017–19. Available at: https://publications.parliament.uk/pa/cm201719/cmselect/cmeduc/343/34307.htm.

House of Lords Economic Affairs Committee (2017) 'Do students get value for money?', Committees, UK Parliament. Available at: https://committees.parliament.uk/committee/175/economic-affairs-committee/news/93635/do-students-get-value-for-money/ (Accessed: 22 August 2021).

Humburg, M., van der Velden, R. and Verhagen, A. (2013) *The Employability of Higher Education Graduates: The Employer's Perspective.* Brussels: European Commission.

Hunt, J. and Nunn, R. (2019) *Is Employment Polarization Informative About Wage Inequality and Is Employment Really Polarizing?* (No. w26064). National Bureau of Economic Research. Available at: https://www.nber.org/papers/w26064 (accessed: 6 April 2022).

Hurst, G. (2019) 'Britons see university fees as poor value', *The Times.* 2 January. Available at: https://www.thetimes.co.uk/article/britons-see-university-fees-as-poor-value-poll-reveals-q8vmk7sks (Accessed: 22 August 2021).

Hutton, W. (2015) 'British capitalism is broken: Here's how to fix it', *The Guardian*, 11 February. Available at: http://www.theguardian.com/business/2015/feb/11/british-capitalism-broken-how-to-fix-it (Accessed: 24 August 2021).

Isopahkala-Bouret, U. (2015) ' "It's considered a second class thing": The differences in status between traditional and newly established higher education credentials', *Studies in Higher Education*, 40(7), pp 1291–1306.

Jack, A. (2019) 'Spiralling costs, high debt and Brexit: Can UK universities survive?', *Financial Times*, 5 February. Available at: https://www.ft.com/content/46582248-133a-11e9-a581-4ff78404524e (Accessed: 22 August 2021).

Jackson, D. and Chapman, E. (2012) 'Non-technical competencies in undergraduate business degree programs: Australian and UK perspectives', *Studies in Higher Education*, 37(5), pp 541–567.

Jackson, M. (2001) 'Non-meritocratic job requirements and the reproduction of class inequality: An investigation', *Work, Employment and Society*, 15(3), pp 619–630.

Jackson, M. (2006) 'Personality traits and occupational attainment', *European Sociological Review*, 22(2), pp 187–199.

Jackson, M. (2007) 'How far merit selection? Social stratification and the labour market 1', *The British journal of sociology*, 58(3), pp. 367–390.

Jackson, M., Erikson, R., Goldthorpe, J.H. and Yaish, M. (2007) 'Primary and secondary effects in class differentials in educational attainment: The transition to A-level courses in England and Wales', *Acta Sociologica*, 50(3), pp 211–229.

Jacob, M. and Klein, M. (2019) 'Social origin, field of study and graduates' career progression: Does social inequality vary across fields?', *The British Journal of Sociology*, 70(5), pp 1850–1873.

Jacob, M., Klein, M. and Iannelli, C. (2015) 'The impact of social origin on graduates' early occupational destinations: An Anglo-German comparison', *European Sociological Review*, 31(4), pp 460–476.

Jacobs, D. and Dirlam, J.C. (2016) 'Politics and economic stratification: Power resources and income inequality in the United States', *American Journal of Sociology*, 122(2), pp 469–500.

Jacobs, D. and Myers, L. (2014) 'Union strength, neoliberalism, and inequality: Contingent political analyses of U.S. income differences since 1950', *American Sociological Review*, 79(4), pp 752–774.

James-MacEachern, M. (2018) 'A comparative study of international recruitment: Tensions and opportunities in institutional recruitment practice', *Journal of Marketing for Higher Education*, 28(2), pp 247–265.

Jarratt, A. (1985) *Report of the Steering Committee for Efficiency Studies in Universities*. London: HMSO.

Jarvis, P. (2013) *Universities and Corporate Universities: The Higher Learning Industry in Global Society*. London: Routledge.

Jenkins, A., Jones, L. and Ward, A. (2001) 'The long-term effect of a degree on graduate lives', *Studies in Higher Education*, 26(2), pp 147–161.

Jessop, B. (2017) 'Varieties of academic capitalism and entrepreneurial universities: On past research and three thought experiments', *Higher Education*, 73(6), pp 853–870. Available at: http://www.jstor.org/stable/26448730 (Accessed: 23 August 2021).

Jessop, B., Fairclough, N. and Wodak, R.P. (eds) (2008) *Education and the Knowledge-Based Economy in Europe*. Rotterdam: Sense Publishers.

Jian, G. (2008) 'Identity and technology: Organizational control of knowledge-intensive work', *Qualitative Research Reports in Communication*, 9(1), pp 62–71.

John, P. and Fanghanel, J. (eds) (2015) *Dimensions of Marketisation in Higher Education*. London: Routledge.

Johnson, J. (2017a) 'Securing value for money in higher education', *Reform*. Available at: https://reform.uk/research/securing-value-money-higher-education (Accessed: 22 August 2021).

Johnson, J. (2017b) 'Speech to UUK annual conference'. Available at: https://webarchive.nationalarchives.gov.uk/ukgwa/20170908183004/https://www.gov.uk/government/speeches/jo-johnson-speech-to-uuk-annual-conference (Accessed: 24 August 2021).

Jones, O. (2020) 'Market economics has driven universities into crisis – and we're all paying the price', *The Guardian*, 14 February. Available at: http://www.theguardian.com/commentisfree/2020/feb/14/market-universities-crisis-staff-strike (Accessed: 22 August 2021).

Jongbloed, B. (2003) 'Marketisation in higher education, Clark's triangle and the essential ingredients of markets', *Higher Education Quarterly*, 57(2), pp 110–135.

Jonsson, J.O. (1992) *Towards a Merit-Selective Society?* Stockholm: Swedish Institute for Social Research.

Jost, J.T., Pelham, B.W., Sheldon, O. and Ni Sullivan, B. (2003) 'Social inequality and the reduction of ideological dissonance on behalf of the system: Evidence of enhanced system justification among the disadvantaged', *European Journal of Social Psychology*, 33(1), pp 13–36.

Kalleberg, A.L. (2013) *Good Jobs, Bad Jobs: The Rise of Polarized and Precarious Employment Systems in the United States, 1970s to 2000s*. New York: Russell Sage Foundation.

Karlson, K.B. (2019) 'College as equalizer? Testing the selectivity hypothesis', *Social Science Research*, 80, pp 216–229.

Karlson, K.B. and Birkelund, J.F. (2019) 'Education as a mediator of the association between origins and destinations: The role of early skills', *Research in Social Stratification and Mobility*, 64, 100436.

Katz, L.F. and Murphy, K.M. (1992) 'Changes in relative wages, 1963–1987: Supply and demand factors', *The Quarterly Journal of Economics*, 107(1), pp 35–78.

Keeley, B. (2007) *Human Capital: How What You Know Shapes Your Life*. Paris: OECD.

Keep, E. (2020) 'Employers, the ghost at the feast', *Journal of Education and Work*, 33(7–8), pp 500–506.

Keep, E. and Mayhew, K. (2010) 'Moving beyond skills as a social and economic panacea', *Work, Employment and Society*, 24(3), pp 565–577.

Kelly, P., Fair, N. and Evans, C. (2017) 'The engaged student ideal in UK higher education policy', *Higher Education Policy*, 30(1), pp 105–122.

Kernohan, D. (2020a) 'The nine worst policy debacles of the last decade', *Wonkhe*. Available at: http://wonkhe.com/blogs/the-9-worst-policy-debacles-of-the-last-decade/ (Accessed: 21 August 2021).

Kernohan, D. (2020b) 'An extra year of LEO data shows the impact of graduate background on earnings', *Wonkhe*. Available at: https://wonkhe.com/blogs/an-extra-year-of-leo-data-shows-the-impact-of-graduate-background-on-earnings/ (Accessed: 26 August 2021).

Kernohan, D. (2022) 'Who benefits from higher education study?', *Wonkhe*. Available at: https://wonkhe.com/blogs/who-benefits-from-higher-education-study/ (Accessed: 26 August 2021).

Kim, C. (2015) 'New color lines: Racial/ethnic inequality in earnings among college-educated men', *The Sociological Quarterly*, 56(1), pp 152–184.

Klein, M. (2021) 'Who benefits from attending elite universities? Family background and graduates' career trajectories', *Research in Social Stratification and Mobility*, 72, p 100585 doi: 10.1016/j.rssm.2021.100585.

Kleinknecht, A., Kwee, Z. and Budyanto, L. (2016) 'Rigidities through flexibility: Flexible labour and the rise of management bureaucracies', *Cambridge Journal of Economics*, 40(4), pp 1137–1147.

Knight, P.T. and Yorke, M. (2002) 'Employability through the curriculum', *Tertiary Education and Management*, 8(4), pp 261–276.

Komljenovic, J. (2020) 'Commodifying higher education: The proliferation of devices for making markets', in Callender, C., Locke, W. and Marginson, S. (eds) *Changing Higher Education for a Changing World*, first edition. London: Bloomsbury Academic, pp 191–204.

Kornelakis, A. and Petrakaki, D. (2020) 'Embedding employability skills in UK higher education: Between digitalization and marketization', *Industry and Higher Education*, 34(5), pp 290–297.

Kristal, T. and Cohen, Y. (2017) 'The causes of rising wage inequality: The race between institutions and technology', *Socio-Economic Review*, 15(1), pp 187–212.

Lacity, M. and Willcocks, L. (2016) 'A new approach to automating services', *MIT Sloan Management Review*, Fall 2016. Available at: https://sloanreview.mit.edu/article/a-new-approach-to-automating-services/ (Accessed: 24 August 2021).

Lambert, H. (2019) 'The great university con: How the British degree lost its value', *The New Statesman*. Available at: https://www.newstatesman.com/politics/education/2019/08/great-university-con-how-british-degree-lost-its-value (Accessed: 22 August 2021).

Lammy, D. (2009) *Speech at Universities UK annual conference*. Department for Business, Innovation & Skills (BIS). Available at: https://webarchive.nationalarchives.gov.uk/ukgwa/20091016192430mp_/http://www.bis.gov.uk/universities-uk-annual-conference (Accessed: 23 August 2021).

Laurison, D. and Friedman, S. (2016) 'The class pay gap in higher professional and managerial occupations', *American Sociological Review*, 81(4), pp 668–695.

Lažetić, P. (2020) 'The gender gap in graduate job quality in Europe: A comparative analysis across economic sectors and countries', *Oxford Review of Education*, 46(1), pp 129–151.

Leicht, K.T. and Fennell, M. (2011) *Professional Work: A Sociological Approach*, first edition. Malden, MA: Wiley-Blackwell.

Leitch Review of Skills (2006) *Prosperity for All in the Global Economy: World Class Skills*. London: HMSO.

Lessard-Phillips, L., Boliver, V., Pampaka, M. and Swain, D. (2018) 'Exploring ethnic differences in the post-university destinations of Russell Group graduates', *Ethnicities*, 18(4), pp 496–517.

Lester, J.N., Lochmiller, C.R. and Gabriel, R.E. (2017) *Discursive Perspectives on Education Policy and Implementation*. Cham: Palgrave Macmillan.

Levy, F. (2018) 'Computers and populism: Artificial intelligence, jobs, and politics in the near term', *Oxford Review of Economic Policy*, 34(3), pp 393–417.

Levy, F. and Murnane, R. (1992) 'U.S. earnings levels and earnings inequality: A review of recent trends and proposed explanations', *Journal of Economic Literature*, 30(3), pp 1333–181.

Lin, K.-H. and Tomaskovic-Devey, D. (2013) 'Financialization and U.S. income inequality, 1970–2008', *American Journal of Sociology*, 118(5), pp 1284–1329.

Littler, J. (2017) *Against Meritocracy: Culture, Power and Myths of Mobility*. London and New York: Routledge.

Liu, Y. and Grusky, D.B. (2013) 'The payoff to skill in the third industrial revolution', *American Journal of Sociology*, 118(5), pp 1330–1374.

Livingstone, D.W., Adams, T.L. and Sawchuk, P. (2021) *Professional Power and Skill Use in the 'Knowledge Economy': A Class Analysis*. Leiden and Boston: Brill and Sense.

Lolich, L. (2011) '...and the market created the student to its image and likening: Neo-liberal governmentality and its effects on higher education in Ireland', *Irish Educational Studies*, 30(2), pp 271–284.

Lucas, S.R. (2001) 'Effectively maintained inequality: Education transitions, track mobility, and social background effects', *American Journal of Sociology*, 106(6), pp 1642–1690.

Lynch, K. (2006) 'Neo-liberalism and marketisation: The implications for higher education', *European Educational Research Journal*, 5(1), pp 1–17.

Lynch, K. (2015) 'Control by numbers: New managerialism and ranking in higher education', *Critical Studies in Education*, 56(2), pp 190–207.

Macfarlane, B. (2011) 'The morphing of academic practice: Unbundling and the rise of the para-academic', *Higher Education Quarterly*, 65(1), pp 59–73.

Maisuria, A. and Cole, M. (2017) 'The neoliberalization of higher education in England: An alternative is possible', *Policy Futures in Education*, 15(5), pp 602–619.

Malin, N. (ed) (2000) *Professionalism, Boundaries and the Workplace*. London and New York: Routledge.

Mandelson, P. (2009) *Higher Education and Modern Life*. London: Department for Business, Innovation & Skills (BIS). Available at: https://webarchive. nationalarchives.gov.uk/ukgwa/20091016192736mp_/http://www.bis. gov.uk/higher-education-and-modern-life (Accessed: 23 August 2021).

Mandler, P. (2020) *The Crisis of the Meritocracy: Britain's Transition to Mass Education since the Second World War*. New York: Oxford University Press.

Marginson, S. (1997) *Markets in Education*. St. Leonards: Allen & Unwin.

Marginson, S. (2006) 'Dynamics of national and global competition in higher education', *Higher Education*, 52(1), pp 1–39. Available at: https://www.jstor.org/stable/29735003 (Accessed: 27 August 2021).

Marginson, S. (2007) 'The new higher education landscape', in Marginson, S. (ed) *Prospects of Higher Education: Globalization, Market Competition, Public Goods and the Future of the University*. Rotterdam: Sense Publishers, pp 29–77.

Marginson, S. (2015) ' "The landscape of higher education research 1965–2015. Equality of opportunity: The first fifty years", SRHE 50th anniversary colloquium, 26 June'. Available at: https://www.srhe.ac.uk/downloads/SimonMarginsonKeynote.pdf (Accessed: 6 April 2022).

Marginson, S. (2016) 'High participation systems of higher education', *The Journal of Higher Education*, 87(2), pp 243–271.

Marginson, S. (2019) 'Limitations of human capital theory', *Studies in Higher Education*, 44(2), pp 287–301.

Marginson, S. and Considine, M. (2000) *The Enterprise University: Power, Governance and Reinvention in Australia*. Cambridge and New York: Cambridge University Press.

Markovits, D. (2019) *The Meritocracy Trap*. London: Allen Lane.

Marks, A. and Scholarios, D. (2008) 'Choreographing a system: Skill and employability in software work', *Economic and Industrial Democracy*, 29(1), pp 96–124.

Marshall, G., Swift, A. and Roberts, S. (1997) *Against the Odds? Social Class and Social Justice in Industrial Societies*. Oxford and New York: Clarendon Press and Oxford University Press.

Mason, G. (2020) 'Higher education, initial vocational education and training and continuing education and training: where should the balance lie?', *Journal of Education and Work*, 33(7–8): 468–490.

Mason, G., Williams, G. and Cranmer, S. (2009) 'Employability skills initiatives in higher education: What effects do they have on graduate labour market outcomes?', *Education Economics*, 17(1), pp 1–30.

Mathers, M. (2021) 'Too many young people going to university, says education charity chief', *The Independent*, 9 August. Available at: https://www.independent.co.uk/news/education/education-news/england-wales-ni-university-students-b1899383.html (Accessed: 27 August 2021).

Mautner, G. (2010) *Language and the Market Society: Critical Reflections on Discourse and Dominance*. New York: Routledge.

May, T. (2016) 'Britain, the great meritocracy: Prime Minister's speech', *GOV.UK*. Available at: https://www.gov.uk/government/speeches/britain-the-great-meritocracy-prime-ministers-speech (Accessed: 26 August 2021).

Mayer, C. (2019) *Principles for Purposeful Business*. London: The British Academy. Available at: https://www.thebritishacademy.ac.uk/publications/future-of-the-corporation-principles-for-purposeful-business/ (Accessed: 24 August 2021).

McAfee, A. and Brynjolfsson, E. (2012) 'Big data: The management revolution', *Harvard Business Review*, 90(10), pp 60–68.

McCaig, C. (2018) *The Marketisation of English Higher Education: A Policy Analysis of a Risk-based System*. Bingley: Emerald.

McCowan, T. (2015) 'Should universities promote employability?', *Theory and Research in Education*, 13(3), pp 267–285.

McCowan, T. (2017) 'Higher education, unbundling, and the end of the university as we know it', *Oxford Review of Education*, 43(6), pp 733–748.

McGettigan, A. (2013) *The Great University Gamble*. New York: Pluto.

McGuinness, S., Pouliakas, K. and Redmond, P. (2018) 'Skills mismatch: Concepts, measurement and policy approaches', *Journal of Economic Surveys*, 32(4), pp 985–1015.

McGuinness, S., Pouliakas, K. and Redmond, P. (2017) *How Useful is the Concept of Skills Mismatch?* Geneva: Skills and Employability Branch International Labour Office.

McKie, A. (2021) 'Elite UK universities take lion's share of bump in recruitment', *Times Higher Education*, 10 August. Available at: https://www.timeshighereducation.com/news/elite-uk-universities-take-lions-share-bump-recruitment (Accessed: 27 August 2021).

McKinsey Global Institute (2017) *A Future that Works: Automation, Employment, and Productivity. Executive Summary*. McKinsey. [online] Available at: https://www.mckinsey.com/~/media/mckinsey/featured%20insights/Digital%20Disruption/Harnessing%20automation%20for%20a%20future%20that%20works/MGI-A-future-that-works-Executive-summary.ashx (Accessed: 6 April 2022).

McQuaid, R.W. and Lindsay, C. (2005) 'The concept of employability', *Urban Studies*, 42(2), pp 197–219.

Merrill, B., Finnegan, F., O'Neill, J. and Revers, S. (2020) '"When it comes to what employers are looking for, I don't think I'm it for a lot of them": Class and capitals in, and after, higher education', *Studies in Higher Education*, 45(1), pp 163–175.

Middleton, C. (2000) 'Models of state and market in the "modernisation" of higher education', *British Journal of Sociology of Education*, 21(4), pp 537–554.

Mijs, J.J.B. (2016) 'The unfulfillable promise of meritocracy: Three lessons and their implications for justice in education', *Social Justice Research*, 29(1), pp 14–34.

Miller, H. (1998) 'Managing academics in Canada and the United Kingdom', *International Studies in Sociology of Education*, 8(1), pp 3–24.

Mincer, J. (1958) 'Investment in human capital and personal income distribution', *Journal of Political Economy*, 66(4), pp 281–302.

Mishel, L., Shierholz, H. and Schmitt, J. (2013) 'Don't blame the robots: Assessing the job polarization explanation of growing wage inequality', EPI-CEPR working paper. Economic Policy Institute. Available at: https://www.epi.org/publication/technology-inequality-dont-blame-the-robots/ (Accessed: 6 April 2022).

Mitnik, P.A., Cumberworth, E. and Grusky, D.B. (2016) 'Social mobility in a high-inequality regime', *The Annals of the American Academy of Political and Social Science*, 663(1), pp 140–184.

Moisio, S. (2018) *Geopolitics of the Knowledge-based Economy*. London: Routledge.

Mok, K.H. and Neubauer, D. (2016) 'Higher education governance in crisis: A critical reflection on the massification of higher education, graduate employment and social mobility', *Journal of Education and Work*, 29(1), pp 1–12.

Mokyr, J., Vickers, C. and Ziebarth, N.L. (2015) 'The history of technological anxiety and the future of economic growth: Is this time different?', *Journal of Economic Perspectives*, 29(3), pp 31–50.

Molesworth, M., Nixon, E. and Scullion, R. (2011) *The Marketisation of Higher Education and the Student as Consumer*. London: Routledge.

Montresor, G. (2019) 'Job polarization and labour supply changes in the UK', *Labour Economics*, 58, pp 187–203.

Moore, R. (2021) The free-market gamble: has Covid broken UK universities? *The Guardian*. 17 January. Available at: https://www.theguardian.com/education/2021/jan/17/free-market-gamble-has-covid-broken-uk-universities (Accessed: 6 April 2022).

Moreau, M. and Leathwood, C. (2006) 'Graduates' employment and the discourse of employability: A critical analysis', *Journal of Education and Work*, 19(4), pp 305–324.

Morgan, J. (2013) 'Business schools were "used as a cash cow", says Willetts', *Times Higher Education*, 1 October. Available at: https://www.timeshighereducation.com/news/business-schools-were-used-as-a-cash-cow-says-willetts/2007850.article (Accessed: 22 August 2021).

Morley, L. (2001) 'Producing new workers: Quality, equality and employability in higher education', *Quality in Higher Education*, 7(2), pp 131–138.

Morley, L. and Aynsley, S. (2007) 'Employers, quality and standards in higher education: Shared values and vocabularies or elitism and inequalities?', *Higher Education Quarterly*, 61(3), pp 229–249.

Morrish, L. and Sauntson, H. (2013) ' "Business-facing motors for economic development": An appraisal analysis of visions and values in the marketised UK university', *Critical Discourse Studies*, 10(1), pp 61–80.

Moss, P. and Tilly, C. (2003) *Stories Employers Tell: Race, Skill and Hiring in America*. New York: Russell Sage Foundation

Moutsios, S. (2010) 'Power, politics and transnational policy-making in education', *Globalisation, Societies and Education*, 8(1), pp 121–141.

Mouw, T. and Kalleberg, A.L. (2010) 'Occupations and the structure of wage inequality in the United States, 1980s to 2000s', *American Sociological Review*, 75(3), pp 402–431.

Muddiman, E. (2017) 'Instrumentalism amongst students: A cross-national comparison of the significance of subject choice', *British Journal of Sociology of Education*, 39(5), pp 607–622.

Murphy, R. (1988) *Social Closure: The Theory of Monopolization and Exclusion*. Oxford and New York: Oxford University Press.

Murphy, R., Scott-Clayton, J. and Wyness, G. (2019) 'The end of free college in England: Implications for enrolments, equity, and quality', *Economics of Education Review*, 71, pp 7–22.

Naidoo, R. (2016) 'Choice in the learning market: Tokenistic ritual or democratic education?', in John, P. and Fanghanel, J. (eds) *Dimensions of Marketisation in Higher Education*. London: Routledge, pp 38–47.

Naidoo, R. and Jamieson, I. (2005) 'Empowering participants or corroding learning? Towards a research agenda on the impact of student consumerism in higher education', *Journal of Education Policy*, 20(3), pp 267–281.

Naidoo, R. and Williams, J. (2015) 'The neoliberal regime in English higher education: Charters, consumers and the erosion of the public good', *Critical Studies in Education*, 56(2), pp 208–223.

Naidoo, R., Shankar, A. and Veer, E. (2011) 'The consumerist turn in higher education: Policy aspirations and outcomes', *Journal of Marketing Management*, 27(11–12), pp 1142–1162.

National Audit Office (2017) *The Higher Education Market: National Audit Office (NAO) Report*. National Audit Office. Available at: https://www.nao.org.uk/report/the-higher-education-market/ (Accessed: 22 August 2021).

National Committee of Inquiry into Higher Education (NCIHE) (1997) *Higher Education in the Learning Society*. London: HMSO.

Newfield, C. (2011) *Unmaking the Public University: The Forty-Year Assault on the Middle Class*. Cambridge, MA: Harvard University Press.

Newson, J.A. and Buchbinder, H. (1988) *The University Means Business: Universities, Corporations and Academic Work*. Toronto: Garamond Press.

Newton, O., Laczik, A. and Percy, C. (2017) *Our Plan for Higher Education*. London: The Edge Foundation.

Nixon, E. and Scullion, R. (2021) 'Academic labour as professional service work? A psychosocial analysis of emotion in lecturer–student relations under marketization', *Human Relations*. doi: 10.1177/00187267211022270.

Nixon, E., Scullion, R. and Hearn, R. (2018) 'Her majesty the student: Marketised higher education and the narcissistic (dis)satisfactions of the student-consumer', *Studies in Higher Education*, 43(6), pp 927–943.

Nixon, J., Marks, A., Rowland, S. and Walker, M. (2001) 'Towards a new academic professionalism: A manifesto of hope', *British Journal of Sociology of Education*, 22(2), pp 227–244.

Noordegraaf, M. (2016) 'Reconfiguring professional work: Changing forms of professionalism in public services', *Administration & Society*, 48(7), pp 783–810.

Nunley, J.M., Pugh, A., Romero, N. and Seals, R.A. (2017) 'The effects of unemployment and underemployment on employment opportunities: Results from a correspondence audit of the labor market for college graduates', *ILR Review*, 70(3), pp 642–669.

O'Brien, T. and Guiney, G. (2018) *Staff Wellbeing in Higher Education*. London: Education Support Partnership.

O'Donovan, N. (2020) 'From knowledge economy to automation anxiety: A growth regime in crisis?', *New Political Economy*, 25(2), pp 248–266.

Oesch, D. and Piccitto, G. (2019) 'The polarization myth: Occupational upgrading in Germany, Spain, Sweden, and the UK, 1992–2015', *Work and Occupations*, 46(4), pp 441–469.

Office for National Statistics (ONS) (2018) *Trends in Self-employment in the UK*. Available at: https://www.ons.gov.uk/employmentandlabourmarket/peopleinwork/employmentandemployeetypes/articles/trendsinselfemploymentintheuk/2018-02-07 (Accessed: 24 August 2021).

Office for National Statistics (ONS) (2019) *Overeducation and Hourly Wages in the UK Labour Market: 2006 to 2017*. Available at: https://www.ons.gov.uk/economy/nationalaccounts/uksectoraccounts/compendium/economicreview/april2019/overeducationandhourlywagesintheuklabourmarket2006to2017 (Accessed: 25 August 2021).

Office for National Statistics (ONS) (2021) *Graduates' Labour Market Outcomes during the Coronavirus (COVID-19) Pandemic: Occupational Switches and Skill Mismatch*. Available at: https://www.ons.gov.uk/employmentandlabourmarket/peopleinwork/employmentandemployeetypes/articles/graduateslabourmarketoutcomesduringthecoronaviruscovid19pandemicoccupationalswitchesandskillmismatch/2021-03-08 (Accessed: 24 August 2021).

Office for Students (OfS) (2019) *Office for Students' Value for Money Strategy 2019 to 2021*. London: OfS.

Office for Students (OfS) (2020) *Grade Inflation 'Remains a Significant and Pressing Issue' – New OfS Analysis*. London: OfS. Available at: https://www.officeforstudents.org.uk/news-blog-and-events/press-and-media/grade-inflation-remains-a-significant-and-pressing-issue-new-ofs-analysis/ (Accessed: 22 August 2021).

Ogbonna E. and Harris, L.C. (2004) 'Work intensification and emotional labour among UK university lecturers: An exploratory study', *Organization Studies,* 25(7), pp 1185–1203.

Ogg, T., Zimdars, A. and Heath, A. (2009) 'Schooling effects on degree performance: A comparison of the predictive validity of aptitude testing and secondary school grades at Oxford University', *British Educational Research Journal,* 35(5), pp 781–807.

Oh, B. and Kim, C. (2020) 'Broken promise of college? New educational sorting mechanisms for intergenerational association in the 21st century', *Social Science Research,* 86, p 102375 doi: 10.1016/j.ssresearch.2019.102375.

Okay-Somerville, B. and Scholarios, D. (2013) 'Shades of grey: Understanding job quality in emerging graduate occupations', *Human Relations,* 66(4), pp 555–585.

Okay-Somerville, B. and Scholarios, D. (2017) 'Position, possession or process? Understanding objective and subjective employability during university-to-work transitions', *Studies in Higher Education,* 42(7), pp 1275–1291.

O'Reilly, J., Leschke, J., Ortlieb, R., Seeleib-Kaiser, M. and Villa, P. (eds) (2019) *Youth Labor in Transition: Inequalities, Mobility, and Policies in Europe.* New York: Oxford University Press.

Organisation for Economic Co-operation and Development (OECD) (1996) *The Knowledge-Based Economy.* Brussels: OECD.

Organisation for Economic Co-operation and Development (OECD) (2001) *OECD Glossary of Statistical Terms: Human Capital Definition.* Available at: https://stats.oecd.org/glossary/detail.asp?ID=1264 (Accessed: 24 August 2021).

Organisation for Economic Co-operation and Development (OECD) (2014) *OECD Employment Outlook 2014.* Brussels: OECD (OECD Employment Outlook). doi: 10.1787/empl_outlook-2014-en.

Ozga, J. (2009) 'Governing education through data in England: From regulation to self-evaluation', *Journal of Education Policy,* 24(2), pp 149–162.

Palfreyman, D. and Tapper, T. (2014) *Reshaping the University: The Rise of the Regulated Market in Higher Education.* Oxford: Oxford University Press.

Parkin, F. (1979) *Marxism and Class Theory: A Bourgeois Critique.* New York: Columbia University Press.

Payne, G. (2017) *The New Social Mobility: How the Politicians Got It Wrong.* Bristol: Policy Press.

Pegg, A., Waldock, J., Hendy-Isaac, S. and Lawton, R. (2012) *Pedagogy for Employability.* York: Higher Education Academy.

Pfeffer, F.T. and Hertel, F.R. (2015) 'How has educational expansion shaped social mobility trends in the United States?', *Social Forces,* 94(1), pp 143–180.

Piff, P.K., Kraus, M.W. and Keltner, D. (2018) 'Unpacking the inequality paradox: The psychological roots of inequality and social class', in J.M. Olson (ed), *Advances in Experimental Social Psychology*. New York: Elsevier, pp 53–124.

Piketty, T. (2014) *Capital in the Twenty-first Century*. Cambridge, MA: The Belknap Press of Harvard University Press.

Piketty, T. (2019) *Capital and Ideology*. Cambridge, MA: Harvard University Press.

Piketty, T. (2020) *Capital and Ideology*, illustrated edition. Cambridge, MA and London: Harvard University Press.

Ponnert, L. and Svensson, K. (2016) 'Standardisation: The end of professional discretion?', *European Journal of Social Work*, 19(3–4), pp 586–599.

Posselt, J.R. and Grodsky, E. (2017) 'Graduate education and social stratification', *Annual Review of Sociology*, 43(1), pp 353–378.

Potts, M. (2005) 'The consumerist subversion of education', *Academic Questions*, 18(3), pp 54–64.

PricewaterhouseCoopers (PWC) (2017) *UK Economic Outlook March 2017*. Available at: https://www.pwc.co.uk/economic-services/ukeo/pwcukeo-slides-final-march-2017-v2.pdf (Accessed: 6 April 2022).

Psacharopoulos, G. (1994) 'Returns to investment in education: A global update', *World Development*, 22(9), pp 1325–1343.

Purcell, K. and P. Elias (2004) *Seven Years On; Graduate Careers in a Changing labour Market*. London: HECSU.

Rahim, N., Lepanjuuri, K., Day, F., Piggott, H., Hudson, R. and Lubian, K. (2017) *Research on the Sharing Economy*. 453 HMRC report. London: HM Revenue and Customs.

Rammell, B. (2007) *House of Commons – Innovation, Universities, Science and Skills – Minutes of Evidence*. Available at: https://publications.parliament.uk/pa/cm200708/cmselect/cmdius/114/7112802.htm (Accessed: 23 August 2021).

Ravenelle, A.J. (2019) *Hustle and Gig: Struggling and Surviving in the Sharing Economy*, first edition. Oakland: University of California Press.

Reay, D. (2017) *Miseducation: Inequality, Education and the Working Classes*. Bristol: Policy Press.

Reich, R.B. (1991) *The Work of Nations: Preparing Ourselves for 21st-century Capitalism*, first edition. New York: A.A. Knopf.

Reisel, L. (2013) 'Is more always better? Early career returns to education in the United States and Norway', *Research in Social Stratification and Mobility*, 31, pp 49–68.

Richardson, H. (2019) 'Job applications "filtered by university ranking"', *BBC News*, 18 September. Available at: https://www.bbc.com/news/education-49728941 (Accessed: 21 December 2021).

Richmond, T. (2018) 'A degree of uncertainty: An investigation into grade inflation in universities', *Reform*. Available at: https://reform.uk/the-reformer/degree-uncertainty-investigation-grade-inflation-universities (Accessed: 22 August 2021).

Rivera, L.A. (2012) 'Hiring as cultural matching: The case of elite professional service firms', *American Sociological Review*, 77(6), pp 999–1022.

Rivera, L.A. (2015) *Pedigree: How Elite Students get Elite Jobs*. Princeton and Oxford: Princeton University Press.

Roberts, C., Parkes, H., Statham, R. and Rankin, L. (2019) *The Future Is Ours: Women, Automation and Equality in the Digital Age*. London: IPPR. Available at: https://www.ippr.org/files/2019-07/the-future-is-ours-women-automation-equality-july19.pdf (Accessed: 6 April 2022).

Romer, P.M. (1990) 'Endogenous technological change', *Journal of Political Economy*, 98(5), pp S71–S102.

Römgens, I., Scoupe, R. and Beausaert, S. (2020) 'Unraveling the concept of employability, bringing together research on employability in higher education and the workplace', *Studies in Higher Education*, 45(12), pp 2588–2603.

Roscoe, P. (2014) *I Spend, Therefore I Am: The True Cost of Economics*. London: Viking.

Rosenfeld, J. (2021) *You're Paid What You're Worth: And Other Myths of the Modern Economy*. Cambridge, MA: Harvard University Press.

Ruggera, L. and Barone, C. (2017) 'Social closure, micro-class immobility and the intergenerational reproduction of the upper class: A comparative study: Social closure and micro-classes', *The British Journal of Sociology*, 68(2), pp 194–214.

Sainsbury of Turville (2006) *The Race to the Top: A Review of Government's Science and Innovation Policies*. London: DIUS.

Sakamoto, A. and Wang, S.X. (2017) 'Occupational and organizational effects on wages among college-educated workers in 2003 and 2010', *Social Currents*, 4(2), pp 175–195.

Salter, D.B. and Salter, B. (2014) *The State and Higher Education: State & Higher Education*. London: Routledge.

Sandel, M.J. (2020) *The Tyranny of Merit: What's Become of the Common Good?* New York: Farrar, Straus and Giroux.

Sang, K., Powell, A., Finkel, R. and Richards, J. (2015) '"Being an academic is not a 9–5 job": Long working hours and the "ideal worker" in UK academia', *Labour & Industry*, 25(3), pp 235–249.

Saunders, D.B. (2010) 'Neoliberal ideology and public higher education in the United States', *Journal for Critical Education Policy Studies*, 8(1), pp 41–77.

Saunders, P. (1997) 'Social mobility in Britain: An empirical evaluation of two competing explanations', *Sociology*, 31(2), pp 261–288.

Saunders, P. (2000) *Unequal But Fair?: A Study of Class Barriers in Britain*. London: Institute for the Study of Civil Society.

Savage, M. (2021) *The Return of Inequality: Social Change and the Weight of the Past*. Cambridge, MA: Harvard University Press.

Sayer, R.A. (2005) *The Moral Significance of Class*. Cambridge and New York: Cambridge University Press.

Schlogl, L. and Sumner, A. (2020) *Disrupted Development and the Future of Inequality in the Age of Automation*. Cham: Palgrave Pivot.

Scholz, T. (2016) *Uberworked and Underpaid: How Workers Are Disrupting the Digital Economy*, first edition. Cambridge and Malden, MA: Polity.

Schomburg, H. and Teichler, U. (2006) *Higher Education and Graduate Employment in Europe: Results from Graduate Surveys from Twelve Countries*. Dordrecht: Springer.

Schram, S.F. (2015) *The Return of Ordinary Capitalism: Neoliberalism, Precarity, Occupy*. Oxford and New York: Oxford University Press.

Schultz, T.W. (1959) 'Investment in man: An economist's view', *Social Service Review*, 33(2), pp 109–117.

Schultz, T.W. (1960) 'Capital formation by education', *Journal of Political Economy*, 68(6), pp 571–583.

Schultz, T.W. (1961) 'Investment in human capital', *The American Economic Review*, 51(1), pp 1–17.

Schultz, T.W. (1971) *Investment in Human Capital: The Role of Education and of Research*. New York: Free Press.

Schultz, T.W. (1975) 'The value of the ability to deal with disequilibria', *Journal of Economic Literature*, 13(3), pp 827–846.

Sellgren, K. (2019a) 'Half of students get degree place with lower grades', *BBC News*, 28 November. Available at: https://www.bbc.com/news/education-50576198 (Accessed: 22 August 2021).

Sellgren, K. (2019b) 'University a "false promise" for too many youngsters', *BBC News*, 7 January. Available at: https://www.bbc.com/news/education-46781569 (Accessed: 21 August 2021).

Sen, A., Bowles, S. and Durlauf, S. (2000) 'Merit and justice', in Arrow, K.J. (ed) *Meritocracy and Economic Inequality*. Princeton: Princeton University Press, pp 5–16.

Sewell, P. and Dacre Pool, L. (2010) 'Moving from conceptual ambiguity to operational clarity: Employability, enterprise and entrepreneurship in higher education', *Education + Training*, 52(1), pp 89–94.

Shapiro, H.T. (2005) *A Larger Sense of Purpose: Higher Education and Society*. Princeton: Princeton University Press.

Shattock, M. (2008) 'The change from private to public governance of British higher education: Its consequences for higher education policy making 1980–2006', *Higher Education Quarterly*, 62(3), pp 181–203.

Shattock, M. (2012) *Making Policy in British Higher Education: 1945–2011*. Maidenhead: Open University Press.

Shattock, M. and Horvath, D.A. (2021) *The Governance of British Higher Education: The Impact of Governmental, Financial and Market Pressures*. London: Bloomsbury Academic.

Shepherd, S. (2018) 'Managerialism: An ideal type', *Studies in Higher Education*, 43(9), pp 1668–1678.

Shields, R. and Watermeyer, R. (2020) 'Competing institutional logics in universities in the United Kingdom: Schism in the church of reason', *Studies in Higher Education*, 45(1), pp 3–17.

Simons, M. and Masschelein, J. (2009) 'The public and its university: Beyond learning for civic employability?', *European Educational Research Journal*, 8(2), pp 204–217.

Sissons, P. (2021) 'The local low skills equilibrium: Moving from concept to policy utility', *Urban Studies*, 58(8), pp 1543–1560.

Skidmore, C. (2019) 'Universities minister gives speech at Universities UK conference', *GOV.UK*. Available at: https://www.gov.uk/government/speeches/universities-minister-gives-speech-at-universities-uk-conference (Accessed: 23 August 2021).

Slaughter, S. and Cantwell, B. (2012) 'Transatlantic moves to the market: The United States and the European Union', *Higher Education*, 63(5), pp 583–606.

Smyth, E. and McCoy, S. (2011) 'The dynamics of credentialism: Ireland from bust to boom (and back again)', *Research in Social Stratification and Mobility*, 29(1), pp 91–106.

Souto-Otero, M. (2010) 'Education, meritocracy and redistribution', *Journal of Education Policy*, 25(3), pp 397–413.

Spence, M. (1973) 'Job market signaling', *The Quarterly Journal of Economics*, 87(3), pp 355–374.

Spitz-Oener, A. (2006) 'Technical change, job tasks, and rising educational demands: looking outside the wage structure', Journal of Labor Economics, 24(2), 235–270.

Spring, J.H. (2015) *Economization of Education: Human Capital, Global Corporations, Skills-based Schooling*. New York and London: Routledge.

Staton, B. (2021a) 'English universities face upheaval as financial strains hit jobs', *Financial Times*, 23 May. Available at: https://www.ft.com/content/6a30e430-95cf-4eec-a435-b7b98077ce23 (Accessed: 22 August 2021).

Staton, B. (2021b) 'Funding for arts courses and London universities to be slashed', *Financial Times*, 20 July. Available at: https://www.ft.com/content/937ee941-a808-40ac-b83e-429d0a7ae5d8 (Accessed: 22 August 2021).

Staton, B. (2021c) 'UK universities braced for squeeze on places ahead of A-level results', *Financial Times*, 6 August. Available at: https://www.ft.com/content/f69860dc-1e68-48ec-9b0f-e67e0c9cc9ce (Accessed: 27 August 2021).

Staton, B. (2021d) 'Covid leaves students with a bitter financial legacy', *Financial Times*, 9 July. Available at: https://www.ft.com/content/c173f c57-0abc-4dbb-aa01-17672798af32 (Accessed: 27 August 2021).

Steffy, K. (2017) 'Willful versus woeful underemployment: Perceived volition and social class background among overqualified college graduates', *Work and Occupations*, 44(4), pp 467–511.

Steier, F. (2003) 'The changing nexus: Tertiary education institutions, the marketplace and the state', *Higher Education Quarterly*, 57(2), pp 158–180.

Stiglitz, J. (1975) 'The theory of "screening," education, and the distribution of income', *American Economic Review*, 65(3), pp 283–300.

Suleman, F. (2018) 'The employability skills of higher education graduates: Insights into conceptual frameworks and methodological options', *Higher Education*, 76(2), pp 263–278.

Sullivan, A., Parsons, S., Wiggins, R., Heath, A. and Green, F. (2014) 'Social origins, school type and higher education destinations', *Oxford Review of Education*, 40(6), pp 739–763.

Sullivan, A., Parsons, S., Green, F., Wiggins, R.D. and Ploubidis, G. (2018a) 'Elite universities, fields of study and top salaries: Which degree will make you rich?', *British Educational Research Journal*, 44(4), pp 663–680.

Sullivan, A., Parsons, S., Green, F., Wiggins, R.D. and Ploubidis, G. (2018b) 'The path from social origins to top jobs: Social reproduction via education', *The British Journal of Sociology*, 69(3), pp 776–798.

Sum, N.-L. and Jessop, B. (2013) *Towards a Cultural Political Economy: Putting Culture in its Place in Political Economy*. Cheltenham: Edward Elgar.

Summerfield, F. and Theodossiou, I. (2017) 'The scarring effects of recessions: Over-education and macroeconomic conditions at graduation', *Economic Inquiry*, 55(3), pp 1370–1387.

Susskind, R. and Susskind, D. (2015) *The Future of the Professions: How Technology Will Transform the Work of Human Experts*. Oxford: Oxford University Press.

Tang, R., Tang, Y. and Wang, P. (2020) 'Within-job wage inequality: Performance pay and job relatedness', NBER Working Papers, 27390. Available at: https://www.nber.org/papers/w27390 (Accessed: 26 August 2021).

Teixeira, P.N. (2011) 'Eppure si Muove: Marketisation and privatisation trends in the EHEA', *Journal of the European Higher Education Area*, 4, pp 57–72.

Teixeira, P.N. (2014) 'Gary Becker's early work on human capital: Collaborations and distinctiveness', *IZA Journal of Labor Economics*, 3(1), p 12. doi: 10.1186/s40172-014-0012-2.

Themelis, S. (2008) 'Meritocracy through education and social mobility in post-war Britain: A critical examination', *British Journal of Sociology of Education*, 29(5), pp 427–438.

Thijssen, J.G.L., Van der Heijden, B.I.J.M. and Rocco, T.S. (2008) 'Toward the employability-link model: Current employment transition to future employment perspectives', *Human Resource Development Review*, 7(2), pp 165–183.

Tholen, G. (2013) 'The social construction of competition for graduate jobs: A comparison between Great Britain and the Netherlands', *Sociology*, 47(2), pp 267–283.

Tholen, G. (2014) *The Changing Nature of the Graduate Labour Market: Media, Policy and Political Discourses in the UK*. Basingstoke: Palgrave Macmillan.

Tholen, G. (2015) 'What can research into graduate employability tell us about agency and structure?', *British Journal of Sociology of Education*, 36(5), pp 766–784.

Tholen, G. (2017a) *Graduate Work: Skills, Credentials, Careers, and Labour Markets*. Oxford: Oxford University Press.

Tholen, G. (2017b) 'The changing opportunities of professionalization for graduate occupations', *Comparative Sociology*, 16(5), pp 613–633.

Tholen, G. (2019) 'The limits of higher education institutions as sites of work skill development, the cases of software engineers, laboratory scientists, financial analysts and press officers', *Studies in Higher Education*, 44(11), pp 2041–2052.

Tholen, G. and Brown, P. (2017) 'Higher education and the myths of graduate employability', in Waller, R., Ingram, N. and Ward, M. (eds) *Higher Education and Social Inequalities: University Admissions, Experiences, and Outcomes*. London: Routledge, pp 152–166.

Tholen, G., Relly, S.J., Warhurst, C. and Commander, J. (2016) 'Higher education, graduate skills and the skills of graduates: The case of graduates as residential sales estate agents', *British Educational Research Journal*, 42(3), pp 508–523.

Thornton, M. (2013) 'The mirage of merit: Reconstituting the "ideal academic"', *Australian Feminist Studies*, 28(76), pp 127–143.

Thurow, L. (1975) *Generating Inequality*. New York: Basic Books.

Tolofari, S. (2005) 'New public management and education', *Policy Futures in Education*, 3(1), pp 75–89.

Tomaskovic-Devey, D. and Lin, K.-H. (2011) 'Income dynamics, economic rents, and the financialization of the U.S. economy', *American Sociological Review*, 76(4), pp 538–559.

Tominey, C. (2022) 'Students should apply for refunds on their fees – at the end of the day, they're consumers', *The Telegraph*, 21 January. Available at: https://www.telegraph.co.uk/education-and-careers/2022/01/21/students-should-apply-refunds-fees-end-day-consumers/ (Accessed: 24 January 2022).

Tomlinson, M. (2007) 'Graduate employability and student attitudes and orientations to the labour market', *Journal of Education and Work*, 20(4), pp 285–304.

Tomlinson, M. (2017) 'Student perceptions of themselves as "consumers" of higher education', *British Journal of Sociology of Education*, 38(4), pp 450–467.

Tomlinson, M. and Holmes, L. (eds) (2017) *Graduate Employability in Context: Theory, Research and Debate*, first edition. London: Palgrave Macmillan.

Tomlinson, M., Enders, J. and Naidoo, R. (2020) 'The teaching excellence framework: Symbolic violence and the measured market in higher education', *Critical Studies in Education*, 61(5), pp 627–642.

Torche, F. (2011) 'Is a college degree still the great equalizer? Intergenerational mobility across levels of schooling in the United States', *American Journal of Sociology*, 117(3), pp 763–807.

Torvik, R. (2002) 'Natural resources, rent seeking and welfare', *Journal of Development Economics*, 67(2), pp 455–470.

Trow, M. (1973) *Problems in the Transition from Elite to Mass Higher Education*. Berkeley: Carnegie Commission on Higher Education.

Trowler, P. (2001) 'Captured by the discourse? The socially constitutive power of new higher education discourse in the UK', *Organization*, 8(2), pp 183–201.

UK Commission for Employment and Skills (UKCES) (2010) *Employability Skills: A Research and Policy Briefing*. London: UKCES.

Universities UK (2015) *Supply and Demand For Higher Level Skills*. Available from: https://www.universitiesuk.ac.uk/policy-and-analysis/reports/Documents/2015/supply-and-demand-for-higher-level-skills.pdf (Accessed: 6 April 2022).

University and College Union (UCU) (2012) *Choice Cuts: How Choice has Declined in Higher Education*. London: UCU. Available at: https://www.ucu.org.uk/media/5054/Choice-cuts--UCU-report-February-2012/pdf/Choice_cuts.pdf (Accessed: 6 April 2022).

van de Werfhorst, H.G. (2011) 'Skills, positional good or social closure? The role of education across structural–institutional labour market settings', *Journal of Education and Work*, 24(5), pp 521–548.

van de Werfhorst, H.G. and Andersen, R. (2005) 'Social background, credential inflation and educational strategies', *Acta Sociologica*, 48(4), pp 321–340.

van Zanten, A. (2015) 'A family affair: Reproducing elite positions and preserving the ideals of meritocratic competition and youth autonomy', in van Zanten, A., Ball, S.J. and Darchy-Koechlin, B. (eds) *World Yearbook of Education 2015*. London: Routledge, pp 19–42.

Vanderburg, W.H. (2004) 'The intellectual assembly line is already here', *Bulletin of Science, Technology & Society*, 24(4), pp 331–341.

Verhaest, D. and Van der Velden, R. (2013) 'Cross-country differences in graduate overeducation', *European Sociological Review*, 29(3), pp 642–653.

Vernon, J. (2018) 'The making of the neoliberal university in Britain', *Critical Historical Studies*, 5(2), pp 267–280.

Vican, S., Friedman, A. and Andreasen, R. (2020) 'Metrics, money, and managerialism: Faculty experiences of competing logics in higher education', *The Journal of Higher Education*, 91(1), pp 139–164.

Vogtenhuber, S. (2018) 'The institutional conditions of inequality in credential and skill attainment and their impact on occupational placement', *Research in Social Stratification and Mobility*, 55, pp 13–24.

Volscho, T.W. and Kelly, N.J. (2012) 'The rise of the super-rich: Power resources, taxes, financial markets, and the dynamics of the top 1 percent, 1949 to 2008', *American Sociological Review*, 77(5), pp 679–699.

Walker, I. and Zhu, Y. (2013) 'The impact of university degrees on the lifecycle of earnings: Some further analysis', BIS Research Paper Number 112. Available at: https://assets.publishing.service.gov.uk/government/uplo ads/system/uploads/attachment_data/file/229498/bis-13-899-the-imp act-of-university-degrees-on-the-lifecycle-of-earnings-further-analysis. pdf (Accessed: 6 April 2022).

Warhurst, C. and Thompson, P. (2006) 'Mapping knowledge in work: Proxies or practices?', *Work, Employment and Society*, 20(4), pp 787–800.

Warriner, D. and Anderson, K.T. (2017) 'Discourse analysis in educational research', in King, K.A., Lai, Y.-J. and May, S. (eds) *Research Methods in Language and Education*. Cham: Springer, pp 297–309.

Watts, R. (2017) *Public Universities, Managerialism and the Value of Higher Education*. London: Palgrave Macmillan.

Weale, S. (2019) 'UK universities brace for last-minute fight for A-level students', *The Guardian*, 10 August. Available at: http://www.theguard ian.com/education/2019/aug/10/uk-universities-brace-for-last-minute-fight-for-a-level-students (Accessed: 22 August 2021).

Weale, S. (2020a) 'Universities brace for government scrutiny after Policy Exchange report', *The Guardian*, 1 March. Available at: http://www.theg uardian.com/education/2020/mar/01/universities-government-scrutiny-policy-exchange (Accessed: 21 August 2021).

Weale, S. (2020b) 'Proportion of students in England awarded first-class degrees soars', *The Guardian*, 19 November. Available at: http://www.theg uardian.com/education/2020/nov/19/students-england-awarded-first-class-degrees-grade-inflation (Accessed: 22 August 2021).

Weale, S., Adams, R. and Hall, A. (2021) 'London South Bank University staff sound alarm over drop in courses', *The Guardian*, 25 May. Available at: http://www.theguardian.com/education/2021/may/25/london-south-bank-university-staff-sound-alarm-over-drop-in-courses (Accessed: 22 August 2021).

Weber, M. (1978) *Economy and Society: An Outline of Interpretive Sociology*. Berkeley: University of California Press.

Western, B. and Rosenfeld, J. (2011) 'Unions, norms, and the rise in U.S. wage inequality', *American Sociological Review*, 76(4), pp 513–537.

Wilby, P. (2020) 'Academic freedom is precious – so why have UK universities sold out to China?', *The Guardian*, 11 August. Available at: http://www.theguardian.com/education/2020/aug/11/academic-freedom-is-precious-so-why-have-uk-universities-sold-out-to-china (Accessed: 21 August 2021).

Willetts, D. (2010) 'Speech at HEFCE Annual Conference', Department for Business, Innovation and Skills. Available at: https://webarchive.natio nalarchives.gov.uk/ukgwa/20120405115346mp_/http://www.bis.gov. uk/news/speeches/david-willetts-hefce-annual-conference (Accessed: 23 August 2021).

Willetts, D. (2017) *A University Education*. Oxford: Oxford University Press.

Williams, G. (1997) 'The market route to mass higher education: British experience 1979–1996', *Higher Education Policy*, 10(3–4), pp 275–289.

Williams, G. (2013) 'A bridge too far: An economic critique of marketization of higher education', in Callender, C. and Scott, P. (eds) *Browne and Beyond: Modernizing English Higher Education*. London: IOE Press, pp 57–72.

Williams, J. (2013) *Consuming Higher Education: Why Learning Can't be Bought*. London: Bloomsbury.

Williams, M. (2004) 'The higher education market in the United Kingdom', in Teixeira, P., Jongbloed, B.B., Dill, D.D. and Amaral, A. (eds) *Markets in Higher Education: Rhetoric or Reality?* Dordrecht: Springer Netherlands, pp 241–269.

Williams, M. (2013) 'Occupations and British wage inequality, 1970s–2000s', *European Sociological Review*, 29(4), pp 841–857.

Wilson, H., Daugherty, P. and Bianzino, N. (2017) 'The jobs that artificial intelligence will create', *MIT Sloan Management Review*, 85(4), pp 14–17. Available at: https://sloanreview.mit.edu/article/will-ai-create-as-many-jobs-as-it-eliminates/ (Accessed: 24 September 2021).

Wilson, R., Barnes, S.-A., May-Gillings, M., Patel, S. and Bui, H. (2020) *Working Futures 2017–2027: Long-run labour market and skills projections for the UK*. London: Department for Education.

Wilton, N. (2011) 'Do employability skills really matter in the UK graduate labour market? The case of business and management graduates', *Work, Employment and Society*, 25(1), pp 85–100.

Winterbotham, M., Kik, G., Selner, S., Menys, R., Stroud, S., Whittaker, S. and Hewitt, J.H. (2020) *Employer Skills Survey 2019: UK (excluding Scotland) Findings*. London: Department for Education. Available at: https://assets.publishing.service.gov.uk/government/uploads/system/uploads/attachment_data/file/925744/Employer_Skills_Survey_2019_research_report.pdf (Accessed: 25 August 2021).

Witteveen, D. and Attewell, P. (2020) 'Reconsidering the "meritocratic power of a college degree"', *Research in Social Stratification and Mobility*, 66, p 100479, doi: 10.1016/j.rssm.2020.100479.

Wooldridge, A. (2021) *The Aristocracy of Talent: How Meritocracy Made the Modern World*. London: Allen Lane.

World Bank (2007) *Building Knowledge Economies: Advanced Strategies for Development*. Washington, DC: World Bank.

World Economic Forum (WEF) (2020) *The Future of Jobs Report 2020*. Available at: https://www.weforum.org/reports/the-future-of-jobs-report-2020/ (Accessed: 24 August 2021).

Wright, R. (2019) 'Workplace automation: How AI is coming for your job', *Financial Times*, 29 September. Available at: https://www.ft.com/content/c4bf787a-d4a0-11e9-a0bd-ab8ec6435630 (Accessed: 24 August 2021).

Wright, S. and Ørberg, S. (2017) 'Universities in the competition state: Lessons from Denmark', in Wright, S. and Shore, C. (eds) *Death of the Public University? Uncertain Futures for Higher Education in the Knowledge Economy*. New York: Berghahn Books, 69–89.

Wright, S. and Shore, C. (eds) (2017) *Death of the Public University? Uncertain Futures for Higher Education in the Knowledge Economy*. New York: Berghahn Books.

Wu, C.-H., Luksyte, A. and Parker, S.K. (2015) 'Overqualification and subjective well-being at work: The moderating role of job autonomy and culture', *Social Indicators Research*, 121(3), pp 917–937.

Xie, Y., Killewald, A. and Near, C. (2016) 'Between- and within-occupation inequality: The case of high-status professions', *The Annals of the American Academy of Political and Social Science*, 663(1), pp 53–79.

Yorke, M. (2006) *Employability in Higher Education: What it is – What it is not*. York: The Higher Education Academy.

Yorke, M. and Knight, P.T. (2006) *Embedding Employability into the Curriculum: Learning & Employability Series 1*. York: The Higher Education Academy.

Young, M. (1958) *The Rise of the Meritocracy 1870–2033: An Essay on Education and Society*. London: Thames & Hudson.

Zaloom, C. (2019) *Indebted: How Families Make College Work at Any Cost*. Princeton: Princeton University Press.

Zhou, X. (2019) 'Equalization or selection? Reassessing the "meritocratic power" of a college degree in intergenerational income mobility', *American Sociological Review*, 84(3), pp 459–485.

Zuboff, P.S. (2019) *The Age of Surveillance Capitalism: The Fight for a Human Future at the New Frontier of Power*. London: Profile Books.

Zwysen, W. and Longhi, S. (2018) 'Employment and earning differences in the early career of ethnic minority British graduates: The importance of university career, parental background and area characteristics', *Journal of Ethnic and Migration Studies*, 44(1), pp 154–172.

Zwysen, W., Di Stasio, V. and Heath, A. (2021) 'Ethnic penalties and hiring discrimination: Comparing results from observational studies with field experiments in the UK', *Sociology*, 55(2), pp 263–282.

Index

References in **bold** type refer to tables.

A

academics, impact of marketisation on 20, 22–23, 25, 117, 118
Acemoglu, D. 76
adaptability 107
AI (artificial intelligence) 34, 76, 77, 78
A-level examinations 121–122
Anderson, K.T. 30, 31
apprenticeships, degree-level 47, 48, 123, 124
Araki, S. 88
artificial intelligence (AI) 34, 76, 77, 78
Ashton, David 75, 78
Attewell, P. 96, 98
Augar Review 11–12, 25, 48, 66
automation 34, 76–78
  see also artificial intelligence (AI)
autonomy
  academics' loss of 20, 117
  decline of in HE sector 20–21
Avent-Holt, D. 94
Aynsley, S. 89

B

Baldwin, Richard 78
Ball, S.J. 20, 30, 40
Beaudry, P. 84
Becker, Gary 55, 58, 113, 114–115
Belfield, C. 92
Bell, Daniel 32
Blair, Tony 35
  see also Labour Party/governments
Bloome, D. 98
Bol, T. 99
Borgen, N.T. 97, 113
Britton, J. 95
Brooks, R. 29
Brown, P. 75, 78, 97, 106, 110, 112, 116
Brown, R. 5, 106
Brown, W. 6, 115
Browne Review 2010 9, 17, 34, 36, 39, 42, 50, 59, 61–62, 119
Burrell, J. 78

C

Cambridge University, public bond deals 17
Cameron, David 40
cap on student numbers 1, 17, 24

capitalism
  and graduate earnings 93
  and graduate work 71–75
Caplan, Bryan 86
Cappelli, P. 99–100
CBI (Confederation of British Industry) 47
class *see* social class, and labour market outcomes
Coates, K. 7
coding elite 78
Cohen, Y. 93
commercialisation 5, 23–24
commodification 5, 12, 23–26, **27**, 75, 121
Commons Education Committee 18
  see also House of Commons Education Committee
competition, in the HE sector 3, 6, 9, 16, 25–26, 41–42, 59, 64–65, 117
Confederation of British Industry (CBI) 47
Conservative Party/governments 7, 9–12, 16, 119
COVID-19 pandemic 17, 121–124
Cowburn, A. 122
credentialism 87–89, 90, 105
cultural capital, and labour market outcomes 96–97

D

DBIS (Department for Business, Innovation and Skills)
  Fulfilling our Potential: Teaching Excellence, Social Mobility and Student Choice (2015) 47–48, 51–52, 60–61, 62, 67
  Higher Ambitions: The Future of Universities in a Knowledge Economy (2009) 46–47, 49–50, 60, 62, 108
  Students at the Heart of the System (2011) 9–10, 41, 47, 59
  Success as a Knowledge Economy: Teaching Excellence, Social Mobility and Student Choice (2016) 10, 28, 41, 42, 47–48, 52–53, 57, 61, 64–66
Dearing Report *see* NCIHE (National Committee of Inquiry into Higher Education)
Dearing, Ronald 7
debt
  private borrowing by universities 17
  see also student loans

degree inflation 63
degree-level apprenticeships 47, 48, 123, 124
Delaney, J. 83
Dellot, B. 78
demand
  for domestic students 17
  for graduates 32–33, 81–83
Department for Business, Innovation and Skills (DBIS) *see* DBIS (Department for Business, Innovation and Skills)
Department for Education and Skills (DfES) *see* DfES (Department for Education and Skills)
Department for Education (DfE) *see* DfE (Department for Education)
Department of Innovation, Universities and Skills (DIUS) *see* DIUS (Department of Innovation, Universities and Skills)
DES (Department of Education and Science)
  Higher Education: Meeting the Challenge (1987) 35
Destinations of Leavers from Higher Education (DLHE) data 52
DfE (Department for Education) 1
  Graduate Outcomes (LEO): Outcomes in 2016 to 2017 (2019) 91
  Value for Money in Higher Education: Seventh Report of Session 2017–19 (2018) 66–67
DfES (Department for Education and Skills)
  The Future of Higher Education (2003) 8, 35, 36, 38–39, 40, 44–45, 46, 57, 58, 59
Di Stasio, V. 88
disability, and labour market outcomes 111
discourse analysis 30–31
DIUS (Department of Innovation, Universities and Skills)
  Higher Education at Work: High Skills, High Value (2008) 37, 39–40, 41, 45–46, 51
DLHE (Destinations of Leavers from Higher Education) data 52
Donelan, Michelle 1, 102
drop-out rates 18, 122
Drucker, Peter 32

E

earnings *see* graduate earnings
economy, role of HE in 12, 28–29
  graduate labour market 28–29
  HE policy 29–31, 34–37
  international competition 37–40
  and the KBE (knowledge-based economy) 31–34, 35, 37, 42

knowledge work 33–34
methodology 30–31
private economic benefits of HE 57–58, 67
Education Reform Act 1988 21, 23
egalitarianism 104
elite education, and labour market outcomes 97
Elliott, Larry 75
EMI (Effectively Maintained Inequality) hypothesis 98
employability 41, 62, 107–109, 115, 116, 120
  dark side of 109–111
  employability skills 45–46, 47, 51, 107
employers
  value of education for 113–114
  see also employability; graduate labour market
entry requirements, lowering of 25
equalising effect of HE 97–98
equality of opportunity 102–103, 105
  see also social mobility
ethnicity, and labour market outcomes 94, 111

F

Fairclough, N. 30
family origin, and labour market outcomes 96–98, 104, 111
Fazackerley, A. 1
FE (further education) colleges 4, 11
Felstead, A. 79
female graduate earnings 91, 94
  see also gender, and labour market outcomes
Ferlie, E. 21
Fernández-Macías, E. 79
Fiel, J.E. 98
financial crisis, 2008 119
Fleming, P. 73–74, 115
Foroohar, R. 93
Foucault, M. 115
Fourcade, M. 78
Fourth Industrial Revolution 34
Frank, R.H. 106
freelance working 72–73
Friedman, S. 98
Fulfilling our Potential: Teaching Excellence, Social Mobility and Student Choice (2015), DBIS 47–48, 51–52, 60–61, 62, 67
Funding Councils 7
Further and Higher Education Act 1992 7
further education (FE) colleges 4, 11
Future of Higher Education (2003), DfES 8, 35, 36, 38–39, 40, 44–45, 46, 57, 58, 59

G

gender, and labour market outcomes 91, 94, 111
Gibbs, P. 121
gig economy 72–73
globalisation 22
Gmiyah, Sam 43
Goldin, C. 72
Goldthorpe, J.H. 103, 104, 113
Goodhart, David 105–106
grade inflation 26
graduate earnings 1, 13, 69, 91–93, 99–100, 119
  economic context of 93
  gender differences in 91, 94, 111
  lack of relationship with educational investment 112
  Longitudinal Educational Outcomes data set 18
  organisational and occupational variations 94
  private economic benefits of HE 57–58, 67
  social factors in 94–98
  see also graduate labour market; graduate premium; graduate work
graduate employability *see* employability
graduate labour market 3–4, 12–13, 28–29, 40–42, 49–54, 70, 81, 89–90, 119
  demand for graduates 32–33, 81–83
  destination data 52
  graduate jobs 84–85
  overqualification 48, 62, 83–84
  professional work 85–86
  signalling and credentialism 86–89
  skill utilisation 84
  see also graduate earnings; graduate premium; graduate work
Graduate Outcomes (LEO): Outcomes in 2016 to 2017 (2019), DfE 91
graduate premium 58, 61–62, 64, 65, 68, 69, 70, 86, 91, 92, 95, 99–100, 116
  see also graduate earnings; graduate labour market; graduate work
graduate underemployment 62
graduate underutilisation 87
graduate unemployment 62
graduate work 3–4, 12–13, 28–29, 31, 43–49, 53–54, 70–71, 101, 119
  and capitalism 71–75
  and employability 41, 62, 107–111, 116, 120
  and HCT 111–116
  and meritocracy 101–107, 116
  nature of knowledge work 78–80
  and technology 75–78
  see also graduate earnings; graduate labour market; graduate premium
graduates
  demand for 32–33, 81–83
  private economic benefits of HE 57–58, 67
Green, F. 84, 91
Grusky, D.B. 92

H

Hazelkorn, E. 22–23
HCT (Human Capital Theories) 13, 31, 37, 55–57, 67–69, 91, 100
  critiques of 111–116
  and employers' requirements from education 113–114
  human capital investment 3, 4
  and humankind 114–116
  informed choice and labour market tailoring 58–61
  lack of realism in 114
  lack of relationship between graduate earnings and educational investment 112
  and marketisation 63–67, 90
  and non-standard employment 73–74
  private economic benefits of HE 57–58, 67
  and productivity 112–113
  and rationality 113
  skills 61–63, 68
HE (higher education)
  competition in 3, 6, 9, 16, 25–26, 41–42, 59, 64–65, 117
  decline of autonomy in 20–21
  impact of COVID-19 pandemic on 17, 121–124
  policy background 6–12
  relationship with the state 2, 21
  wider social purposes of 120–121
  see also marketisation of HE
Hecht, K. 106
Henseke, G. 91
Hesketh, A. 110
Higher Ambitions: The Future of Universities in a Knowledge Economy (2009), DBIS 46–47, 49–50, 60, 62, 108
Higher Education Act 2004 8–9
Higher Education and Research Act 2017 10–11
Higher Education at Work: High Skills, High Value (2008), DIUS 37, 39–40, 41, 45–46, 51
Higher Education in the Learning Society (1997) (NCIHE/Dearing Report) 7–8, 35, 36–37, 38, 40, 43–44, 50–51, 53, 57, 58–59, 62, 64
Higher Education Market: National Audit Office (NAO) Report 2017 18, 23
Higher Education: Meeting the Challenge (1987), DES 35

Higher Education Policy Institute 18, 123
Holloway, J. 30, 31
Holmes, C. 91
homo economicus 58, 113
Horowitz, J. 84
House of Commons Education Committee 49
see also Commons Education Committee
House of Lords Economic Affairs Committee 18
Human Capital Theories (HCT) *see* HCT (Human Capital Theories)
humankind, and HCT (Human Capital Theories) 114–116
Humburg, M. 85
Hunt, J. 79
Hurley, J. 79
Hutton, W. 74

I

inequality 113
meritocracy, and the unjust legitimisation of inequality 105–106
see also social factors, and labour market outcomes
informed choice for students 58–61, 67–68
international competition 37–40
international student market 17, 25
interpersonal skills 85
IoT (Internet of Things) 76
Isopahkala-Bouret, U. 89
IT professionals 78

J

Jackson, M. 103
Jarratt Report 23
Jessop, B. 34
Johnson, Jo 18, 63
Jongbloed, B. 5, 15

K

Kalleberg, A.L. 94
Katz, L.F. 72
KBE (knowledge-based economy) 3, 12, 13, 31–33, 37, 42, 43, 53–54, 70
Keep, E. 33
Kelly, P. 30
Kernohan, D. 9
Kleinknecht, A. 79
knowledge society 32
see also knowledge-based economy (KBE)
knowledge work 33–34, 78–80
see also knowledge-based economy (KBE)
knowledge-based economy (KBE) 3, 12, 13, 31–33, 37, 42, 43, 53–54, 70
Knowledge-Based Economy (OECD) 33
Kristal, T. 93

L

labour market *see* graduate labour market
Labour Party/governments 2, 8–9, 16, 35–37, 123
Lambert, H. 26
Lammy, David 36
Lampl, Sir Peter 118
language
discourse analysis 30–31
Lauder, H. 75, 78
Laurison, D. 98
Leitch Review of Skills
Prosperity for All in the Global Economy: World Class Skills (2006) 40–41, 45
Levy, F. 77
lifelong learning 11
Liu, Y. 92
Local Education Authorities
funding of tuition costs 7
London South Bank University 24
Longhi, S. 94
Longitudinal Educational Outcomes data set 18
low-value courses 11, 18, 66, 122
Lynch, K. 22, 23–24, 121

M

maintenance grants 7, 8, 10, 11, 15–16
male graduate earnings 91, 94
see also gender, and labour market outcomes
managerialism 12, 18–23, **27**, 85
Manchester University, public bond deals 17
Mandelson, Peter 35–36, 46
Marginson, S. 56, 114, 119
market segments 25
marketing 26
marketisation of HE 12, 13–14, 117–119
future of 121–124
and HCT (Human Capital Theories) 63–67, 90, 101
impact on academics 20, 22–23, 25, 117, 118
introduction and overview 1–6
policy background 6–12
and the purposes of HE 120–121
resistance to 118, 123
markets 24–26, 41–42, 106
Markovits, Daniel 97
Marshall, Alfred 55
Marshall, G. 105
Mason, G. 109
May, Theresa 101–102
Mayhew, K. 91
McCaig, C. 11, 68
McCowan, T. 25, 110
McGuinness, S. 83

McKinsey Global Institute 80, 93
meritocracy 101–103, 116
  nature of merit 106–107
  achievability of through educational
    policy 104–105
  and the unjust legitimisation of
    inequality 105–106
Middleton, C. 20
Mijs, J.J.B. 106
Mincer, Jacob 55
Mitnik, P.A. 97
modernisation thesis 102
Morgan, J. 23
Morley, L. 89
Morse, Amyas 23
Mouw, T. 94

N

Naidoo, R. 19
National Audit Office (NAO)
  *The Higher Education Market: National
    Audit Office (NAO) Report* 2017 18, 23
National Student Information data 24
National Union of Students (NUS) 47
NCIHE (National Committee of Inquiry
    into Higher Education)
  Higher Education in the Learning Society
    (1997) (Dearing Report) 7–8, 35,
    36–37, 38, 40, 43–44, 50–51, 53, 57,
    58–59, 62, 64
'neoliberal economy' 74–75
neoliberalism 4, 21, 28, 115, 119
New Labour *see* Labour Party/
    governments
New Public Management (NPM) 21
new technologies *see* technology
Newfield, C. 33, 54
niches 25
non-standard employment 72–74
Northern Ireland; devolved HE policy 4
NPM (New Public Management) 21
Nunn, R. 79
NUS (National Union of Students) 47

O

O'Brien, Neil 2
O'Donovan, N. 34
OECD (Organisation for Economic
    Co-operation and Development)
  The Knowledge-Based Economy 33
OFFA (Office for Fair Access) 8
OfS (Office for Students) 1, 10, 18, 26,
    67, 122
  value for money 17–18
ONS 77, 83
Osborne, George 10
outsourcing
  and technology 78
  of university functions 25

overqualification 48, 62, 83–84, 87
ownership, of companies 74
Oxford University, public bond deals 17

P

performativity 20–21
personal capital 111
platform workers 72–73
post-1992 universities 17
postgraduate market 16
postgraduate taught courses, costs of 16
post-industrial society 32
precarious employment 72–74, 85–86
private borrowing by universities 17
privatisation 5
productivity
  lack of relationship with
    earnings 112–113
  productivity gap 44, 48–49, 75
professions
  graduate labour market 85–86
  vocational education and training for 107
*Prosperity for All in the Global Economy:
    World Class Skills* (2006) (Leitch
    Review of Skills) 40–41, 45
public bond deals 17
public mission, of HE 121
public service reform 21

Q

quasi-markets 20, 21
  see also markets
queuing theory 88, 110

R

ranking 1, 21–23
rationality, and HCT 113
Reay, Diane 104
redbrick universities 31–32
redundancies 24
REF (Research Excellence Framework) 22
responsibilisation 74
Restrepo, P. 76
Robbins Report 1963 29
Rosenfeld, J. 94
'Routine-Biased Technical Change' 72
Russell Group universities 17

S

Sakamoto, A. 94
Sandel, Michael 105
SBTC (skill-biased technological
    change) 71–72, 79, 82, 83
Schram, S.F. 74–75
science, technology, engineering and
    mathematics (STEM) subjects 11, 46,
    48, 65
Scotland; devolved HE policy 4
screening 86–87

Shapiro, H.T. 121
sharing economy 72–73
Shattock, Michael 29
Shepherd, S. 19
Shultz, Theodore 55
signalling theory 86–89, 90, 113
Skidmore, Chris 28
skill-biased technological change
  (SBTC) 71–72, 79, 82, 83
skills 45–49, 84, 88, 107–108, 114
  demand for 32–33, 40–42
  and employability 45–46, 47, 51, 107,
    108, 109–110
  as a form of human capital 55–56
  interpersonal skills 85
  role of HE in 13
  SBTC (skill-biased technological
    change) 71–72, 79, 82, 83
  skills gap 44–45, 49, 51
Smith, Adam 55
social class, and labour market
  outcomes 95–97, 104, 111
social closure 88–89
social factors, and labour market
  outcomes 94–98, 103, 110–111, 113
social justice 102, 105
social mobility 97–98, 102–103, 104,
  118
  see also meritocracy
social networks, and labour market
  outcomes 96–97, 111
Souto-Outero, M. 112–113
state, the
  and employability 108
  relationship with the HE sector 2,
    21, 122
STEM (science, technology, engineering
  and mathematics) subjects 11, 46,
  48, 65
student choice 21, 41–42, 64–65, 117
  informed choice 58–61, 67–68
  policy developments 8, 9
student housing, income from 17
student loans 16
  policy developments 8, 9, 11
  repayment reform proposals 123
student numbers, cap on 1, 17, 24
student recruitment 24–25
students
  as consumers 24
  HE as an investment by 2, 57–58,
    67–68, 69
  and informed choice 58–61, 68–69
Students at the Heart of the System (2011),
  DBIS 9–10, 41, 47, 59
Success as a Knowledge Economy: Teaching
  Excellence, Social Mobility and Student
  Choice (2016), DBIS 10, 28, 41, 42,
  47–48, 52–53, 57, 61, 64–66

Susskind, D. 85
Susskind, R. 85
Sutton Trust 118

T

Tang, R. 94
Teaching and Higher Education
  Act 1998 8
Teaching Excellence and Student
  Outcomes Framework (TEF) 10–11,
  18, 22, 24–25, 52, 67
teaching grants 16
teaching quality 10, 25, 60, 62, 65, 66,
  67, 68
technology 13
  and graduate work 71–72, 75–78
  SBTC (skill-biased technological
    change) 71–72, 79, 82, 83
technoscientific capitalism 72
TEF (Teaching Excellence and Student
  Outcomes Framework) 10–11, 18, 22,
  24–25, 52, 67
Teixera, P.N. 58
Thatcher, Margaret 7, 21, 23, 35
  see also Conservative Party/governments
Third Way 35
Toffler, Alvin 32
Tolofari, S. 21
Tominey, C. 1
tuition costs, Local Education Authority
  funding of 7
tuition fees 1, 15–16, 25–26, 47, 59–60
  and the COVID-19 pandemic 122
  opposition to 123
  policy developments 8, 9, 10
  see also user-pay finance

U

UKCES (UK Commission for
  Employment and Skills) 107–108
unemployment/underemployment of
  graduates 62
universities see HE (higher education)
University Grants committees 21
University of Central Lancashire 26
University of Leicester 24
University of Liverpool 24
University of the West of England 26
user-pay finance 12, 15–18, **27**
  see also tuition fees

V

value for money 17–18, 66–67
Value for Money in Higher Education: Seventh
  Report of Session 2017–19 (2018),
  DfE 66–67
Van de Werfhorst, H.G. 88
Van Zanten, A. 106
Vanderburg, W.H. 78–79

vice-chancellors, role of 21
vocational education and training 45, 92,
    107, 114, 124
  degree-level apprenticeships 47, 48,
    123, 124

W

Wales; devolved HE policy 4
Wang, S.X. 94
wealth, and labour market outcomes
    96–97, 98
Weber, Max 88
Wilby, Peter 2
Willetts, David 23, 42

Williams, G. 19
Williamson, Gavin 122
Witteveen, D. 96, 98
work *see* graduate work

Y

Yorke, M. 108
Young, M. 102

Z

zero-hours contracts 73–74
Zhou, X. 98
Zhu, Y. 84
Zwysen, W. 94

www.ingramcontent.com/pod-product-compliance
Lightning Source LLC
Chambersburg PA
CBHW070932030426
42336CB00014BA/2646